I0866557

The Sailor

The Sailor

Franklin D. Roosevelt and the Transformation of American Foreign Policy

David F. Schmitz

UNIVERSITY PRESS OF KENTUCKY

Copyright © 2021 by The University Press of Kentucky

Scholarly publisher for the Commonwealth,
serving Bellarmine University, Berea College, Centre
College of Kentucky, Eastern Kentucky University,
The Filson Historical Society, Georgetown College,
Kentucky Historical Society, Kentucky State University,
Morehead State University, Murray State University,
Northern Kentucky University, Transylvania University,
University of Kentucky, University of Louisville,
and Western Kentucky University.
All rights reserved.

Editorial and Sales Offices: The University Press of Kentucky
663 South Limestone Street, Lexington, Kentucky 40508-4008
www.kentuckypress.com

Library of Congress Cataloging-in-Publication Data
Names: Schmitz, David F., author.
Title: The sailor : Franklin D. Roosevelt and the transformation of American foreign policy / David F. Schmitz.
Other titles: Franklin D. Roosevelt and the transformation of American foreign policy
Description: Lexington, Kentucky : University Press of Kentucky, [2021] | Series: Studies in conflict, diplomacy, and peace | Includes bibliographical references and index.
Identifiers: LCCN 2020053146 | ISBN 9780813180441 (hardcover) | ISBN 9780813180465 (pdf) | ISBN 9780813180458 (epub)
Subjects: LCSH: United States—Foreign relations—1933–1945. | Roosevelt, Franklin D. (Franklin Delano), 1882–1945. | United States—Politics and government—1933–1945. | World War, 1939–1945—United States. | Internationalism—History—20th century. | Lend-lease operations (1941–1945)
Classification: LCC E806 .S3488 2021 | DDC 973.917092—dc23

This book is printed on acid-free paper meeting
the requirements of the American National Standard
for Permanence in Paper for Printed Library Materials.

Manufactured in the United States of America.

ASSOCIATION of UNIVERSITY PRESSES

Member of the Association
of University Presses

To Polly

Who enhances it all

Contents

Preface

The post–World War II world was shaped more by Franklin D. Roosevelt than anyone else. The Roosevelt world was created in response to the dual crises of the Great Depression and World War II. The internationalist policies Franklin Roosevelt pursued in response to the upheavals of the 1930s and 1940s set off a great debate about the role of the United States in the world from the mid-1930s through the war years. Roosevelt saw the proper role of the United States as a world leader with its power and influence extended globally, basing its defense on preparedness and collective security, and cooperating with allies through multilateral international organizations to promote and protect American values and institutions. In FDR's vision of a postwar world, peace, prosperity, and American security would be obtained through the Good Neighbor Policy, the Atlantic Charter, and the four freedoms that emerged from the challenges posed by fascism and militarism in the 1930s and which guided the fighting of World War II.

Franklin Roosevelt saw World War II as one war with many parts. He was the only person in the position to confront all aspects and theaters of the war and to have the knowledge and ability to engage each of the vexing international issues. He understood how the complex political, military, and strategic problems were interrelated, and what was needed to secure a stable, peaceful, and prosperous world order. His "great design"[1] was pursued in a manner to avoid the mistakes of the Treaty of Versailles. The maintenance of the alliance with Great Britain after World War II was critical but not sufficient to achieve the goals of postwar peace and prosperity. That would take the continuation of the Grand Alliance with the Soviet Union, the rebuilding of Germany and Japan, the establishment of multilateral international economic institutions, and an end to colonial empires.

As Arthur M. Schlesinger Jr. noted in 1994, the contrast between Roosevelt and the other leaders during World War II was stark. "The world we live in today is Franklin Roosevelt's world," Schlesinger wrote. It was not the world of Adolf Hitler, whose "thousand-year Reich turned out to have a brief and bloody run of a dozen years," or the world of Joseph Stalin that had just recently collapsed with the end of the Soviet Union. Nor was it the one envisioned by Winston Churchill that maintained Europe's empires.[2] Roosevelt was determined to do all he could to eliminate any chance of a revival of fascist militarism and set the course for international economic cooperation to prevent future wars. The president understood that Russia was crucial for winning the war and would emerge as a great power; the only way to peace was by engaging it as a partner in the postwar world. Finally, FDR foresaw the end of Europe's colonial empires and that China would also emerge as a great power. He, therefore, sought a Third Way between imperialism and revolution to bring forward a pro-Western nationalism.

This work is an interpretive analysis of Franklin Roosevelt's overall approach to and the making of American foreign policy. Its purpose is to explain FDR's worldview, his beliefs about the United States and its interests, the president's understanding of the issues that confronted America, and how these shaped the policies he developed to address the crises of the 1930s and the Second World War. Given the significance of Roosevelt's diplomacy, it is surprising that there is only a single, one-volume study of the entirety of FDR's foreign policy, Robert Dallek's *Franklin D. Roosevelt and American Foreign Policy, 1932–1945*.[3] While still valuable in its encyclopedic treatment of Roosevelt's diplomacy, it is dated due to the availability of new sources and a significant volume of scholarship on various aspects of Roosevelt's foreign policy over the forty years since its publication. It also sets out the prevailing view that Roosevelt was an isolationist who became, due to pressures outside the Western Hemisphere, a reluctant interventionist in world affairs.[4] By extension, most scholars have seen little continuity in Roosevelt's thinking or coherence in his approach to the world. Thus, most works concentrate on either the 1930s or the World War II years. This study challenges these assumptions.

Introduction

Sailor

> As with sailing, so with politics: make your cloth too taut and your ship will dip and heel, but slacken off and trim your sails, and things head up again.
>
> —Euripides, *Orestes*

In 1916, Assistant Secretary of the Navy Franklin D. Roosevelt was on the destroyer USS *Flusser* off the coast of Maine conducting an inspection of American naval ships. Sailing near Campobello Island, where the Roosevelt family spent most summers, the review was interrupted when a heavy fog, common to the area, set in. Familiar with the local waters and conditions, Roosevelt took command of the vessel from Lieutenant William F. "Bull" Halsey Jr. and steered the ship through Lubec Narrows, the straight between Campobello and the mainland. Roosevelt had sailed many smaller boats in these difficult waters, but he had never commanded a destroyer. Halsey was naturally concerned about the fate of his ship: "The fact that a white-flannelled yachtsman can sail a catboat out to a buoy and back is not guarantee that he can handle a high-speed destroyer in narrow waters. A destroyers' bow may point directly down the channel, yet she is not necessarily on a safe course. She pivots around a point near her bridge structure, which means that two-thirds of her length is aft of the pivot, and that her stern will swing in twice the arc of her bow. As Mr. Roosevelt made his first turn, I saw him look aft and check the swing of our stern. My worries were over; he knew his business."[1]

This event captures much that is important for understanding Roosevelt and his foreign policy. Roosevelt was an avid and accomplished sailor. On the waters of the Hudson River and off the coasts of Maine and Campobello

Island, New Brunswick, he learned to read the sea and tides, and how to understand the rocks, channels, currents, winds, coastlines, and challenges of often dangerous waters. The ability to tack is crucial to sailing; it taught FDR at a young age patience and flexibility, and that there was more than one route to a final destination. What mattered was arriving at your goal, more than the exact course taken. Sailing is a complex endeavor; one has to weigh options and choices, be versatile in the face of weather and changing sea conditions, and handle many tasks while making compromises and tradeoffs to reach final decisions.[2]

His taking command of the USS *Flusser* foreshadows even more about the future president. It expressed Roosevelt's confidence in himself and his ability to judge situations and take risks. He acted in a manner that he believed was required of him, sure that he was right to take control. Roosevelt was already, at the age of thirty-four, a well-established Wall Street lawyer and politician with connections to the most powerful members of both parties. This included President Theodore Roosevelt, his distant cousin and uncle of his wife Eleanor, and President Woodrow Wilson, who had appointed him assistant secretary of the navy, the same post the Republican Roosevelt had once held.

While Roosevelt was not guided by a particular philosophy, and his pragmatic approach to the issues and challenges that confronted the nation defied easy labels, he held a patrician's sense of the obligation of service and duty that guided him while in office. This outlook was married to a great confidence in himself and optimism about the future, both his own and that of the nation. When asked once to define his political philosophy he declared, "I am a Christian and a Democrat—that's all."[3] These were the two central points of his worldview. An Episcopalian, Roosevelt believed in a benevolent and loving God that rewarded those who were good. His belief in democracy and Christianity shaped how he understood others and events, and were his starting points for thinking about the world. He was confident that if good people were in charge, the ultimate outcome of events was bound to be right. As a result, he had a Whig view of history, which saw humans progressing to better material and spiritual positions, greater rational thought, and more freedom.

Franklin Roosevelt set his sights on the presidency from a young age. Educated at Groton, Harvard, and Columbia, he was exposed to world issues early on, read widely on foreign policy and history (his undergraduate major), and adopted at an early age an internationalist perspective to his thinking on world issues. As a law clerk right out of Columbia University Law School he worked for a Wall Street firm, handling cases in the municipal courts. Greenville Clark, a fellow clerk, recalled Roosevelt talking about his future. "I remember him saying with engaging frankness that he wasn't going to practice law forever, that he intended to run for office at the first opportunity, and that he wanted to be and thought he had a very real chance to be President."[4] In this effort to gain experience and a national reputation, FDR saw himself following much of the same route, in terms of the offices he sought, as Theodore Roosevelt. He would be elected to the New York Assembly, serve as assistant secretary of the navy, and become governor of New York. To Franklin Roosevelt, this appeared "eminently reasonable."[5]

It would take Roosevelt's level of confidence, strength, and vision to confront the long-standing policy of hemispheric defense that guided American foreign policy into the 1930s. George Washington's warning in his Farewell Address against the nation tying itself to any foreign countries, and Thomas Jefferson's caution against entangling alliances, served as guideposts for almost 150 years. Woodrow Wilson's "great departure" in World War I notwithstanding,[6] prior to Roosevelt's presidency the concept of defense in the United States meant protecting the territorial sovereignty of the nation secured by the two oceans—codified in the nation's commitment to the Monroe Doctrine, which warned Europe against efforts to reclaim colonies in the Western Hemisphere and pledged that the United States would remain neutral in European affairs—and defending the rights of neutrality at sea. The perceived failure of Wilson at Versailles and the coming of the Great Depression served to entrench millions of Americans in their support for this traditional approach to defending the nation through nonintervention and neutrality, often referred to by the misnomer of isolationism.[7]

Roosevelt found the traditional policy inadequate, out-of-date, shortsighted, and dangerous, and he challenged and eventually overcame these existing ideas. In the process, he established internationalism as the dominant paradigm for American foreign policy and developed the concept of "national security" as its expression. As David M. Kennedy has argued, safeguarding individual security from the unregulated economy was the central purpose of Roosevelt's New Deal programs,[8] but for Roosevelt, security at home was only possible with national security abroad. He told the nation in a fireside chat on April 14, 1938, that "you and I agree that security is our greatest need." The president assured his listeners that he was doing all he could to "attain that security." In doing so, he pointed out that he was "thinking not only of the immediate economic needs of the people . . . but also . . . of our democracy and of the recent trend in other parts of the world away from the democratic ideal."[9]

The Great Depression and World War II were defining moments in American history, marking the full emergence of the United States as a world power. At the center of this transition was Franklin D. Roosevelt. Roosevelt's foreign policy was based on his belief that the United States had to be a world leader, and that as a great power the only way to secure peace and prosperity was through preparedness, defense in depth, collective security, cooperation with allies, and the creation of an international environment conducive to American interests and values as expressed through multilateral, international organizations. He set these views out for the American people through his speeches and fireside chats. As we know from his secretary, Marguerite A. "Missy" LeHand, Roosevelt worked diligently on these talks and they fully expressed his own ideas and words. After receiving input on and/or drafts of a speech he would read the material and then put it aside and write "a completely new draft." He would then edit it, working with his staff and experts. "When the final draft is complete," she noted, "there can be no doubt that it is the President's own speech and that every word and punctuation has been carefully gone over by him."[10]

The policies he pursued in response to the dual crises of the 1930s and 1940s brought forth a great debate over the role of the United States in the world; it transformed how Americans thought about their nation and international relations, and shaped wartime diplomacy and planning for the postwar world. Guided by his commitment to an internationalist perspective and his belief in American exceptionalism, Roosevelt developed an interlocking set of ideas and policies that first produced a debate about neutrality and preparedness and then guided the United States into World War II and served to mobilize support for the war while establishing an American responsibility for the postwar world. While the president's victory in the 1940 election marked the beginning of the decline of the political strength of noninterventionism, the critical moment came in the period between Roosevelt's reelection to a third term in office and Pearl Harbor. It was then that FDR fully set out his view of the United States as the arsenal of democracy, proclaimed his war goals around the protection of the four freedoms—freedom from want, freedom from fear, freedom of speech, freedom of religion—secured passage of the Lend-Lease Act, and announced the principles of the Atlantic Charter. These steps framed Roosevelt's vision of internationalism and the postwar role of the United States.

Attending Groton was the perfect match for Roosevelt and his ambitions. A school established for the sons of America's elite families, under the direction of the Episcopal minister Endicott Peabody, it inculcated a vision of society led by men of the highest Christian character. Service to the community, nation, and the world was seen as an obligation of those who were best able to reform the social order and maintain progress. Groton's mission statement proclaimed that "every endeavor will be made to cultivate manly Christian character, having regard to moral and physical as well as intellectual development."[11] Peabody made the themes of character and service central to the curriculum, extracurricular activities, and all of his sermons.

Theodore Roosevelt summarized the philosophy of Groton, and the reason why he was in politics, when he declared: "Much has been given you, therefore we have the right to expect much from you."[12] Franklin Roosevelt agreed wholeheartedly with that view and carried these lessons with him his whole life. As president, in 1941 he took the time to write to Peabody, whom he greatly admired, to say that "I count it among the blessings of my life that it was given to me in formative years to have the privilege of your guiding hand and the benefit of your inspiring example."[13]

These ideas reinforced Franklin Roosevelt's natural optimism about the future. He believed the United States was an exceptional country and the nation a progressive force in history. In terms of foreign policy, he saw the United States and its democratic institutions as being in conflict with older systems of class structure, arbitrary power, and repressive political systems, and he believed that Washington had to play a leadership role in the world to provide stability, balance, guidance, and a proper world order. American interests and values could only be protected and flourish in a world that was becoming more liberal. Eschewing the Social Darwinist and essentialist racial attitudes that were so common to people of his class and background, Roosevelt thought all people could adopt the American way of life if given the opportunity.

He was, therefore, an anti-imperialist who supported free trade because he considered empires antidemocratic and saw them as obstacles to liberal progress and sources of international disorder due to the inevitable backlash against colonial rule. In Roosevelt's linear view of history, colonial systems disrupted the natural development of nations, guided by providence, toward a better world. Roosevelt noted in 1926 that "I well remember my old schoolmaster, Mr. Peabody, teaching us that material and spiritual progress has had its periodic ups and downs, but that the up-curves are always the longer, and that the net advance is certain in the end."[14] It was up to individuals who knew the lessons of history to shape that better future, and it was the job of the nations they led to provide protection and paternalistic guidance to those less advanced. Roosevelt saw himself as that type of leader and the United States as the ideal nation to guide the world.

Roosevelt's love of sailing and the sea carried over to his passion for the Navy and naval history, central features of his character. From the time he was young and read Theodore Roosevelt's *The Naval War of 1812* and Alfred Thayer Mahan's two seminal works, *The Influence of Sea Power on History 1660–1773* and *The Interest of America in Sea Power, Present and Future*,[15] FDR was a serious student of naval history, theories of warfare, and strategy. It was clear to him that the Navy provided a greater security reach to U.S. power and defense in depth. He owned an extensive collection of maps, naval prints, paintings, drawings, manuscript letters, documents, logbooks, pamphlets, and books related to the American Navy since 1775.[16] These studies gave him a global view of strategy, a sense of the interconnectedness of the world, and an expansive understanding of what he would come to call national security that combined territorial defense with efforts to extend American values and ideals in the world.

This is not to say that Roosevelt just took his ideas on foreign policy from Theodore Roosevelt, Mahan, and Woodrow Wilson. In part, there has been too much effort to try to pigeonhole FDR in that manner. Franklin Roosevelt's foreign policy was his own, and is best understood by examining his words and actions. He saw the world in a different way from earlier presidents, and he faced challenges and crises that were distinct from those confronted by his predecessors in residence at 1600 Pennsylvania Avenue. The rise of the fascist challenge that led to World War II certainly demanded responses that could not be found by simply emulating or even adapting previous thinking and policies. In the process, Roosevelt redefined the way the nation saw its national interests as related to the rest of the world and changed the concept of defense to one of national security.

Warren Kimball has provided the best guidance for thinking about FDR's foreign policy and understanding the complexity of the nation's thirty-second president, and his work on Roosevelt and World War II remains an essential starting place. Kimball posited that one has to understand the "broader consistency that shaped [FDR's] policies—his assumptions" about the United States and that guided his thinking on the world. These concepts were the "fundamental starting point for the tactics and strategy" FDR used, and must be recognized in order to understand his decision making and policies.[17]

Too much also has been made of negative comments by contemporaries of Roosevelt who claimed that he was an intellectual lightweight. Friends at Harvard saw FDR as lacking depth, calling him "the 'featherduster' because of supposedly shallow and priggish qualities,"[18] someone with a good personality but with more charisma than substance, a lightweight who got by on his looks, charm, and connections. Endicott Peabody remembered FDR as satisfactory "but not brilliant," and Supreme Court Justice Oliver Wendell Holmes saw him as "a second-class intellect" who had a first-class temperament. Senator Henry Cabot Lodge found the then assistant secretary of the navy "well-meaning . . . but light." The columnist Walter Lippmann summarized these negative assessments of FDR as a hale and hearty country club fellow with little substance, writing that he was "a perfectly estimable person with no discernable qualifications for the burdens of the presidency."[19]

Similar to the efforts to portray Roosevelt's contributions as just a later version of earlier presidents' policies, these interpretations miss the measure of the man. Franklin Roosevelt, as he would prove many times, consistently foiled those who underestimated him. Prior to becoming president and being reelected three times, FDR was elected twice to the New York Assembly as a Democrat from an overwhelming Republican district, served successfully as assistant secretary of the navy during World War I, secured his party's vice presidential nomination in 1920 based on his performance in Washington, emerged in the 1920s, after being stricken by polio, as the foreign policy spokesman for the Democrats, and was elected twice as governor of New York. Roosevelt's command of issues, his strategic vision, political instincts, and unprecedented achievements demonstrate that his was both a first-class mind and temperament.

Frances Perkins, Roosevelt's secretary of labor, did not have a high opinion of FDR when they first met in 1910, noting that "no one who saw him in those years would have been likely to think of him as a potential President of the U.S.A"; but she came to see Roosevelt as "the most complicated human being I ever knew." This is the most accurate one-line summation of Roosevelt there is. She credited this complexity for the future president's drive to achieve, sympathy for others, insight into problems, and imagination, which allowed him to succeed in the face of crises. His ability to see events and issues from multiple perspectives simultaneously and his willingness to change course help explain Roosevelt's ability to tolerate "apparent contradiction" in his views and actions, a trait "which so exasperated those associates of his who expected 'crystal clear'" decisions. As Perkins further noted, "The core of Roosevelt's character was viability—a capacity for living and growing" that guided his approach to governing and made him "essentially adaptable to new circumstances."[20] To understand Roosevelt and his foreign policy is to unpack that complexity.

When he became president, Franklin Roosevelt believed that the United States, based on its reliance upon hemispheric defense and political noninvolvement in Europe, was inadequately prepared to meet threats to the nation's interests in the world and to its borders. The United States needed to adopt a global perspective on its security, one that extended the concept of its defense beyond its coastlines and a narrow definition of the Monroe Doctrine, and instead was based on a strategy of national security that placed its front lines for protection across the Atlantic and Pacific Oceans. But, Roosevelt argued, it would take more than just force to keep the nation safe. Only the spreading of American values and institutions would bring real security to the nation, which made ideology as important a component of policy as geopolitical concerns.

Central to his justifications and conceptualization of this policy were FDR's understanding of American exceptionalism and his conviction that he needed to promote and defend American values—such as freedom, democracy, and self-determination—and institutions globally to insure the nation's safety. Roosevelt believed that American values were universal and that other people desired them and would adopt them if they had the opportunity. He was an internationalist who consistently worked to expand America's role in the world through multilateral institutions and collective security, and he held to the conviction that foreign nations benefited from their relationship with the United States.

Facing an unprecedented domestic crisis that tested the nation's institutions and values when he took office in March 1933, Roosevelt initially devoted most of his attention and efforts during his first term in office to finding a solution to the Great Depression. By the end of the decade, that concern was directly connected to the escalating threats from Nazi Germany and Imperial Japan. In response to the international crisis of the 1930s, Roosevelt confronted long-standing sentiment against American intervention in foreign wars. People from all parts of the United States favored neutrality and noninterventionism, based on traditional policies such as the Monroe Doctrine and hemispheric defense, and reinforced by their disillusionment with American participation in World War I. Over the course of his presidency, Roosevelt gradually overcame the sentiment of nonintervention and moved the nation to adopt his internationalist definition of America's role in the world and national security. In doing so, the president reshaped the public's understanding of the national interest and defense, within a framework of American exceptionalism, as it came to accept the necessity for war in Europe and Asia in the defense of American interests, and he established the basis for post–World War II American foreign policy.

In the 1930s and early 1940s, Americans debated and fought over the meaning of American exceptionalism, the extent of the U.S. role in the world, and the use of its political and military power as an instrument of policy. The passage of the Neutrality Acts of 1935 and 1937 marked the high point of the noninterventionist position. By 1940, however, as Roosevelt won reelection for an unprecedented third term in office, his internationalist view of the United States as a world leader, with its defense based on preparedness and collective security, took hold and guided the United States into and through World War II. Roosevelt's Quarantine Speech in October 1937 was the start of this shift. In it, the president set out the basis for increased American involvement abroad and the doctrine of just war as the basis for national security.[21] As war broke out in Asia, Germany's revisions of the Versailles Treaty and increasing belligerency exposed the shortcomings of the noninterventionist position and led to efforts by Roosevelt to increase American aid to Great Britain and to redefine American foreign policy around an expanded internationalist definition of national security and preparedness for war. Roosevelt, invoking the arguments of just war and the defense of democracy against totalitarianism, slowly but surely moved the nation away from a limited view of hemispheric defense and neutrality toward intervention against German and Japanese aggression in the defense of national security and American values. The fulcrum of this effort and key moment for Roosevelt in defining national security came in the period of December 1940 to March 1941. The president's pronouncement that the United States was the "great arsenal of democracy" on December 29, 1940, and the upholder of the four freedoms on January 6, 1941, set out the ideological justifications for American involvement in the conflict. The passage of lend-lease in March 1941 marked the final triumph for the internationalist position.[22] With the Japanese attack on Pearl Harbor, the American people prepared to take up the burden and sacrifices of World War II. Thus, Roosevelt moved the nation beyond a view of hemispheric defense, increased trade, and neutrality to support an internationalism that accepted the risks of intervention globally, political alliances, and the necessity of the use of American power abroad as the only means to provide both prosperity and peace.

An examination of the whole period of Roosevelt's presidency, with a focus on the context and continuity for the crucial decisions of 1939–1941, and how they were implemented during World War II, demonstrates that FDR was consistent in his outlook on international affairs, if not always in his actions, and that he moved as quickly as he thought politically possible to change the direction of American foreign policy. As a result, Roosevelt's decisions and actions leading up to World War II formed the critical juncture in America's relations with the world in twentieth century U.S. foreign policy. Moreover, they not only brought the nation into the war but they also shaped the thinking of the next generation of American leaders and Cold War policy after it.

The global economic crisis during the 1930s and then World War II tested all of Roosevelt's skills, his lifelong study of international relations, and his abilities as a strategic thinker. Certainly he made compromises, missteps, and mistakes as he confronted the complex issues of that time. His training as a sailor helped him navigate and correct course when his actions came up short, and those skills were put to use many times as the fortunes of the war and the difficulties of working with his allies demanded that the president politically tack and rethink positions. As Roosevelt stated in 1932, facing shifting conditions and finding different routes was "the fun of sailing. If you're headed for somewhere and the wind changes, why you just change your mind and go somewhere else."[23] Given the enormity of the international crisis he faced, FDR had to consistently adjust his policies even while he remained committed to his core internationalist positions and was confident that he could find a solution. Rexford Tugwell, an original member of Roosevelt's Brain Trust, observed that "there never was a prominent leader who was more determined about his objectives and never one who was more flexible about his means."[24] Roosevelt was optimistic, flexible in terms of method, held internationalist beliefs, and was convinced that the survival of the nation was at stake during World War II; these were critical to his successes as president and made him the most important figure in twentieth-century United States foreign policy.

1

Exceptionalism and Internationalism

In one of the first speeches he gave as a member of the New York state legislature, in March 1912, Roosevelt made clear his progressive view of history, the need for American leadership in the world, and his concern about balance at home and abroad. For the past thousand years, Roosevelt argued, the struggle to "obtain individual freedom" had been the "great and fundamental question in the economic life of people" in "almost every European and American country." From the American Revolution forward, this had taken the form of the struggle for representative government and the guarantee of liberty for the individual that a republic brought about. What was now needed was the "liberty of the community" to correct the imbalances of power and wealth that were emerging in American society. "To state it plainly," Roosevelt declared, "competition has been shown to be useful up to a certain point, but co-operation, which is the thing that we must strive for today, begins where competition leaves off. This is what the founders of the republic were groping for." The example he used was the conservation of land, and the need to conserve resources and protect areas such as forests from being overcut. To allow a person or company to use up all of the natural resources of the land was a destruction of the liberty and rights of the community, "and by liberty, we mean happiness and prosperity." Some, Roosevelt noted, would "hold up their hands in horror" at this idea "and say 'Unamerican' or 'dangerous,'" but it was just using regulation for the common good. If "we call the same identical process co-operation these same old fogies will cry out 'well done.'" This was an early statement of the mature economy theory, the idea that the challenges facing the nation stemmed from adjusting to the changes wrought by industrialization; here, FDR set out much of the framework by which he understood the problems of the nation and the connection between domestic and international events, as well as his vision of good government.[1]

This analysis drew upon Theodore Roosevelt's views on the need to regulate big business and to place the national need ahead of individual and parochial interests. Speaking just two years earlier, the former president had declared that "we are face to face with new conceptions of the relations of property to human welfare." No longer could private property trump all other interests. "The man who wrongly holds that every human right is secondary to his profit must now give way to the advocate of human welfare, who rightly maintains that every man holds his property subject to the general right of the community to regulate its use to whatever degree the public welfare may require it."[2]

Drawing from the same perspective, FDR would place his emphasis on creating and sustaining balance in society, a position that would be crucial to how he understood international relations as well as domestic economic problems. When he was president, he noted that he saw it as his "job to make the essence of democracy" work for all citizens. The problem was how to make a government that was created for an agrarian society work in one that now had large cities, big corporations, and a large percentage of the population that worked for someone else. The role of the president was "to make what changes have to be made without sacrificing the basic freedoms of individuals, without making government itself too strong while making it strong enough to keep private concentrations of wealth and power from depriving people of their rights, or treating people as commodities in the marketplace." Thus, the government had to act as a broker, balancing the different and competing demands. Fundamentally, government had to ensure there was "work and security" for all, what Roosevelt called the "spiritual values" of society. Only when these were secure could people really be free.[3] Moreover, for this to happen, Americans had to understand that there was a direct connection between foreign policy and their domestic well-being and that peace and prosperity did not depend only on reform at home but also on the international environment in which the United States existed.

Roosevelt's political ambitions took a big step when, at just thirty-one years old, he was named assistant secretary of the navy in 1913. The appointment was ideal for Roosevelt; it put him in Washington and gave him the opportunity to work with and impress the most powerful people in the Democratic Party while he built a national profile and reputation in a position he was well-qualified to hold. As Roosevelt reportedly said at the time of his appointment, "All my life I have loved ships and been a student of the Navy, and the Assistant Secretaryship is the one place, above all others, I would love to hold."[4] He gained invaluable experience and knowledge during his eight years in office, which included visits to the Panama Canal, to nations in the Caribbean, and to Europe during and immediately after the Great War, where he played a significant role in the mobilization of American forces and the successes of the navy against Germany. Moreover, Roosevelt came to understand the importance of public opinion in the making of foreign policy, and during this time he saw his various ideas about America and the world coalesce into a clear internationalist position while he maintained his understanding of the need for flexibility and patience in pursuing important goals.

In what was a minor speech in his first year as assistant secretary of the navy, about the long-forgotten Battle of Oswego during the French and Indian Wars, Roosevelt framed the event in a manner that revealed a great deal of his worldview and served as a prescient foreshadowing of the situation he would confront in the late 1930s. It was also one of his first articulations of his conception of American exceptionalism: the view that American society was distinct from and better than other nations; that freedom, liberty, and constitutional government had indeed created a New World, as compared to the corruption and persistent strife of the Old World in Europe; and that it was an obligation of the United States to use its favored position to lead. As Roosevelt recalled the battle, on the one side stood the French, rulers of a vast territory in North America, held together by an impressive organization of trading posts that gave them influence far beyond their numbers. What was hidden by their efficiency was that "they were the representatives of a tottering monarchy, a discredited form of government" that was staving off its eventual defeat from the "inevitable conflict between the past and the future." The French would score early victories due to the British Colonies' "lack of preparation for armed conflict," decentralized governance, and internal divisions. "At last, of course, the awakening came," Roosevelt surmised, "the giant child began at last to realize his strength. The Colonies exceeded New France in numbers, in wealth, in resources" and, once mobilized, prevailed. While they lacked unity, victory was possible because the British Colonies "were sound." The internal bickering and lack of preparation for war was overcome due to the "inherent soundness of the foundation." The people's ideals and democratic spirit "carried them to victory." The lesson for Roosevelt was clear. The United States had to be more aware of potential dangers and better able to respond to threats. "Conflict, like everything else in modern civilization, is so complicated that preparation is essential. That is why we have our navy, our army . . . and that is why some of us think ahead." The long-ago conflict between the British and French colonies, Roosevelt concluded, "cannot fail to inspire us to better things."[5]

Immediately upon taking his office, Roosevelt began advocating for a U.S. naval expansion to meet the nation's security demands. He did not present this concern as just the addition of ships to protect the coast. Rather, he cast the need as part of his view that national defense involved more than just preventing foreign troops from landing on American soil. It meant controlling the seas through defense in depth by confronting any enemy as far from the nation's shores as possible, protecting American access to markets, defending strategic points such as the Panama Canal, the Philippines, Hawaii, and other islands in the Pacific, and maintaining vital trade routes in the Atlantic and Pacific Oceans. National security meant security at home, defense of national interests abroad, and the development of an international environment conducive to American values and institutions.

In January 1915, Roosevelt set out a strategic vision based on his understanding of geography, the interconnectedness of the world, and the need to broaden the tenets of the Monroe Doctrine. "If we believe in the maintenance of the Monroe Doctrine," the assistant secretary of the navy declared, "America has very direct interests inside a line which I will draw very roughly." Using a large map and pencil, Roosevelt illustrated his point. "Starting up here at the North Pole . . . and coming on down through the . . . Atlantic Ocean . . . and around Cape Horn, and up this way around American Samoa, and then up here and around Guam . . . then around the Philippines, then up here past the Aleutian Islands and back to the Pole." As he concluded, "that is some territory" the navy had to defend. The best way to do so was for the navy "to meet the enemy with an overpowering force as far away from our coast as possible to prevent him from coming within striking distance." It had to be able to defend interests "that lie beyond the limits of the continental United States." Employing Mahan's most famous phrase, Roosevelt stated that this could only be properly achieved through "the control of the seas" and preparedness.[6]

When war broke out in Europe during the summer of 1914, Roosevelt immediately saw Germany as the clear enemy and a threat to American security, material interests, and political values. He wrote Eleanor Roosevelt on August 1 that the war in Europe would be "a complete smash up," and that "these are history-making days. It will be the greatest war in the world's history." It would inevitably impact the United States, and he was afraid that Secretary of the Navy Josephus Daniels and Secretary of State William Jennings Bryan had no conception of what was unfolding and what it would demand from the nation. Writing to his wife again the next day, FDR stated that he hoped England would quickly join with France to defeat Germany, but that he expected "a long drawn-out struggle." He was frustrated that people like Daniels and Bryan thought the United States, as a neutral, "can go about our business as usual." They did not understand the interconnectedness of the United States with Europe, the meaning of the disruption of trade, and the importance of a world system compatible to American interests. A German victory, although not a direct threat since it would not lead to an invasion of the east coast, would still hurt the security of the country by forcing it to operate in a world dominated by autocratic power and hostile governments. It was Roosevelt's job to begin naval preparations for what was to come.[7]

Preparedness would quickly become Roosevelt's central concern and a crucial part of his overall definition of national defense. While he soon concluded that the United States had to become a belligerent to ensure an Allied victory, FDR had to walk a fine line in which he publicly supported Wilson's policy of neutrality while he made the case for a larger navy to protect American security. He was frustrated by the lack of discussion within the administration on how to respond to German provocations, and by the fact that many of Wilson's advisors "prevent discussion of the future steps because it is a disagreeable subject." Moreover, he feared the president was not even talking to military officers. In December 1915, writing in the *Nation's Business*, Roosevelt defended increased military spending as "purely defensive" and necessary for the protection of the nation. The public needed to understand that naval defense meant being able to "control for defensive purposes those portions of the ocean in which a country is immediately interested" as well as trade routes and access to other parts of the world. The current naval expansion, he opined, was not as large as experts believed necessary, but was still a positive first step "in defining the true requirements of national safety."[8]

From Roosevelt's perspective, the purpose of the naval buildup was national security. "The broad idea of national defense is to protect not merely the continental interests of this nation, but all of its interests, wherever they may be, to keep our territory over the sea, to preserve our international policies and trade." Thus, he continued to push for a larger navy, even though the nation was neutral, to defend those interests. "An adequate navy is notice served by the United States upon the nations of the world that war shall never again be fought upon American soil." By fall 1916, Roosevelt was insisting to Secretary Daniels that "we've got to get into this war."[9]

As tensions grew between the United States and Germany, Roosevelt became more frustrated with Wilson's policy of neutrality. In the hope that he might prod the former history professor to bolder action he sent Wilson a gift on January 1, 1917: a memorandum that Secretary of State James Monroe had written to President James Madison over 100 years earlier in the midst of the War of 1812, which Roosevelt personally owned. What Monroe wrote in 1814 captured Roosevelt's own thoughts to a great extent even while it represented the past the assistant secretary of the navy sought to avoid. Roosevelt wrote to Wilson that the note was "in many ways so interestingly parallel to the events of the day" that he thought the president would want to have it. Monroe's central point was that "a war in Europe . . . has long been found to spread its calamities into the remotest regions. Even the U.S., just and pacific as their policy is, have not been able to avoid the alternative of either submitting to the most destructive and ignominious wrongs from European Belligerents, or of resisting them by an appeal to the sword." Submission, or neutrality, "too long protracted, would have no other effect than to encourage and accumulate aggressions, until they should become altogether intolerable" and made the ultimate fighting "more slow and difficult."[10] As the message suggested, there was little doubt that Wilson's assistant secretary of the navy sought to push him toward intervention on the side of the Allies.

After the German announcement of unrestricted submarine warfare, Roosevelt believed that war was inevitable. He asked Wilson in early March 1917 if he could bring the naval fleet home to be "fitted out for war" in preparation. The president turned down Roosevelt's request, stating "I cannot allow it." As the assistant secretary was leaving, Wilson called him back to explain his decision. "I don't want to do anything," the president said. "I do not want the United States to do anything in a military way, by way of war preparations, that would allow the definitive historian in later days . . . to say that the United States had committed an unfriendly act" toward Germany.[11]

The experiences of the war would bring some modifications to Roosevelt's views regarding the best use of the navy and military strategy. The battleship-based fleet, the centerpiece of Mahan's thinking, and the naval buildup Roosevelt had advocated, culminated in the Wilson administration's July 1916 Big Navy Act, which called for the rapid building of ten battleships and six battle cruisers. German submarine warfare and the devastating shipping losses in the Atlantic, however, forced a shift to the construction of more destroyers; a more flexible navy was required to meet a different threat than the one anticipated. Roosevelt was quick to see the implications of changes in technology and weapons, and what the consequences were for the navy. As he acknowledged as early as 1915 in an article, "The Future of the Submarine," he thought he "knew much about naval strategy and warfare. But I have come very quickly to realise [*sic*] that I did not."[12] He now understood the threat submarines posed to moving both supplies and troops to Europe and saw that success in combatting them would be a key to victory.

Once the United States entered the war, Roosevelt worked to ensure that the navy played a central role in the military victory. The German resumption of unlimited submarine warfare took a terrifying toll on Allied shipping and threatened to isolate American supplies and troops. Speaking in July 1917, Roosevelt told an audience in upstate New York that if the Germans kept up their current rate of sinking supply ships, the United States would be in the position of having trained an army that it could not get to France.[13] His fear prompted him to warn Wilson that the elimination of submarines "must of necessity be a vital factor in winning the war."[14] Given this, one of FDR's biggest achievements as assistant secretary of the navy was advocating for and implementing the North Sea Mine Barrage, a fence of over fifty-six thousand mines set across the North Sea designed to bottle up German submarines and isolate those that were already out in the ocean. It was implemented in 1918 with much greater success than thought possible by those who opposed Roosevelt's idea. In conjunction with the increasing supply of American destroyers, it allowed the United States and the United Kingdom to coordinate their efforts and ensure the continued flow of supplies and American troops from the fall of 1917 to the end of the war.

During the summer of 1918, Roosevelt traveled to Europe to coordinate naval strategy with the Allies, and he went to France to visit with American marines and witness the fighting firsthand. While there he viewed the devastation at Verdun, saw the massive cemeteries and destruction of the land, and came under fire from German artillery. He wrote of the "thousands and thousands of graves tightly packed together" so close to the front and of how "this earth has been churned by shells, and churned again" so that the "trench systems and forts and roads have been swallowed up in a brown chaos." Equally disturbing was the large number of casualties still being taken by Allied and American troops, the exhaustion of the people throughout France, and the struggle for survival. He had witnessed total war up close and the costs it exacted. These experiences would shape his immediate thinking about how to structure the peace agreements after the war so as to produce stability and create order in the postwar world. He knew these would have to go beyond mere military methods if they were to bring real peace and security.

After the Great War, Roosevelt set out the lessons he believed needed to be learned to properly guide American foreign policy. Most of these stemmed from his belief in American exceptionalism and would remain central to his thinking on foreign policy. The war cemented his conviction that the United States, as a global power, had to be a world leader. It had to rethink its conception of security to properly be a force for order and peace, and the best ways to accomplish this were by joining the League of Nations, working cooperatively and through collective security with other countries, and spreading democratic ideals and institutions.

As a central component of Roosevelt's postwar internationalism, he linked progressivism at home with support of the League of Nations and American world leadership, and he linked opposition to the League with reactionary domestic policies. Addressing the Democratic National Committee on May 25, 1919, he argued that the Republicans had lost "sight of the great ideals for which we have fought this war" and that they would abandon the task of peace with the job only half done. Since 1916, the Republicans had become the party "devoted to the policies of conservatism and reaction, to the principles of little Americanism and jingo bluff." For democracy to succeed and flourish, it must be, Roosevelt declared, a "progressive Democracy," guided by a sane liberalism of "common sense idealism, constructivism [and] progress." The Republicans' understanding of defense, security, and American interests was "self-seeking, narrow, material" and was stuck in the nineteenth century. The Democrats knew, in contrast, that progress at home was linked to peace and prosperity abroad and that those could only be assured through American world leadership.[15] Domestic affairs and international relations were inseparable. Concomitantly, support for self-determination, disarmament, and the peaceful resolution of disputes abroad would help promote the spread of democracy and American institutions and ideals, which would bring stability, order, and the emergence of governments conducive to a peaceful international system.

These points remained central to the vision of American foreign policy that FDR articulated over the next two years. For example, speaking in Worcester, Massachusetts, on June 25, 1919, the assistant secretary of the navy argued that while many were slow to see the need for the United States to enter "into the war for civilization" and the "duty we owe to other peoples and nations," it was becoming "clear as the sun that the United States would commit a grievous wrong to itself and to all mankind if it were even to attempt to go backwards towards an old Chinese wall policy of isolation." In the years ahead, there would be challenges to peace and world order, and "the United States cannot escape an important, perhaps, even a controlling voice."[16]

Nine days later in a Fourth of July oration in Syracuse, New York, Roosevelt invoked the necessity for the American way of progress, ingenuity, and ideals to guide international relations and bring about lasting peace. As was fitting for the occasion of his address, FDR proclaimed that the American "principles of the equal rights of men, of justice to the weak as well as the strong, of government by consent of the governed as set forth in our constitution are being recognized by all the great nations on earth as the most wonderful doctrine for the guidance of human conduct that has ever been devised." In the process, "the world today is remaking its old laws and revising its old treaties with our constitution as its text book. Since last Fourth of July the stars in our flag have shone with a brightness amid the darkness of foreign battlefields that no planet's ever equalled [*sic*]." The United States had demonstrated that its system worked better than any other and that it was able to create more wealth and power than all others through its innovations and industrial might; thus, all "boasting as to what we could do in war has ceased to be boasting and became a mere recital of deeds achieved."[17]

He used the examples of his own contribution of the deadly mine barrier in the North Sea and the incredible output of U.S. shipbuilding during the war as demonstrations of the type of American innovation and leadership that the world needed in order to maintain a real and lasting peace, as contrasted to what the British called "a patched-up peace."[18] He recalled that after being "told by experts of other nations" that a minefield in the sea was impossible, he then had watched it "stretch out, nevertheless, day by day, catching the enemy's barbarous boats from time to time in its fatal tentacles, until . . . it stretched in lines that almost met from shore to shore." Similarly, the navy, employing American ingenuity, had overcome "apparently insoluble problems of construction in one-third the time the most rash and optimistic expert allocated" to build ships and guns and have the "thrill of thankful and joyful relief as each convoy laden with troops passed safely through the harbor's mouth, thanks to the unwearying vigilance of our tireless gray destroyers."[19]

These ideas, more than the specifics of the Treaty of Versailles, led Roosevelt to support the League of Nations. He set out his fundamental position on the issue of the League in a July 18, 1919, speech in Poughkeepsie, New York. If the Senate refused to ratify the treaty it would be "throwing away the benefits of the war and of victory." Given the bitterness of the conflict, the millions of lives lost, and the damages inflicted, "the great surprise is that anything at all came out of the Paris conference," much less something as significant as the League of Nations, which provided mechanisms for discussion and arbitration of international conflicts, disarmament, and collective security for all nations against aggressors. In addition, if the United States failed to ratify the Treaty of Versailles and join the League, Roosevelt declared that he would be forced "as a matter of national protection" to recommend a new naval construction program over three years with a cost of at least $600,000,000. In the process, the United States would lose the "confidence of the nations of the world" and its position as a world leader. But if the League was adopted, "future generations will look to us and call us blessed" for the peace it would bring, and "we will have given the world something to stand beside the Magna Carta and the federal constitution."[20]

During the presidential campaign of 1920, Roosevelt consistently drew upon this framework, particularly emphasizing the uniqueness of the U.S. role in the world, the need for collective security, and the importance of accepting a new way of looking at the world and not wasting the victory achieved in 1918. In his formal acceptance of the Democratic Party's vice presidential nomination on August 9 at his home in Hyde Park, New York,

Roosevelt contrasted what he saw as the two different visions of how to ensure American security and its proper role in the world. Both were based on notions of American exceptionalism, yet each drew different conclusions from the unique nature of the American experience. One was a naïve, fortress approach where the American people "shut our eyes . . . close our ports, build an impregnable wall of costly armaments, and live, as the Orient used to live, a hermit nation" stuck in the past. This view saw Europe as unredeemable and America as best served by staying out of its affairs. The other looked to the future with open eyes, recognizing "that modern civilization has become so complex and the lives of civilized men so interwoven with the lives of other men in other countries as to make it impossible to be in the world and not of it." To that end, the Democrats offered a peace treaty that would allow the United States to take up its proper role in the world as a leader in the effort to make sure the Great War led to a real peace.[21]

On a campaign stop in Milwaukee, Wisconsin, on August 12, Roosevelt argued that a new theory of international law had emerged from the Great War. "The chief gain—I like to think—an even greater gain in the long run than the actual winning of the war, has been a complete change in the theory of international law." It was now clear that cooperation and collective security were necessary for peace and prosperity. While individual societies had banded together to protect themselves from the "gun-toter or the man who tries to control things by physical force," what FDR called the law of the community, the law of the individual state, pirates, and aggressors "could still carry on their nefarious business without calling down on themselves the wrath of the civilized world. Under the old theory of international law, it was presumed that when one nation attacked another the rule for all the other nations to follow was the rule of neutrality." That would change under the League of Nations: "The nation which plans to attack another can assume with fair probability that *all* the other nations will be against it—not neutral as in the old days." The international community would demand that the aggressor "shall *show cause* why it did not observe the law of nations, the law of decency, the law of the twentieth century."[22]

If this new international law had been in place, Roosevelt opined, Germany in 1914 would have "known beyond question" that if it attacked France and Belgium it "could not count upon such neutrality." All of the world would have united. "Who can doubt that such a clear front presented by the civilized world would not have caused the strongest power to hesitate?" The new international law would work, he declared, because "there can be no neutrality as between right and wrong!" Although the United States had tried to stay on the sidelines, hoping the war would have no impact and that it could conduct business as if nothing had changed, it finally realized its mistake. Under the League, "that sane commonsense" would have triumphed right away. No nation could expect victory against the united will of the rest of the world.[23]

For Roosevelt, the United States had nothing to fear from joining the League of Nations as it would enhance its security, peace, and world order, bring a reduction in arms, and allow all nations to peacefully progress and prosper. He linked the purposes of the League directly to his understanding of American exceptionalism. The American people had to realize that their ideals were universal and were at the center of the peaceful aims of the League, and that the United States was at its best and most successful when it was influencing world events. "The American flag," Roosevelt declared in September, "is a spirit, a thing intangible yet very real in the message it carries." Freedom, democracy, and progress were "not for the American people alone but for countless millions in every other part of the world. It has been an expression of the composite ideals and the great spiritual purposes of an unselfish nation." The American Revolution was about more than independence. "It was a successful attack on despotism; and it was followed by the establishment of a new but successful form of democratic-republican government." Since 1776, it had inspired other peoples to seek their own freedom, as demonstrated by those nations in Latin America who modeled their governments after Washington's.[24]

In all of its relations with the world since its independence, Roosevelt argued that the United States had stood for the doctrines of peace and freedom. He cast the Monroe Doctrine as an early internationalist policy of collective security to protect weaker nations from empires, as the "first expression of self-determination for nations, the first championing of new and relatively weak states against the power of imperialism and despotism." Europe was deterred from any action as it understood the United States was "doing more than just thinking of our own self-protection" when it came to international affairs. The same was true for the American defense of freedom of the seas. It "was not a policy of selfishness, but was of importance to all nations who used the ocean highways." The final example for Roosevelt was the war with Spain. He argued that the United States had fought to free Cuba and give it independence. Well before 1914, then, the American flag's "message continued to give hope to the downtrodden in other lands and to progressively minded people everywhere." All nations understood "that the American flag carried a new message of hope, that it represented a great people opposed to aggression and willing to change the existing conditions of mistrust and competitive armament."[25]

The Great War, therefore, was not fought just to defeat the Kaiser. Roosevelt saw it as a continuation of the fight for freedom at home that had marked the nation from its outset and an opportunity to create a new international system. Peace and security would not come from platitudes, mere goodwill, or the old diplomacy of balance of power. A new approach was necessary, one that would allow nations to act early and "would prevent the causes of trouble and not wait till trouble itself had come to a head." The people of Europe knew this could only come about with the United States in the lead just as they knew victory would finally come against the Central Powers with the arrival of the American flag.[26]

That promise, Roosevelt was sure, could only be kept if the United States joined the League. Victory had appeared to redeem the promise of the flag, that "the relations between nations was to be put on a new basis." As FDR saw it from his visits to Europe in 1918 and 1919, the ideals and values of the United States were "spreading through the world" and "we were proud that we could have the opportunity to point the way to world peace, not mere cessation of conflict but the peace of permanence." That was the hope of the world, that the United States could lift from future generations the horror of war. Europeans wanted the United States to join the League of Nations and to lead; "they ask that America help in the name of humanity. They ask that they be given again the inspiration of our flag." To not join the League, Roosevelt concluded, would be to forget the history of the nation and to reject its proper role in the world.[27]

Because of this, he was convinced that the world expected, and the United States had an obligation, to deliver something new in the wake of the carnage of the Great War, to provide "an agreement between nations which for the first time in history put international relations on the same scale and plane that the relations between individuals had been since the days of Christianity." Thus, the controversial Article X of the League Covenant, which guaranteed the territorial integrity of all nations, "is an extension of the Monroe Doctrine, the purpose is to prevent from happening again the thing which happened to Belgium in 1914," with this exception: instead of the United States standing alone as the guarantor against external aggression, it would be all nations. None of this, to Roosevelt, would "in any way weaken or lessen or change our rights under our Constitution or the rights of our Congress to declare war or to send our boys overseas," just as the Monroe Doctrine did not change any of that.[28]

It was time, Roosevelt concluded, for American leadership in the world to spread American ideals and create a new set of rules for international relations in the twentieth century. That was not idealism; it was a necessity for national security. It was inconceivable to FDR that anyone would want to return to the approaches and thinking that existed in 1914, "back to the days of armament and bloodshed of generation after generation." It was time to take a new step and for "the splendid force of America, the moral force of America, [to] restore this nation to the leadership of the world." The rest of the world was waiting. Roosevelt envisioned the United States as "the keystone of the arch" that would build a permanent peace. All the American public needed to make this happen was to have the same faith in America that had shaped its great history and placed it in the position to accept the role of world leadership that destiny had brought forward.[29]

The ticket of James Cox and Roosevelt was defeated decisively and the United States never joined the League. Still, his time as assistant secretary of the navy and as vice presidential candidate was crucial in shaping and sharpening Roosevelt's views on foreign policy and his internationalist ideas. The Great War had confirmed his view that the United States could not act unilaterally in the world, that its prosperity and protection were linked to Europe and Asia as well as the Western Hemisphere. Roosevelt, therefore, continued to support free trade, low tariffs, and the Open Door policy versus closed trading systems or nationalistic approaches. He understood more than he had in 1912 the weakness of relying on a policy of hemispheric defense, the need for collective security, and the correctness of his opposition to colonial empires. European imperialism was a source of instability, conflict, and rivalry in addition to being antiliberal and undemocratic. While he retained a paternalistic outlook toward Central America and the Caribbean during the 1920 campaign, famously stating that the United States was "the big brother to these little republics" and that he had written Haiti's constitution, FDR also believed that the United States had the right to declare to the world: "We are an unselfish nation, with a mission in the world. We care about the rights of the downtrodden people, we care about the rights of small nations that cannot defend themselves against aggression."[30] Roosevelt now linked progress and reform at home with his firm belief in American exceptionalism to form a progressive internationalism that understood the dangers of autocratic power and militarism and that sought to spread American ideals and democracy in the name of security as well as morality.

The aftermath of the Great War led to an inward turn by the United States as it sought, in the words of President Warren Harding, a return to normalcy. While it was not the time of isolationism that myth holds, the 1920s nonetheless witnessed a strong desire by many Americans to spurn international commitments and return to a reliance on neutrality for security. Along with the Senate's rejection of the Treaty of Versailles, a postwar Red Scare sought to purge America of foreign ideas and radical, un-American influences while continuing the wartime emphasis on one hundred percent Americanism. In 1924, Congress passed restrictive immigration laws that cut off the flow of people across the Atlantic; restrictions on Southern and Eastern European immigration were added to those already existing against the Chinese and Japanese. The coming of the Great Depression served to reinforce these nationalist trends as the 1930 Smoot–Hawley tariff restricted imports in an effort to protect American jobs. Few people were publicly advocating for a greater role by the United States in world affairs.

In the face of these political winds, Roosevelt never abandoned his fundamental internationalist perspective. Indeed, his sense of American exceptionalism was the source of his internationalism. He saw the failure to recognize that fundamental changes had occurred in the last part of the nineteenth century as the reason that others held onto a misunderstanding of America's interest and considered hemispheric defense the best means to peace, security, and prosperity. It would require patience and a different approach to achieve his goals. In 1921, he took a lead role in establishing the Woodrow Wilson Foundation, designed to honor the former president and promote his ideals, particularly in the area of foreign policy; and a few years later he chaired the committee that led to the establishment of the Walter Hines Paige School of International Relations at Johns Hopkins University.

Roosevelt was out of the public eye for over a year as he fought to regain the use of his legs after being stricken by polio in August 1921. He would never be able to walk again on his own without the use of leg braces and assistance from others. Still, FDR's irrepressible optimism and faith in God carried him through the struggle without complaints. While it is true he later told Frances Perkins that when he first became ill he was completely distraught and wondered why God had turned away from him, these thoughts quickly passed. In many ways, his true character was fully on display: his patience, strength, energy, ability to adjust and adapt, self-confidence, and belief that he was destined to do great things. Armed with these qualities, he gave no thought to abandoning his career as a politician, with his aim still on the White House.[31] With the assistance of his wife, Eleanor, and his closest aid Louis Howe, Roosevelt soon reengaged with Democratic Party politics; he made a stunning return at the 1924 Democratic Convention by walking to the podium to nominate New York Governor Al Smith.

As part of his return, Roosevelt wrote an article on American relations with Japan in 1923. In that same year he also produced an unpublished "Plan to Preserve World Peace." Combined with his 1926 address at Milton Academy and a 1928 article in the journal *Foreign Affairs*, these pieces provided the most extended expressions of his thinking on foreign policy before he became president. His essay, "Shall We Trust Japan?" indicated Roosevelt's willingness to go against conventional thinking while seeking to use negotiation and cooperation to overcome international conflict. His answer to his title's question was, in brief, yes; all of the factors that caused tensions between the two nations—China, trade, immigration, and naval competition—"have been removed" or were "on the road to eventual elimination." First and foremost, Japan had agreed to the Washington Naval Treaty and to the limitations on each nation's naval building to a strict ratio of tonnage on capital ships—5 for the United States and the United Kingdom and 3 for Japan—and the broader Washington System based on collective security. In the process, the United States recognized Japan's legitimate security concerns and need for markets and raw materials. As Roosevelt noted, these actions "involved some national sacrifice, of prestige, of political ambition, of dignity" on Japan's part. Tokyo was able to do so because the United States, while upholding the Open Door policy and its pledge to maintain Chinese territorial integrity, recognized "that there is a real necessity to Japan of the markets and raw products" of China. Thus, each nation found it could protect its interests through an international system of cooperation rather than conflict.[32]

These positive developments provided the basis for a change of attitude toward Japan and "a magnificent opportunity" for the United States to take a leadership role in fostering international cooperation. There was a great demand and "deep belief," Roosevelt claimed, "that we owe a little something to mankind as a whole, the demand for the quieting of the troubled waters" in the world. If nations went looking for offense from others it could be easily found. But improved relations with Tokyo demonstrated that Washington could use a different approach to secure each nation's interests. If the United States "in all good faith confidently expect from Japan cooperation in world upbuilding, we shall go far toward insuring peace."[33] This, if successful, would serve as a model for easing similar tensions elsewhere in the world.

As for Roosevelt's "Plan," it was drafted in response to a competition for a $100,000 American Peace Award for the best essay on how the United States could help maintain peace. It served as his first effort to rethink the shortcomings and problems of the League of Nations and to recast it to make U.S. involvement in such an organization politically possible. The key, for Roosevelt, was to find a way for the United States to be involved with an international organization committed to the maintenance of world peace. As he would note in 1925, "I don't care how many restrictions or qualifications" were placed on American participation. "I seek an end and do not care a rap about methods of procedure."[34] The purpose, he wrote, was not to meddle in the regional affairs of other nations or to "give to the representatives of other peoples the right to compel us to enter upon undertakings calling for or leading up to the use of armed forces without our full and free consent, given through our constitutional procedures." Still, it was vital that America participate in such an organization "in a serious and continuing effort to eliminate the causes of war." This was necessary and justified "by the record of our history, by our own best interests, and chiefly by our high purpose to help mankind to better things." His innovations were to imagine a "Society of Nations" with an executive committee of nations that had the great powers on it for renewable terms of ten years.[35] The idea would reemerge as the United Nations Security Council. Given the lack of originality and the impracticality of his ideas being implemented at the time, it is not surprising that Roosevelt shelved the piece.

While not a foreign policy address, Roosevelt's talk on May 18, 1926, at the dedication of the Alumni War Memorial at the Milton Academy, set out the link between his progressive view of history and the ultimate success of internationalism. Beginning with the question "Quo Vadis—Wither Bound?" Roosevelt expressed his characteristic optimism as he used St. Peter's famous question to Jesus, "Where are you going?" to challenge the students to lead. He invoked what he called the "laws of the history of progress" as "the truest value of the study of history." He opined that the only danger facing the nation was inaction, that it "may suffer from too long a period of the do-nothing or reactionary standards" of the Republican Party. That inaction would block the necessary period of "liberal or even radical" change necessary to move people forward toward greater prosperity and peace. The trends in all areas of life were moving to "the greater unification of mankind." Thus, the "isolation of individual nations will be as difficult in this future as would be the isolation of" individual American states from each other; as the laws of progress moved small communities into nations, "alliances between nations" become "a permanent congress of nations." Roosevelt declared that he saw "many rays of light in that future" and that the "true service" of America to mankind "will not come until all the world recognizes all the rest of the world as one big family."[36] In his first inaugural address as governor of New York, he made the same point, stating that "our civilization cannot endure unless we, as individuals, realize our personal responsibility to and dependence on the rest of the world."[37]

In 1928, FDR was tapped to provide the Democratic Party view on foreign policy in the journal *Foreign Affairs*. The thesis of his article was a familiar one from him, that the United States was an exceptional nation destined for world leadership. Given this, the spirit of America equaled internationalism. As Roosevelt noted in his first sentence, in the "century and a half of national life there have been outstanding periods when American leadership has influenced the thought and action of the civilized world towards international good will and peace." Unfortunately, he continued, there were rare periods, such as the past eight years under Republican rule, when American policy "has been negative and sterile" and brought opposition from the world. His article served as a critique of what he saw as a wrong interpretation of American exceptionalism that led to unilateralism, imperialism, and neutrality, and to policies based on the notion that the United States could secure its interests by acting alone.[38]

An examination of the Declaration of Independence and the Constitution, Roosevelt opined, clearly showed that the Founding Fathers wanted the United States to serve as an example to mankind, as it did for the new republics formed in Latin America. The Monroe Doctrine, while partially designed out of "self-protection," was also "influenced by an ideal" and had been promulgated to defend the right of self-determination and the spread of democratic government. Guided by this peaceful intent and desire to assist freedom, the United States adopted an anti-imperial position and "high moral purpose" in its international relations, as exemplified by the Open Door policy toward China and efforts to educate those who came under American tutelage, such as the Filipinos. This positive policy culminated in President Woodrow Wilson's October 1913 speech in Mobile, in which he promised that the United States would "never again seek one additional foot of territory by conquest" and would make sure that no "material interests [were] made superior to human liberty and national opportunity."[39]

Although the outbreak of the Great War had interrupted further development of these ideas in the Western Hemisphere, Roosevelt argued, it had also brought forth a new vision for the relationship among nations through a peace without victory where "through an association of nations the world could in the days to come avoid armed conflict and substitute reason and collective action for the age-old appeal to the sword." Beginning in 1919, the Republican Party rejected this view and turned the nation away from a positive policy, the only exception being the 1921–1922 Washington Naval Conference, which was abandoned once Secretary of State Charles Evans Hughes left office in 1925. Otherwise, the Republicans had made policy based on the "desirability of an isolated national existence or a national development heedless of the welfare, prosperity and peace of the other peoples of the world." Through action such as Secretary of State Frank Kellogg's efforts to outlaw war, an approach "that has failed for two thousand years," they were replacing deeds with mere words and cooperation with high tariffs and debt collection so that the United States could "eat our cake and have it too."[40]

Roosevelt saved his most scathing criticisms for the Republicans' policy toward the Americas, most notably the recent intervention into Nicaragua. In what Roosevelt characterized as a return to "Dollar Diplomacy," he argued that even if some U.S. interventions produce positive results, the republics in Latin America "disapprove our intervention almost unanimously." As a result of sending Marines to Managua, Washington "had fewer friends in the Western Hemisphere" than ever before and "has allowed dislike and mistrust . . . to grow into something like positive hate and fear." Foreshadowing his Good Neighbor Policy, and his repudiation of Theodore Roosevelt's Corollary to the Monroe Doctrine, FDR called for "new principles of a higher law, a newer and better standard in international relations" that would start in the

Americas and serve as an example for the world. It would be based on the respect of other nations' sovereignty and the recognition of the interdependence of nations for their prosperity, peace, and security. It could still happen, Roosevelt noted, that a sister republic might "fall upon evil days; disorder and bad government" might require temporary assistance to return stability and order. Still, it was not the role of Washington to unilaterally intervene. Rather, it was the "duty of the United States to associate itself with other American Republics" in order to analyze the situation and decide upon the best course of action and assistance. "Single-handed intervention by us in the internal affairs of other nations must end; with the cooperation of others we shall have more order in this hemisphere and less dislike."[41]

Roosevelt ended his piece with the declaration that it was time to end the negative interregnum and time for the United States to return to a role of leading the world to "better international understanding and the peaceful settlement of disagreements." With the right leadership, "or more truly, if the spirit behind it is great—the United States can regain the world's trust and friendship and become again of service"; it could reduce the threat of war, promote prosperity, and "for all time renounce the practice of arbitrary intervention in the home affairs of our neighbors." International cooperation, anti-imperialism, and collective security were the cornerstones of Roosevelt's internationalism and represented, he believed, the proper spirit of America.[42]

Due to the Great Depression, foreign policy was not an important issue during the 1932 presidential campaign, and Roosevelt only addressed it once as the primary focus in a speech to the New York Grange on February 2, 1932. His talk that day has drawn attention because he backed away from his endorsement of the United States joining the League of Nations. He recalled his support twelve years earlier as a means to avoid another world war and declared that "for that course I have no apology to make." If the purpose of the League was still the prevention of war and "settlement of international difficulties in accordance with fundamental American ideals," Roosevelt would seek membership. But as it currently existed, Roosevelt argued, the League of Nations envisioned by Wilson to preserve world peace had become a place to resolve "strictly European political national difficulties," and those were issues in which the United States should not play a role.[43]

Throughout the campaign, Roosevelt did emphasize one point related to foreign policy: the necessity of balance in order to redress the problems in

America, restore prosperity, and maintain a healthy society. It is often overlooked that in his speech to the New York Grange, Roosevelt brought up the subject of the League in a discussion of the need for greater markets for American goods. The key problem was that the Smoot–Hawley tariff made it impossible for European, Latin American, or Asian nations to sell their products in the United States and acquire the gold necessary to buy American-made agricultural or manufactured goods. This law, and similar actions taken by other nations to protect their home markets, had created artificial barriers and imbalance in world commerce. Roosevelt argued that it was time "to use a little horse sense" and work out better arrangements with other nations through tariff revisions, reciprocal trade agreements, and a return to the Open Door. "I have good reason to believe that many nations who, like us, are suffering from stoppage of industry, will meet us half way and put all the cards on the table for the purpose of breaking an actual deadlock which has paralyzed world trade and thrown millions here and abroad out of useful work."[44]

When Roosevelt discussed the need for balance, he was not referring to the concept of the balance of power internationally. With the Great War as only the most recent example, Roosevelt rejected that idea as the way to peace. Rather, he was concerned with the imbalances of economic and political power, how they led to the current world crisis, and what type of balance was needed to successfully address it. As he said to the New York Grange, it was the duty of the federal government through the "regulation of inter-state commerce and by working out a sound policy" to restore balance in the economy and ease international tensions to peacefully redress grievances. Balance in domestic and foreign affairs, and the interdependence of the two, was the only way to peace and prosperity.[45]

As his New York Grange speech indicated, an emphasis on balance would be central to Roosevelt's 1932 campaign for the presidency and his belief in the interdependence of domestic and international affairs. Facing the crisis of the Great Depression, Roosevelt sought a rebalancing of power within American society. He presented these ideas most explicitly in his September 23, 1932, speech to the Commonwealth Club of San Francisco. Displaying his usual optimism about America, Roosevelt set out his understanding of "some of the relationships of government and economic life" that would determine the future prosperity and security of the nation. At the center of the nation's history, Roosevelt declared, from the time of the American

Revolution forward, "people sought a balancing—a limiting force" on arbitrary power through the government. This was done "not to destroy individualism but to protect it." Roosevelt invoked Frederick Jackson Turner's frontier thesis to explain American economic growth and freedom, with the safety valve of the West providing "a haven for men to whom the East did not provide a place."[46]

The Industrial Revolution brought an end to this period of American life in the latter part of the nineteenth century and, by the beginning of the twentieth century, had ushered in a period of imbalance. "The history of the last half century," Roosevelt declared, "is accordingly in large measure a history of a group of financial Titans, whose methods were not scrutinized with too much care" as long as they produced economic growth and new goods; they were aided by the federal government, which provided protective tariffs and subsidized railroads and other industries, but did not allow equal opportunity for farmers, labor, or the middle class. Theodore Roosevelt, FDR argued, was the first progressive to see the problems caused by the "malefactors of great wealth"; he sought to break up the concentrations of power and, along with Woodrow Wilson, provided some regulation of the economic system. This approach, although laudable, offered limited success because it did not fully recognize the nature of the economy or place the government in the role of the broker state with the "duty to protect the rights of personal freedom and private property of all its citizens."[47]

Roosevelt was confident the nation could meet the challenges of the day. That was the duty of the government: "to enter and protect the public interest" with "such assistance and balance as government can give." This demanded new approaches to domestic and foreign policy so as to create a system that would prevent future speculative booms and major depressions. "Faith in America, faith in our tradition of personal responsibility, faith in our institutions, faith in ourselves demands that we recognize the new terms of the old social contract," Roosevelt concluded. "We shall fulfill them, as we fulfilled the obligation of the apparent Utopia which Jefferson imagined for us in 1776, and which Jefferson, Roosevelt and Wilson sought to bring to realization. We must do so, lest a rising tide of misery engendered by our common failure, engulf us all. But failure is not an American habit; and in the strength of great hope we must all shoulder our common load."[48] As his San Francisco address demonstrated, FDR took ideas seriously, which is why he consulted so often with intellectuals and created his so-called Brain Trust.

Roosevelt referred to it as his Privy Council, and noted that while he did not have a Brain Trust, he "trusted in brains."[49]

When Roosevelt was elected president in November 1932, the nation and the world were in a state of crisis. On all fronts, the new president faced difficult, complex problems that would test all of his skill and optimism as he faced the dual crises of the Great Depression and renewed aggression abroad. In January 1933, Adolf Hitler came to power in Germany, presenting a direct challenge to the Versailles order and peace in Europe. Simultaneously, the political left was growing stronger in parts of Europe as many questioned the ability of capitalism and liberal democracy to provide a solution to the economic problems. In East Asia, Japan had conquered Manchuria, bringing an end to the Washington System and an end to cooperation between Japan and the other powers. FDR knew that many Americans blamed a lot of the nation's problems on Europe and on American participation in World War I; disillusioned with Versailles, their neutralist sentiment hardened into a determination to avoid any involvement with issues outside of the Western Hemisphere. While Roosevelt, too, wanted to concentrate on problems at home and on domestic reform, he knew the two crises were interrelated and that the United States could not achieve a complete economic recovery, prosperity, and peace without also addressing the problems of the international system. Guided by his internationalist assumptions about the United States and the world, in his first term in office Roosevelt sought avenues to increase U.S. participation in world affairs so as to begin to shape an international environment that would aid the recovery from the Great Depression and provide security for the nation.

2

Constructing an Internationalist Framework, 1933–1936

Few presidents have entered the office in more difficult circumstances than Franklin D. Roosevelt. Abraham Lincoln faced the looming prospect of the Civil War, and George Washington the doubts about the new federal government. One might add Thomas Jefferson and the question as to whether or not the transfer of power between parties would succeed peacefully. The months between the election in November 1932 and inauguration in March 1933 seemed interminable as the economic institutions and social fabric of the nation appeared to be unraveling. Unemployment, bank failures, breadlines, business closings, plummeting agricultural prices, and foreclosures provided the backdrop for Roosevelt's inaugural speech. The depth of the crisis even dented FDR's confidence. On election night, he told his son James, "I'm just afraid I may not have the strength to do this job. After you leave me tonight, Jimmy, I am going to pray that God will help me, that he will give me the strength and the guidance to do this job and to do it right. I hope that you will pray for me, too, Jimmy."[1]

Yet, not even the weight of the Great Depression could deflate Franklin Roosevelt's optimism for long. In his inaugural address on March 4, 1933, he sought to buoy the nation's spirits and change its course by the force of his temperament. Noting the conditions of the country, Roosevelt declared, "This great Nation will endure as it has endured, will revive and will prosper. So, first of all, let me assert my firm belief that the only thing we have to fear is fear itself—nameless, unreasoning, unjustified terror which paralyzes needed efforts to convert retreat into advance." He promised "vigorous action" to put people to work, redress the imbalances in society, regulate and reform the banking system, and raise the value of agricultural goods.[2]

Little attention was given to international affairs. While Roosevelt was concerned by Adolf Hitler coming to power less than two months earlier and Japan's conquest of Manchuria, his attention was by necessity devoted to launching his New Deal program and restoring the American people's confidence and faith in their institutions to solve the nation's economic problems. The president knew that foreign relations could not be ignored, and that long-term prosperity could only be secured in a peaceful world. But his internationalist beliefs were often muted, if not at times compromised, in his first term in office. For example, in his inaugural address he acknowledged that international trade was important, but a secondary concern at the moment. "I shall spare no effort to restore world trade by international economic adjustment," the president declared, "but the emergency at home cannot wait on that accomplishment."[3]

The brief exception in the speech was FDR's specific mention of the Good Neighbor Policy. Commonly understood, and initially implemented, as a new direction for United States policy toward Latin America, Roosevelt cast the concept in global terms. "In the field of world policy I would dedicate this Nation to the policy of the good neighbor—the neighbor who resolutely respects himself and, because he does so, respects the rights of others—the neighbor who respects his obligations and respects the sanctity of his agreements in and with a world of neighbors."[4] In implementing the Good Neighbor Policy, Roosevelt was able to make concrete in the Western Hemisphere his principal conceptions about international relations that would guide American foreign policy through World War II. The president could take the initiative in Latin America without incurring domestic opposition because it was understood as part of America's sphere of influence under the Monroe Doctrine. In doing so, he began to construct a framework of his internationalist vision of national security and America's proper role in the world.

The effort to build a multilateral, cooperative world order that was centered on mutual respect and collective security would be challenged by the emerging political and military threats in Europe and Asia. Roosevelt was well aware of the political restraints on his ability to address the threats from Germany and Japan; therefore, he sought to protect American interests abroad short of direct political involvement outside the Western Hemisphere.

He was unwilling in his first term to raise controversial foreign policy issues and risk incurring the wrath of the proponents of neutrality and nonintervention while he pursued his New Deal initiatives at home. Moreover, while Roosevelt found the Nazi regime repugnant, he thought it was possible to negotiate with Germany, as with other nation states, to reach mutually beneficial agreements. Thus, while he believed the United States should play a leadership role globally to promote peace, prosperity, and liberal values, Roosevelt's initial response to the crises across the Atlantic and Pacific Oceans was to build on traditional approaches, to use trade and economic means to influence events in Europe, and to seek ways to support China in an effort to deter any further Japanese aggression in East Asia.

After his election, Roosevelt avoided President Herbert Hoover's efforts to tie him to the Republican Party's policies in Europe or to agreements about any commissions on war debts or disarmament. He sought to maintain his independence to act and freedom to shift course. Hoover's first request that the president-elect endorse his policies, in a November meeting between the two men, went poorly when Roosevelt refused to promise his support for any actions Hoover might take on war debts. A second attempt by Hoover in December failed to result in even a meeting. Roosevelt took the position that it was the responsibility of those in office to conduct policy. Still, he did not want to shut the door completely to talking with the Hoover administration, and he needed to learn firsthand the status on many issues. Roosevelt, therefore, reached out in late December 1932 to Secretary of State Henry L. Stimson. Remarkably, given the close ties of both of these New Yorkers to Theodore Roosevelt, this meeting, on January 9, 1933, in Hyde Park, was their first. While FDR's one session with Hoover had been tense, the meeting with Stimson was cordial, cooperative, and productive. Talking for six hours, the two men covered the state of the world and American policy and found themselves in substantive agreement on many points.

On Europe, Roosevelt remained circumspect in terms of how he would address its economic problems, war debts, and the ongoing disarmament talks; and he continued to refuse to commit to any course of action the Hoover administration might take. Roosevelt understood the importance of Europe and international trade to the United States, and shared the goal of further arms reductions. He saw the destabilizing impact of remilitarization, but he did not agree with the actions Hoover proposed and saw no short-term fix to the problem that would foster a permanent resolution of the issues. In effect, Roosevelt did not see that applying patches to the existing arrangements would cure the economic problems that beset Europe and wanted to start with a new approach and a comprehensive solution.

Concerning East Asia and Latin America, Roosevelt was more forthcoming and noted his agreement with the policies Stimson had orchestrated. Regarding Japan, the two men discussed ways to protect China and dissuade Japanese leaders from further aggression without causing direct conflict with Tokyo. He told Stimson he "fully approved" of his actions regarding the Manchurian crisis; and, right after their meeting, he publicly endorsed the Stimson Doctrine and the nonrecognition of Japan's control of that Chinese province. Roosevelt also concurred with Stimson's initiative of repudiating the Roosevelt Corollary to the Monroe Doctrine and efforts to remove American forces from Latin American nations in order to reduce tensions and provide for greater cooperation. Stimson's views were directly in line with what Roosevelt and Sumner Welles, an old friend of the president, had been discussing since the mid-1920s and during the 1932 campaign. The Democratic Roosevelt would build upon these actions through the Good Neighbor Policy.[5]

In his policy toward Latin America, FDR took his first bold steps in the area of foreign policy. The Good Neighbor Policy set out to reshape U.S. relations with its hemispheric neighbors and, just as importantly for the president, served as a model and template for thinking about how to resolve international problems. In the implementation of the Good Neighbor Policy, Roosevelt reconceptualized the fundamental assumptions of American foreign policy and national security; he saw this as a way to begin the "education" of the public about the proper role of the United States in the world and how to confront potential threats to the United States and other democracies. Nonintervention in Latin America, Pan-American cooperation, and the promotion of democracy did not directly challenge neutrality, yet these policies provided a concrete manifestation of international cooperation, nonintervention, working through multilateral institutions, and collective security. Roosevelt saw the Good Neighbor Policy not as a defensive posture that relied on the two oceans and neutrality to keep the United States safe, but as the proper understanding of the Monroe Doctrine, in which Washington promoted its values and institutions to proactively shape the world. Neutrality was not only a poor strategy of defense, in Roosevelt's view, it was also an abdication of America's responsibility as a great nation. Because Roosevelt linked the Good Neighbor Policy to the Monroe Doctrine, it remained politically acceptable when it was announced in 1933 and gave him a free hand to shape the policy as he desired.

Because Latin America represented the one area of the world where the United States had extensive political and economic involvement, and where Washington exercised a dominant influence, FDR saw it as the best area for him to start changing the narrative about national security, to work out key concepts, and to put in place the structures of an internationalist foreign policy. The Monroe Doctrine, according to American officials, had created a "special relationship" between the United States and Latin America, and it was seen, as Henry L. Stimson explained in 1931, as the area of the world "most vital to our national safety, not to mention our prosperity."[6] The defeat of Spain in 1898 led to the taking of Puerto Rico and the establishment of a protectorate over Cuba through the Platt Amendment, which allowed for American intervention in Cuban affairs. In the next decade, Theodore Roosevelt secured American control over the Panama Canal Zone and issued the Roosevelt Corollary to the Monroe Doctrine, which declared that the United States had the right to intervene in the nations of Latin America if instability in the region threatened order and American interests, or if the nations to the south failed to meet their international obligations. This exercising of an international police power, as the Republican Roosevelt phrased it, soon led to the dispatch of American forces at different times over the next three decades to Cuba, the Dominican Republic, Haiti, Honduras, Mexico, and Nicaragua and to the establishment of financial protectorates over Cuba, the Dominican Republic, and Haiti.

Recognizing that American actions had aroused more anger than support, Stimson, upon becoming Secretary of State in 1929, sought to bring an end to all U.S. military interventions in Latin America by starting the process of removing the remaining American forces in the region. In December 1928, Undersecretary of State J. Reuben Clark, a prominent international lawyer, sent Secretary of State Kellogg a lengthy memorandum that analyzed the Roosevelt Corollary and concluded that it was a misapplication of the Monroe Doctrine. In early 1930, Stimson published the Clark Memorandum, officially repudiating the Roosevelt Corollary. Although the rejection of Theodore Roosevelt's claim did not completely disavow intervention, it removed the Monroe Doctrine as a justification for it and set the groundwork for the Good Neighbor Policy.

Since his time in the Wilson administration, FDR had modified his position on American policy and desired to see an end to American military intervention in Latin America. In developing what would become the Good Neighbor Policy, Roosevelt worked with Sumner Welles, who would oversee the policy's execution, first as ambassador to Cuba and then as undersecretary of state. Welles had experience in the State Department working in Latin America and, having written a two-volume study of the Dominican Republic during the 1920s, was considered a leading expert on the region. Similar to Roosevelt, he opposed continued U.S. intervention in the Caribbean because it created instability and resentment rather than order. For both men, a new approach to American policy beyond the use of American forces was necessary to eliminate the problems of the area before revolts broke out. The Good Neighbor Policy would treat Latin American countries as sovereign, independent states and would strive to prevent the rise of the conditions that produced revolutions.

In January 1928, Roosevelt suggested to Welles that it would be desirable for the United States, whenever it felt compelled to intervene in the Caribbean, to instead consult with representatives from other Latin American republics. The two men agreed it was imperative that the American people understand that the economic and political interests of the United States and the other nations in the hemisphere "*are inextricably joined* one to the other," rather than continuing to accept the "*delusion* that *we can safeguard our own commercial interests without regard for the economic interests of our neighbors* and at the same time maintain the political friendship" of those nations. If this vision of a Pan-American union was adopted by the United States and recognized by the nations of Latin America as a new policy of cooperation rather than American intervention, it would serve to remove, as Welles stated, "the major portion of the grounds for *suspicion* of the United States which at present exist."[7]

These steps, however, were only remedial measures to end intervention for the purpose of enforcing order. The same efforts at cooperation were even more important to prevent the rise of conditions that led to instability, disorder, and revolution. Prior American policy had been to allow crises to develop and then respond with coercion when a civil war broke out. Both Roosevelt and Welles were convinced that the United States needed to use its power, prestige, and financial resources to help promote prosperity and order and cooperative relations to remedy the conditions that bred unrest. To end the cycle of intervention, there was a need for cooperative diplomacy and for assistance that proactively addressed problems and was based on an understanding that long-term United States interests were best served by promoting economic and political self-determination abroad, rather than consistently resorting to force.

Roosevelt and Welles also concluded that U.S. policy toward Latin America must change in order to challenge neutralist sentiment among the American people and the outdated reliance upon hemispheric defense. Unless the United States adopted a new approach, it could not, in Welles's words, "maintain itself as the greatest force in the world of the future, spiritually and materially." It was imperative that Washington recognize that American policy in the Caribbean Basin "is a record of disaster" that "has resulted in the arousing of well justified apprehensions, suspicions and fear and bitter animosity against the United States throughout all of Latin America." A new policy had to be based on the assurances to all that the United States claimed no greater privileges than any other nation and "possesses no right of intervention in the internal affairs of any other state."[8]

As the keystone of American foreign policy, Washington had to align the national interests of the United States with those of the republics of Latin America while eliminating the obstacles to trade and respecting the rights of every nation's sovereignty. The removal of valid grounds for resentment would allow the United States to gain the confidence and goodwill of the people and leaders of Latin America. Security depended on the "good will of the republics adjacent to the Canal" and the key shipping lanes for the protection of the Panama Canal and the movement of the navy to protect both coasts. In addition, the new policy would lead to the improvement of trade and commerce and would allow the United States to acquire and move goods in time of war. As Welles summarized it, American policy toward Latin America had to acknowledge "the absolute equality in sovereignty of the Latin American nations with ourselves" and also "our own need, politically and commercially, for their support and for their loyal friendship."[9] For his part, Roosevelt stated that the "single-handed intervention by us in the internal affairs of other nations must end; with the cooperation of others we shall have more order in this Hemisphere and less dislike."[10]

With Welles's assistance, these views became part of Roosevelt's campaign in 1932. The Democratic Party platform called for greater cooperation among the American republics and an end of the use of American troops to resolve problems. In particular, while the Democrats affirmed their support of the Monroe Doctrine, "it *will never be interpreted* by this Government as a privilege which it has assumed in order *to interfere* at will in the domestic concerns of the Latin American States."[11]

For Roosevelt, it was now a cardinal principle that the United States had to develop closer relations with the countries of Latin America for both political and commercial reasons, that it had to renounce any use of troops to impose its will, and that tariffs had to be reduced to provide for a greater interchange between North and South America. The system that was developed was certainly not ideal and Roosevelt was forced to make compromises along the way. Most notably, nonintervention did not bring an end to U.S. support for authoritarian regimes that cooperated with Washington, and many dictators quickly learned that working with the Roosevelt administration on security was a means to avoid criticism. The Good Neighbor Policy, nonetheless, provided the starting point for a redirection of American foreign policy toward internationalism.[12]

Roosevelt used his Pan-American Day speech on April 12, 1933, to further develop his thoughts. The Monroe Doctrine, Roosevelt declared, would remain a fundamental tenet of American foreign policy to help provide unity and security for all the nations in Latin America, but it would no longer serve as a justification for interference in any country's domestic affairs. As the president stated, the purpose of the Monroe Doctrine, what he termed "this Pan American doctrine of self-defense," was "directed at the maintenance of independence" of all the nations in the Western Hemisphere. Given the common history and ideals of the twenty-one American republics, Roosevelt believed that each one "must recognize the independence of every other Republic." The well-being of each nation depended on the security and prosperity of the others, and that was the foundation for the Good Neighbor Policy. "Your Americanism and mine," Roosevelt asserted, "must be a structure built of confidence, cemented by sympathy which recognizes only equality and fraternity"; mutual responsibilities, understanding, and obligations were the essential qualities "which constitute a good neighbor."[13] For Roosevelt, all of this, of course, served the interest of the United States, but its importance extended even further. He believed that establishing the Good Neighbor Policy toward Latin America would provide the basis and example for American leadership beyond the Western Hemisphere. It was a crucial starting point in his effort to redefine national security and search for peace through a new international system.

The Good Neighbor Policy was quickly tested in Cuba, where unrest grew throughout 1933. Since 1903, when the Platt Amendment was adopted, the United States had intervened consistently at such moments, sending troops to Cuba four different times over the previous three decades. Events in Havana appeared to invite a fifth round of intervention by American forces to quell the unrest, protect American investments and property, and ensure American control of the key sea lanes to the Panama Canal through its naval base at Guantanamo. Between August 1933, when General Gerald Machado lost power, and January 1934, when Fulgencio Batista installed a government with Washington's support, Cuba had five different presidents in as many months. Having announced the Good Neighbor Policy, Roosevelt could not resort to a military mission. He was determined to demonstrate that his new policy could work to secure American interests, stability, and cooperation with other Latin Americans nations by following a different course of action.

When Welles arrived in Havana he had to find a way to restore stability without resorting to the threat of American intervention. The initial approach to the problem was to negotiate a new trade agreement between the United States and Cuba, on the assumption that an economic revival would bring political stability, quiet the unrest, and serve as a model for the Good Neighbor Policy. After a week in Cuba, Welles was optimistic that both a political agreement among Cuban factions and an economic agreement between Havana and Washington could be reached that would stabilize Cuba and protect American interests. In support of Welles's mediation efforts, and the first formal meeting between Machado's government and opposition parties on July 1, 1933, Roosevelt sent a message expressing his satisfaction that the Cubans were seeking a peaceful solution to their problems.[14] Both the president and the ambassador, however, underestimated the extent of opposition to Machado's continued rule and found it impossible to stem the tide demanding the general's removal. Welles pressured Machado to carry out reforms, but this just aided the opposition and furthered the political stalemate that developed. Although the ambassador reluctantly decided that Machado had to be removed, he faced the problem of how to do this without it appearing to be just another case of American intervention.

On August 4, a general strike spread across Cuba and effectively brought an end to Machado's rule. Welles informed Machado that to salvage the situation short of a revolution he would have to resign. The new government of

Carlos Manuel de Cespedes provided no resolution to the problems as he lacked support from any important groups. After less than a month in office, he was overthrown in September by the "Sergeants Revolution," which installed Professor Ramon Grau San Martin, a leading reformer. Grau, under the slogan "Cuba for Cubans," promised to unilaterally eliminate the Platt Amendment, suspend payments on loans to the United States, and nationalize parts of the sugar industry. In the midst of this upheaval, Washington dispatched twelve ships to the Cuban coast as a precaution to safeguard American citizens, "pending the restoration of normal conditions" by the Cuban government. At the same time, Roosevelt made it clear that there "was no possible question of intervention or of the slightest interference with the internal affairs of Cuba," and that "strict instructions accordingly" were given to the commanders of each vessel.[15]

Having lost control over the situation, Welles now sought pressure from Washington against Grau, and requested that the president withhold recognition of his government. Roosevelt and Secretary of State Cordell Hull agreed to nonrecognition, and, for his part, Welles turned to Fulgencio Batista, a sergeant in the army, encouraging him to oust Grau and restore good relations with the United States. To justify the nonrecognition of Grau's regime, Roosevelt stated that, while Welles's conferences with Cuban leaders had led to some progress, including the release of political prisoners and the end of the censorship of the press, the general strike had pitched the nation into chaos with renewed repression and bloodshed. Roosevelt did not see U.S. support of the Grau government as "a policy of friendship" because it would provide legitimacy to a government that lacked "the support and approval of the people of that Republic." The efforts of Ambassador Welles to negotiate a political settlement and a trade treaty were "by deed," Roosevelt stated, "our intention of playing the part of a good neighbor to the Cuban people," but no progress could be made until there was a government that had popular support and that could maintain order.[16]

Welles returned to Washington in December to take up his position as assistant secretary of state. The turmoil in Cuba was still unresolved, but Washington's refusal to work with Grau had the impact Welles sought. On January 13, 1934, Batista deposed Grau and two days later established Carlos Mendieta as president of Cuba. The United States quickly recognized the new government in Havana. With relations restored, the Roosevelt administration signed a new treaty with Cuba that abrogated the Platt Amendment.

Washington made a new commercial agreement with the Mendieta government that increased Cuba's sugar quota and extended loans to the island and, in August, signed the first Reciprocal Trade Agreement with Havana. Reviewing the recent history of relations, Roosevelt stated that the abandonment of the Platt Amendment "not only strengthened the friendship between Cuba and the United States, but very materially increased the good-will and confidence with which we are regarded by all the other American Republics" and provided "definite proof that the United States was opposed to any further armed intervention in the American countries."[17]

The goodwill gained by the Good Neighbor approach was evident at the meeting of the Pan-American Union in December 1933. Secretary of State Hull led the American delegation to the Seventh International Conference of American States in Montevideo, Uruguay. Unlike American officials at previous meetings, Hull did not have to defend any unpopular policies or actions by the United States. Rather, the United States took the lead in setting the agenda. The secretary of state sought the endorsement of the concept of bilateral reciprocity trade agreements to lower tariffs to bring down trade barriers in the hemisphere based on mutual concessions by all nations. The proposal was adopted amidst an atmosphere of cooperation and friendship, including a pledge by all nations to respect the sovereignty of all the other republics. Upon its conclusion on December 26, Leo S. Rowe, the director general of the Pan-American Union, wrote to Roosevelt that the meeting closed with clear accomplishments to its credit. Although the agreements reached on trade were important, the "outstanding characteristic of the Conference has been the far reaching influence of your declaration of Latin American policy" that garnered the goodwill, confidence, and cooperative spirit of all the other delegations.[18]

Building on these achievements, Roosevelt formally set out the Good Neighbor Policy on December 28, 1933, in an address before the Woodrow Wilson Foundation. He renounced the policy of unilateral United States intervention, declaring that the "definitive policy of the United States from now on is one opposed to armed intervention." He went further and rejected the basis of the Roosevelt Corollary to the Monroe Doctrine when he stated that the "maintenance of constitutional government in other nations is not a sacred obligation devolving upon the United States alone." If there was a failure in orderly processes in a nation that had an impact on others, then it "becomes the joint concern of a whole continent in which we are all neighbors." It was exactly "the comprehension of that doctrine . . . that has made the conference now concluding its labors in Montevideo such a splendid success."[19]

The new policy remained within the framework of hemispheric defense, but the president was looking beyond that toward the rest of the world. Unfortunately, Roosevelt noted growing tension in Europe and Asia, where peace was threatened by leaders who sought territorial expansion. "The superficial observer," the president opined, sees this development stemming from "the growth of the spirit of nationalism." That, however, obscured the real problem. "The danger to world peace lies not in the world population but in the political leaders" of the aggressor nations. A new approach to international threats was needed to counter these challenges to the community of nations. Roosevelt asserted, "I express the views of my countrymen when I state that the old policies, the old alliances, the old combinations and balances of power have proved themselves inadequate for the preservation of world peace." While the United States was not a member of the League of Nations, and Roosevelt made it clear he did not contemplate joining, the United States would work with the League when possible to foster peace. In that spirit, FDR called for a renewal of Woodrow Wilson's quest for a reduction of armaments, nonaggression agreements, and, most importantly, collective security, which the president believed ninety percent of the world's people wanted. "If that other 10 percent . . . can be persuaded . . . to do their own thinking and not be led, we shall have practical peace, permanent peace, real peace throughout the world." This was the course that the United States was setting for the Western Hemisphere and, he was convinced, was the only path to a lasting peace.[20]

In a series of Inter-American conferences, the United States promoted the idea of hemispheric solidarity in the face of the growing crises in Europe and Asia. On January 30, 1936, Roosevelt invited all the nations of the Western Hemisphere to an extraordinary conference in December to "determine how the maintenance of peace among the American Republics can best be safeguarded." The goal was twofold: to codify the basic assumptions of the Good Neighbor Policy and to "advance the cause of world peace, inasmuch as the agreements which might be reached would supplement and reinforce the efforts of the League of Nations" and provide a model for all future efforts "seeking to prevent war." The reason Roosevelt held the conference, he recalled two years later, was that "all of us had been watching with apprehension the recent events in world affairs beyond the sea": violation of treaties, aggression, rearmament and preparations for war, nationalist economic policies, and "the breakdown of democratic institutions." It was imperative to keep this type of discord out of the Western Hemisphere while finding ways toward peace in such stormy waters.[21]

Demonstrating the significance he attached to these efforts, President Roosevelt traveled on the USS *Indianapolis* to visit Brazil and Uruguay and to be present for the opening ceremonies of the Inter-American Conference for the Maintenance of Peace on December 1, 1936, in Argentina. Speaking in Rio de Janeiro on his way to the conference, FDR warned that the cost of war was more than human life and that the stakes went beyond territorial security. War "destroys as well the ideals of individual liberty and of the democratic form of representative government." The contrast between the situation in the Western Hemisphere and the rest of the world was stark. Across both oceans was "a grim picture of armed camps and threats of conflict." Therefore, it was not enough that peace currently prevailed among the American republics. It was "essential that this condition be made permanent" and that "all instrumentalities for the maintenance of peace must be consolidated and reinforced" so as to ensure peace for future generations, and to "present a record which our Hemisphere may give to the world as convincing proof that peace lies always at hand when Nations, serene in their sovereign security, meet their current problems with understanding and good-will."[22]

In an address to the conference in Buenos Aires on December 1, FDR proclaimed that the 1933 announcement of the Good Neighbor Policy had led the American republics at Montevideo to "set an example to the whole world by proclaiming a new spirit, a new day" in hemispheric relations. They gathered again to show a different path to the world. "Beyond the ocean we see continents rent asunder by old hatreds and new fanaticisms" and by demands that injustice be corrected by force in contrast to "resorting to reason and peaceful justice" as was being done in the New World. Through their example, the nations gathered could "help the Old World to avert the catastrophe which impends" by preventing any future wars among themselves and preventing the conditions that give rise to war. This could be done by adhering to democratic processes, political freedom, and respect for the rights of other nations. It was also imperative to acknowledge the "self-evident fact that the welfare and prosperity of each of our Nations depend in large part on the benefits derived from commerce among ourselves and with other

Nations." Peace and prosperity rested on the international exchange of goods. All countries have "felt the evil effects of recent efforts to erect trade barriers of every known kind," and it was "no accident that the Nations which have carried this process farthest are those which proclaim most loudly that they require war as an instrument of their policy."[23]

The Inter-American Conference for the Maintenance of Peace adopted eleven treaties and sixty-two other resolutions and declarations. Among the agreements reached in Argentina was a protocol on nonintervention in other nations, a collective security agreement for all nations to consult in the event of war either in the hemisphere or outside of it, and further movement toward the elimination of trade barriers. Roosevelt saw the Buenos Aires meeting as "proof that in a world which is beset with rumors and threats of war, Governments determined to keep alive the spirit of peace and will to renew mutual trust and faith in treaties can move together in a cooperative search for the means of enduring peace."[24] As the State Department noted, "The national security of each American Republic has now become the common interest of all. Any threat by a non-American power to the peace of any Republic would become the collective concern of all others," at the same time that the fear of intervention by "one American Republic in the domestic affairs of any other has been removed."[25]

In his Annual Message to Congress on January 6, 1937, Roosevelt declared that "in a world unhappily thinking in terms of war," the United States and its neighbors met "in an atmosphere of complete confidence and understanding" to discuss the maintenance of peace. "Here was a great and a permanent achievement" for the security of the nation and hemisphere, and "an example which must have a wholesome effect upon the rest of the world."[26] The next year, speaking at the laying of the cornerstone of the Federal Building at the New York World's Fair, FDR stated that the Fair would be held at a time when all were aware "that the affairs of many parts of the world are, to put it politely, somewhat distraught." It was the good fortune of the Western Hemisphere, thanks to the Good Neighbor Policy, to be removed from the fear and uncertainty about war that troubled the rest of the world. Yet, "we cannot remain unconcerned." The goals of that policy were not "in its inception, or subsequently, limited to one hemisphere." Roosevelt declared that based on its success in the Western Hemisphere, "the American Republics believe that it could succeed in all the rest of the world if the spirit which lies behind it were better understood and more actively strove for in the other parts of the world."[27]

FDR summarized the successes of the Good Neighbor Policy in 1938: it had led to a dramatic improvement of U.S. relations with Latin America and was proof that an internationalist approach to national security could work. "I think I can say that our neighbors in Central and South America had formerly regarded us with resentment and suspicion—resentment because of some of our armed activities in the past often actuated by dollar diplomacy, and suspicion because of our supposed imperialistic designs based upon our superior size and strength." This created fear, antagonism, and distrust. All of that changed due to the Good Neighbor Policy, bringing forth a "new era . . . characterized by confidence and mutual helpfulness." In conferences, exchanges of views, and consultations, Washington demonstrated that "it was intent upon respecting the rights of the other Nations on this hemisphere, and that its conduct toward those neighbors would never be anything which could not be justified under the law of Nations or approved by the conscience of America."[28]

After war broke out in Europe in 1939, the United States joined the other twenty-one republics to issue a declaration of neutrality and proclaim that there was a 300-mile-wide security zone around North and South America. The next year, after the fall of France, Belgium, Holland, and Luxembourg, all the nations of the Americas agreed to a policy that opposed the transfer of a remaining European colony from one nation to another; and, in a "Declaration of Reciprocal Assistance," they reaffirmed collective security by proclaiming that any attack on one state was an act of aggression against all nations. This new Pan-American spirit would be vital during the war as it allowed the United States the use of bases for military operations and provided access to critical raw materials for the war effort. In all, the United States signed base agreements with sixteen nations. This plan for hemispheric defense met no opposition at home and provided Roosevelt with a starting point to define American security needs and meet the challenges posed by Germany and Japan later in the decade.

As he indicated in his inaugural address, Roosevelt viewed the revival of international trade as vital to his foreign policy, both to address the Great Depression and to foster a properly functioning international system. The president was guided by his understanding that finding markets abroad was essential for the United States to maintain prosperity and full employment, and that greater international trade would help ease the conditions that bred aggression and war. To that end, Roosevelt had appointed Cordell Hull as his secretary of state. A senator from Tennessee, Hull was well known for his advocacy of lower tariffs and free trade. Roosevelt, Hull, and Welles all believed that high tariffs and nationalist economic policies had played a central role in spreading and deepening the worldwide economic crisis. Moreover, trade barriers bred the type of distrust and conflict among nations that led to war.

Roosevelt understood that no nation could isolate itself economically. Speaking on May 7, 1933, in his second fireside chat, FDR noted that "the domestic is inevitably and deeply tied in with the conditions in all of the other Nations of the world." Although he conceded that much could be done at home and that it was correct to concentrate on that first to produce, "in all probability, a fair measure of prosperity to return in the United States," he said that it would "not be permanent unless we get a return to prosperity all over the world."[29] Similarly, Hull believed that it was "virtually impossible to develop friendly relations with other nations in the political sphere so long as we provoked their animosity in the economic sphere." In contrast, the free flow of trade raised every nation's standard of living, "thereby eliminating the economic dissatisfaction that breeds war."[30]

Roosevelt's first action in terms of international economic policy, his so-called bombshell message that brought an end to the June 1933 London Economic Conference, appeared, correctly, to many observers to contradict his and Hull's internationalist views on trade. Yet, it was President Hoover who had agreed to American participation in the meeting to discuss trade and arms reduction. Roosevelt had no input in the agenda or influence on what would be discussed. More importantly for Roosevelt, the fiscal policies proposed in London conflicted with his plan to take the U.S. dollar off the gold standard so that he could raise prices on U.S. goods and engage in deficit spending to finance public works projects and spur the economy. While Roosevelt sent Hull as the head of the United States delegation, he did so without providing any instructions and had little confidence that much would be accomplished. The outcome would be a disappointment in many ways to Hull, but Roosevelt prioritized domestic matters over international in 1933.

The conference got off to a poor start when British Prime Minister Ramsey MacDonald brought up the subject of war debts. All nations had agreed prior to the meeting that this subject would not be raised, and for Roosevelt this promised opposition from many in Congress who opposed any further reductions to European debts. When the delegates began discussing a new international monetary system to stabilize currencies that would fix the value of the dollar to a set standard, Roosevelt backed away completely from the proceedings. The president instructed Hull that he "would find it as a catastrophe amounting to a world tragedy" if the conference allowed itself "to be diverted by the proposal of a purely artificial and temporary experiment" related to the monetary exchanges of a few nations, and he refused to accept any international agreement that would "erect probable barriers against our own economic fiscal development."[31] In the middle of the famed hundred days that launched the New Deal, FDR was not going to allow his reform efforts to be constrained by an agreement that would not address the fundamental problems of international commerce or have any positive impact on the economic conditions in the world.

In 1934, Congress passed the Reciprocal Trade Act as a means to lower tariffs, increase trade, and, hopefully, ease the economic crisis and promote stability and peace abroad. It allowed the president to negotiate new agreements with other nations that would lower the tariff by up to fifty percent if that country reciprocated by opening up its market to U.S. goods. These new treaties did not need Congressional approval and could be renewed beyond their original three-year length. Moreover, the most-favored-nation status was extended automatically to other nations that signed similar agreements with the United States. In theory, this would reduce tariffs not just in bilateral trading, but all around the world. American exports would rise by more than $1 billion over the next five years. The desire to use economic arrangements to help solve political problems remained central to the administration's approach to foreign policy, but these alone could never solve the problems the United States confronted in Europe and Asia.

Given the enormity of the international crisis of the 1930s, Roosevelt had to consistently adapt his policies, tacking to deal with the shifting political winds and changing events. In doing so, he knew he had to alter American foreign policy from its traditional moorings of neutral rights, the protection of American shipping, and adherence to the Monroe Doctrine. Roosevelt considered these approaches, which were designed to keep other powers out of the Western Hemisphere, to be outdated in an economically interdependent and industrialized world. FDR found it essential that the nation adopt an internationalist approach to foreign policy to ensure its national security.

The concern over international issues was heightened by the growing appeal and power of fascism on the right and communism on the left, what

FDR termed the new political fanaticisms. These challenges to the status quo and the questioning of the principles of liberalism, capitalism, and democracy had been engendered by the Great Depression throughout the world. There were no clear indications of what direction this upheaval would take, and Roosevelt saw no straight path forward as a number of factors limited his ability to take action. Looking back at World War II, it is hard to understand how leaders thought they could negotiate with Hitler. Few, however, could fully envision the barbarity of the Nazi regime. In contrast, they had clear memories of the destruction and costs of the Great War, and the desire to avert another war was the highest priority of Congress and the American public, as demonstrated by the widespread sentiment against the League of Nations and opposition to the idea of American involvement in European political affairs.

By the 1930s, many questioned what the United States had gained from its participation in the Great War and its departure from the policy of hemispheric defense. The most notable outcomes of the war appeared to be bolshevism in Russia, continued political quarreling in Europe, the emergence of fascism in Europe and militarism in Japan, and an economic depression. Adherents to neutrality also believed in American exceptionalism, but they understood it differently than Roosevelt and thought the nation should only serve as a model and example, without getting involved overseas.

Given this, as tensions grew in Europe, millions of Americans feared involvement in another war that promised, they believed, little that was positive for the United States. This disillusionment was fueled by a series of works, such as the books *Merchants of Death* by Helmuth Carol Engelbrecht and Frank Cleary Hanighen, and George Seldes's *Iron, Blood and Profits*, both published in 1934. These books claimed that the United States had been manipulated into entering the Great War by a conspiracy of bankers, who had lent great sums to the Allies and wanted to protect their investments, and by munitions makers, who benefited from the fighting and government purchases of their deadly products.[32] These "Merchants of Death," noninterventionists argued, would be the only ones to profit from another war.

Another constraint on making foreign policy was the ambivalent response to Hitler's rise to power in Germany and Japan's aggression against China. On the one hand, there was no great enthusiasm for the Nazi Party or Hitler among the vast majority of the American public or U.S. policymakers. The Nazis used violent, unsavory, and antidemocratic tactics, and Hitler threatened to undo the Versailles Treaty and upset the political stability in Europe. On the other hand, American leaders were greatly concerned about the rise of left-wing political movements and the specter of bolshevism spreading in Europe. They had developed a favorable view of fascism in Italy and saw Benito Mussolini's seizure of power as providing stability and conditions conducive for American trade and business and as a force against the spread of communism.[33] As three different social systems, liberal democracy, fascism, and communism, competed for support and were in conflict in Europe, the question for the Roosevelt administration was how to support the democratic nations and deter fascist expansion, while not aiding the political left on the continent.

German and Italian actions, however, did serve to fuel the drive for new legislation to keep America out of war. Germany withdrew from the League of Nations and announced in March 1934 its plans for rearmament. In December of that year, Italy sought to expand its colonial empire and Italian troops clashed with Ethiopian forces, raising the fear of war. Congress was deluged with letters and editorials calling for action to prevent bankers and arms makers from dragging the nation into another war. In response, the Senate established the Special Committee Investigating the Munitions Industry, chaired by Republican Senator Gerald P. Nye of North Dakota. Its work led Congress to pass a series of Neutrality Acts designed to prevent a repeat of the events that led up to the Great War.

The Nye Committee hearings on why the United States went to war in 1917 reached the same conclusion as the sensational publications that led to its formation: that bankers and arms merchants were responsible for American entry into World War I. This understanding became codified in law with the passage of the first Neutrality Act in 1935. Congress, seeking to prevent the United States from fighting World War I again, established a rigid neutrality law and an impartial arms embargo. The legislation stated that if the president found a state of war existed, the shipping of arms to belligerent nations and the transportation of war materials on American ships was prohibited.

Franklin Roosevelt disagreed with all of the assumptions that led to the Neutrality Act. At the same time, the president understood the popularity of the effort. Rather than engage in a direct political battle, his administration sought greater flexibility in the neutrality legislation that would allow the executive to impose an arms embargo against aggressor nations only. This did not mean Roosevelt sought to directly confront the fascist dictators. He and Hull agreed with the goal of keeping the United States out of war if possible, but the president and secretary of state believed that inflexible neutrality could have the opposite effect: it could embolden potential aggressors by removing the fear that America would give support to any nation. Furthermore, such a position, the president noted, "might drag us into war instead of keeping us out."[34] Roosevelt preferred no legislation rather than the impartial embargo Congress proposed and worked behind the scenes to modify the proposed neutrality bill.

By the summer of 1935 it was clear that the neutrality legislation would pass and any direct opposition by the president would lead to a political defeat, possibly derail his domestic legislation, and harm his chances at reelection in 1936. It appeared, as Senator Hiram Johnson declared, that the passage of the Neutrality Act of 1935 marked the "triumph of the so-called isolationists and . . . the downfall, although we may not know it, of the internationalist."[35] The next year a prohibition of loans to belligerents was added. The law was again modified in 1937 to include a "cash and carry" clause. Designed to avoid the problems of loans and the carrying of goods on neutral ships, "cash and carry" would allow nations at war to purchase munitions in the United States only if they paid for them in full and transported them on their own ships. Roosevelt would have to move cautiously, using all of his skills as a political sailor to maneuver in the face of Congressional opposition and public support for neutrality.

After World War I, stability was achieved in East Asia through a series of naval, security, and commercial treaties negotiated by the United States, the United Kingdom, Japan, and other powers. At the center of the 1920s Washington System were the naval treaty that limited the size of each of the powers' fleets and the Nine-Power Treaty. The latter guaranteed Chinese sovereignty over its territory and formally recognized the Open Door policy, which in theory ensured all nations' access to China's markets and foreign trade. The coming of the Great Depression in 1929 undercut the Washington System and, in the process, had a devastating impact on U.S. relations with Japan. As access to American funds evaporated in the wake of the stock market crash, and the Hawley-Smoot tariff cut Japan's exports to the United States in half, the system of cooperation in East Asia quickly unraveled. With Great Britain, France, and Holland closing off their empires to foreign trade,

Japan found itself unable to acquire many of the materials necessary for its economy. As a result, the militarist faction in Japan, which had always questioned the idea of cooperation with the West, gained the upper hand. It set out to create an empire that would be self-sufficient and did not depend on other nations for its prosperity and security. From the Japanese perspective, the United States only supported the Open Door commitment to free trade when it gained from the arrangement and violated it when it served Washington's purposes. The militarists decided that Japan's security was best assured through unilateral action, and in September 1931 Japan began to take control over Manchuria by force.

From the outset, the United States opposed the Japanese conquest and sought to cooperate with the League of Nations on measures to deter Japan's move and support China. President Hoover opposed economic sanctions, fearing that they would lead to war, and it was clear that the League of Nations was not going to take any action. Short of war, there was seemingly little Washington could do to stop Japan. Yet, Secretary of State Stimson did not want to condone Japanese aggression and its violation of the Nine Power Treaty. The only viable option was nonrecognition of Japan's conquest and the mobilization of public opinion in opposition to such actions. The Stimson Doctrine, announced on January 7, 1932, stated that the United States "cannot admit the legality of any situation *de facto* nor does it intend to recognize any treaty or agreement . . . which may impair the treaty rights of the United States . . . including those which relate to the sovereignty, the independence, or the territorial and administrative integrity of the Republic of China, or to the international policy relative to China, commonly known as the open door policy."[36]

Stimson did not believe this declaration would check Japan's aggression or bring about a reversal of its course. But nonrecognition could effectively serve American interests as a moral weapon designed to express the opposition of the United States and its people to the Japanese action. Moreover, he hoped that it would help shape world opinion on the issue and would provide a means to reassure China and others that the United States was not abandoning its interests in East Asia. With the world too divided and unwilling to take action against Japan, the Stimson Doctrine, with its refusal to sanction Japan's dismemberment of China, was the best alternative available to awaken the world to the potential dangers that would lie ahead if aggression was not checked. Certainly, with the mounting economic problems at home, the American public would go no further at that time. Nonrecognition was correct, but it was also insufficient for upholding international agreements and deterring aggression.

How to confront Japan's aggression in Asia was no clearer when FDR became president. Roosevelt, as he had promised Stimson, maintained the policy of nonrecognition of Japan's conquest of Manchuria, but it was uncertain what further action he could take to deter it from further expansion. Trade with Japan was three times greater than with China, and economic sanctions would hurt the United States at a time when it was searching for all the markets it could find. Additionally, cutting off Japan's access to certain products from the United States, such as oil and iron, might only encourage its military to seek further unilateral solutions to its economic problems through expansion in order to gain control of these resources.

While there was no sense of urgency that Japan had to be stopped immediately, it was understood that Japan could challenge American interests and policies and become an enemy of the United States in East Asia and the Pacific. The extent of the problem was set out by American ambassador to Japan, Joseph Grew, in a May 1933 analysis that Hull forwarded to Roosevelt. Grew sought to make clear Japan's military potential and argued that it would be wrong for the United States to underestimate Japan's strength. Japan was, he noted, often seen "as a small, overcrowded nation . . . without natural resources, and largely dependent upon foreign sources for its foodstuffs." With the taking of Manchuria, Japan's empire was larger than the combined territories of Belgium, Denmark, France, Germany, Netherlands, Spain, and Switzerland, and it controlled over 120 million people, almost equal to the population of the United States. Moreover, the Japanese "are intelligent, industrious, energetic, extremely nationalistic, war-loving, aggressive and, it must be admitted, somewhat unscrupulous." Japan could feed its entire people, and had "developed its industries in recent years until it is able to supply itself with all of the necessities of life, and can build all the ships, and make all the airplanes, tanks, guns, ammunition, chemicals, etc., needed to wage a severe war, if it is not too protracted." All of this supported the most "powerful fighting machine in the world today," one "designed for the purpose of keeping Western nations from interfering while Japan carries out its ambitions in Asia."[37]

Japanese leaders, Grew opined, saw Tokyo's control over East Asia as "the nation's natural expansion," something akin to America's own sense of

Manifest Destiny. More dangerous than just the size of the nation or the military was "the national morale and esprit de corps—a spirit which perhaps has not been equaled since the days when the Mongol hordes followed Genghis Khan in his conquest of Asia." Grew concluded by noting that the strength of a nation driven by "great moral determination, fired with national ambition, and peopled by a race with unbounded capacity for courageous self-sacrifice is not easy to overestimate."[38]

Acknowledging this problem, Roosevelt sought ways to put pressure on Japan and aid China. In 1933, Congress granted his request for $50 million credit for China to purchase agricultural products and airplane parts in the United States. In addition, the president authorized the construction of thirty new warships and two aircraft carriers to bring the United States closer to full capacity under the Washington Treaty as the first step toward meeting Japan's growing threat. The administration also pressed Japan on renewing the naval treaty restrictions, which would end in 1936 if one of the signatory nations renounced its provisions by December 1934. Roosevelt was determined that if the limits on navies was to end, the responsibility would be Tokyo's. When Japan did disavow the treaty, Roosevelt was able to obtain in early 1936 a significant increase in naval spending to begin modernizing the American fleet. From 1933 to 1940, the navy grew from 193 commissioned ships to 337, with another 119 under construction, and from 106,000 sailors to 210,000.[39]

The differences between Washington and Tokyo were made clear in April 1934 during the so-called Amau incident. Foreign Office spokesman Amau Eiji announced that Japan alone had the right to preserve the peace and order in East Asia, notably China, and that any further military aid or other efforts to supply China would be viewed as hostile actions toward Japan. In making this statement, Tokyo was renouncing all international agreements related to China, most notably the Open Door, and establishing it as a protectorate of Japan under what it would call the Greater East Asian Co-Prosperity Sphere.

The United States rejected this position and reiterated its support for the Open Door policy and the need for nations to respect the rights of others and adhere to international agreements. As the Far Eastern Division of the State Department noted in a thirty eight page analysis of the problems in relations with Japan, Tokyo was seeking the surrender by the United States and Great Britain of their interests in East Asia and the recognition of "Japan's 'Monroe

Doctrine for Asia'" in preparation for further action against China. The Japanese sought to "promote and facilitate the attainment by Japan of a paramount and dominating position in the Far East"; the United States' response was that nations must adhere to existing agreements and not favor any country in the region. Washington could not accept a policy that provided "the advantage or disadvantage of any."[40]

In May, Japan's ambassador to the United States, Hirosi Saito, met with Cordell Hull to officially present Japan's position. The ambassador told Hull that in Japan it was believed "that the United States in the past had sought to checkmate his country in most all of its plans, ideas or moves in the way of progress externally." In his prepared memorandum that he handed to Hull, Saito requested that the United States recognize Japan's sphere of influence in China in return for Japan's respect for the Monroe Doctrine. The western Pacific "lies within [Japan's] proper and legitimate power to establish a reign of law and order" as the main stabilizing power.[41]

The two men met again to discuss the note and the American response. Saito agreed that the main point was that "his Government did feel that it had a special interest in preserving peace and order in China." Hull responded by setting out the fundamental assumptions behind the Open Door policy. He told the ambassador that it would be "more profitable" for Japan to work cooperatively to "retain the perfect understanding and the friendship of all civilized nations" in order to promote the "welfare of their respective peoples and at the same time meet their duties to civilization and to the more backward populations of the world." The concern was that Japan was seeking an empire and not just a protection of its rights and stability in the region. The latter, Hull argued, was best obtained through international agreements. Given the current world crisis, the secretary of state argued, it was crucial that "civilized countries should be especially vigilant to observe and to preserve both legal and moral obligations." Hull said that nations must "work whole-heartedly together; and that this action of course would, more fully than any other, promote the welfare of the people of each and also best preserve civilization."[42]

This exchange showed how difficult it would be to find common ground for a resolution or a compromise between the two nations. Roosevelt saw Japan's pursuit of a territorial empire as a threat to the United States and to peace, and its withdrawal from the League of Nations and abrogation of the naval treaty at the end of 1934 confirmed American concerns that Tokyo was embarking on a course of expansion that would collide with American interests in East Asia. Stanley Hornbeck, the head of the Far Eastern Division of the State Department, noted that it was now "a fact that the Japanese conceptions today of legality, of morality and of expediency differ from ours."[43] In early 1935, Ambassador Grew provided a two-part analysis of Japan's decisions. Given the prospect of an enlarged Japanese navy, Grew urged that the United States "be adequately prepared to meet all eventualities in the Far East." It was "the general conclusion . . . that there exists in Japan today a definite urge toward economic and political expansion in East Asia and, as a corollary, a growing pressure against the interests of western nations, including the interests of the United States." What Grew termed "the present-day chauvinism in Japan" stemmed from a resentment of the West and a sense of being accorded second class status in international relations. Tokyo believed that Japan occupied "a position which entitles them to the same consideration in the Far East that the British and the French claim in the affairs of Europe or even the United States in the Western Hemisphere, and they intend to assert and maintain this position with all the strength at their command."[44]

There were also internal factors that drove Japanese expansion, notably overpopulation, lack of natural resources, industrialization, and the desire to increase the standard of living on the home islands. "With a larger sphere of activity Japanese industry and commerce will expand further and remove the spectre of restricted markets." Tokyo's position that "if this has to be done at others' expense it cannot be helped" was part of Japan's sense of "manifest destiny" to dominate and protect East Asia and its need for a safety valve for its population. Thus, it was essential to see Japan's actions, Grew noted, "as the reasonable and logical operation of well-nigh irrepressible forces based on the underlying principle of self preservation."[45] Grew, therefore, recommended that the United States' response be based on two concurrent principles that would allow for flexibility in Washington's approach. First, the United States needed a policy of "national preparedness for the purpose of protecting our legitimate interests in the Far East." Second, the ambassador suggested "a sympathetic, co-operative and helpful attitude toward Japan."[46]

Grew's ambivalence reflected overall American policy. The Roosevelt administration worried about Japan's actions, but up to this point no significant U.S. material interest had been harmed. Yet, to do nothing would send the wrong signal that Washington was acquiescing to Tokyo's claims and maneuvers. The path forward was unclear, and domestic opposition to deeper involvement in international disputes further limited any action by the White House. Given this, the administration continued to make its opposition to Japan's emerging policy known to Tokyo and to send aid to China even though that only served to further antagonize Japan. Administration officials were unsure of what other options could be taken. Certainly, in the mid-1930s, no one was proposing going to war, alone or with other nations, over China, nor was Roosevelt willing to concede the Open Door policy to Japan's version of an empire. The president, therefore, sought during his first term to make Tokyo aware of American opposition to further expansion while building up American naval power in the hopes of deterring Japan's plan of dominating East Asia.

The outbreak of the Italo-Ethiopian War in October 1935 forced President Roosevelt to give more attention to the building international crisis in Europe. When Italy invaded Ethiopia on October 3, Roosevelt reacted angrily. He immediately instructed Secretary of State Hull to invoke the recently passed Neutrality Act in order to deny Italy access to American arms, and warned American traders that they conducted business with Italy at their own risk. Hull added a call for a "moral embargo" by American companies on the shipment of war-related items, such as oil, copper, and steel. The administration would not, however, impose a complete embargo, that is, one enforced by the government, which would antagonize Mussolini and hurt his war effort. Washington was afraid that restrictions by the West on Rome might bring about a conflict over resources between Italy and Great Britain in the Mediterranean and possibly lead to a European war.

It was more than Italian domination of Ethiopia that concerned the White House. Roosevelt saw the war as an example of the problems with imperialism. Such naked aggression threatened the general peace and stability of the world. The Italian invasion of Ethiopia prompted Roosevelt to deliver a major foreign policy speech on Armistice Day 1935. He expressed his fear about the consequences of war during such unstable times. People had to come to understand that the "elation and prosperity which may come from a new war must lead—for those who survive it—to economic and social collapse more sweeping than anywhere experienced in the past."[47] Early the next year, Roosevelt wrote that "one cannot help feeling that the whole European panorama is fundamentally blacker than any time," and compared the potential for revolutionary upheaval to that of 1848 and 1917. He concluded that these "may be the last days of the period of peace before a long chaos."[48]

Events in Spain served to deepen this concern. In July 1936, civil war broke out when General Francisco Franco's fascist rebels attacked the republican Popular Front government in Madrid. While the United States joined with Great Britain and France in declaring neutrality, Germany and Italy aided Franco's forces, and the Soviet Union, following its policy of a united front of progressive forces against fascism, provided material assistance to the Loyalists. American nonintervention stemmed from Washington's fear that the war in Spain could spill over the Pyrenees into a wider European conflagration and its desire to avoid cooperating with the left to contain the threat of fascism.

Ever since the founding of the Spanish Republic in 1931, American officials had been skeptical and feared that it was just a matter of time before it would go Bolshevik. The weakness of the new government and its confiscatory policy toward foreign investments led embassy officials in Madrid to believe that the new government represented "a Kerensky interlude" preceding a communist takeover.[49] The formation of the Popular Front government of left parties in early 1936 caused relations between the United States and Spain to break down almost completely before the civil war. The State Department saw the Popular Front as nothing more than a cover-up for Soviet aggression and a different means of bringing about communist takeovers of other nations, what ambassador to the Soviet Union William Bullitt termed the "tactics of the Trojan horse.[50]

The Neutrality Act did not cover a civil war, and there was no legal basis to deny the sale of weapons to the Spanish Republic. Still, given the views of American officials and the fear of strengthening the left, there was never any real chance that the United States would come to the aid of the Loyalists. Summarizing the State Department's position, Undersecretary of State William Phillips noted that "if the government wins . . . communism throughout Europe will be immensely stimulated."[51] Having defined the civil war as a revolt against a communist government, and not the spread of fascism, the solution was to deny arms to the Loyalists. A "moral embargo" on all weapons sales to the Spanish Republic was implemented and neutrality became policy.

Many in the United States opposed this policy, and several thousand would eventually defy the government and go to Spain to fight the spread of fascism. Only after Germany's taking of Austria in 1938 and the conclusion that appeasement was failing did most Americans come to see the Spanish Civil War as part of a larger fascist threat, and the policy as a mistake. President Roosevelt reached the same conclusion; in 1939, American policy was changed to allow the sale of supplies to Spain, too late to help the Loyalist cause.

With tensions mounting in Europe, warfare breaking out on its periphery, and Japan becoming more aggressive, Roosevelt knew that some action was necessary if peace was to be maintained and a general war averted. The president feared another war for good reason, having witnessed the death and destruction of World War I and the upheavals it was still bringing to the world. He did not, however, want foreign policy to become an issue in his reelection campaign and he offered no new plans or ideas on international affairs. If Roosevelt had decided to use the campaign to address the building crises in Europe and Asia, his choices of how to approach the issue were limited. He could side with the popular position of the noninterventionists—maintain strict neutrality, strengthen hemispheric defense, and steer clear of Europe's problems. But Roosevelt saw this as a short-sighted approach that did not promote America's interests and security; it would be an abandonment of his internationalist beliefs and an abdication by the United States of its responsibility as a great nation.

Another option was to embrace the Soviet Union's call for a united front against fascism and attempt to forge a coalition to oppose Germany. This was rejected out of hand for two reasons. First, it was a political impossibility as there would be no support for such a policy. Second, it was contrary to Roosevelt's main goal of avoiding a general war. A popular front against fascism, Roosevelt was sure, would lead to a conflict that would bring massive destruction, social upheaval, and revolution to Europe, exactly what the president was trying to prevent. The question for Roosevelt was how to contain Germany and deter Japan without relying on the Soviet Union and augmenting the influence of the European left, and without going to war.

In this context, the president decided in 1937 on a third option: negotiations with Germany to address the crucial economic issues while seeking to improve relations with Great Britain, and setting out to educate the American public about the dangers the United States faced abroad. Hemmed in by public opinion and Congressional legislation, focused primarily on domestic recovery, and guided by his goals of preventing war and fostering greater international trade and cooperation, Roosevelt sought to redress what were seen as Germany's legitimate grievances in order to reintegrate it through increased trade into an international order compatible with the United States. This built on traditional American policies of the Monroe Doctrine and hemispheric defense, the rights of neutrals, and the open door while it simultaneously began to expand the meaning of national security and what was necessary for the defense of the nation by shifting policy away from neutrality toward cooperation with allies and collective security. In doing so, the president began his long campaign from 1937 to 1941 to overcome noninterventionist sentiment in America.

3

International Crises, 1937–1940

The events of 1936 brought crisis and the specter of war to Europe. In March, German forces reoccupied the demilitarized Rhineland. In May, Italy completed its conquest of Ethiopia. In July, the Spanish Civil War began. These events, combined the next year with Japan's attack on China in July 1937, convinced Roosevelt that the world was rapidly moving toward a general war that would have devastating consequences for all nations. In 1937, with his reelection safely behind him, FDR began his search to find policies that would preserve peace. Simultaneously, the president launched a public campaign that challenged the assumptions of the advocates of neutrality and the nonintervention position, and set out to educate the American people about the dangers the United States faced abroad. The effort to redirect public opinion was designed to gain support for an internationalist foreign policy based on deterrence, preparedness, and close relations with Great Britain. The president sought to convince the public that the nation's security depended as much on developments on the other sides of the two oceans as it did on good relations and security in the Western Hemisphere.

In making the case for an internationalist approach to foreign affairs, Roosevelt and his supporters argued that as a great power the United States had a vital interest in the world's affairs, and that American security was now being threatened by the actions of Germany and Japan. Developments overseas, therefore, were crucial to U.S. national security and prosperity, and it was essential, from Roosevelt's perspective, to protect both the valid and peaceful interests of the nation and its values and institutions abroad. Given this, the United States could not just stand on the sideline as an observer of these events. Instead, it had to become more involved in world affairs to try to shape their direction, and it had to prepare to defend itself in case peace could not be maintained. In sum, the president argued that Germany and Japan not only threatened America's legitimate interests abroad and national security at home, but also represented the antithesis of American values. The rulers in Berlin and Tokyo had destroyed freedom in their own nations and were embarked upon a course of expansion that threatened freedom and liberty in other parts of the world, including the Western Hemisphere and the United States. They were trampling on treaties and international law and showed no signs of restraint in pursuit of their objectives of total power and domination. Democracy and freedom in the United States could not survive, much less flourish, in such a world.

Roosevelt considered the problems in Europe the greatest danger to the United States, due to the extent of American interests, the capacity of German power, and the threat to American values. At the same time, though, these growing global threats were interconnected and influenced all other regions of the world. The reasons for conflict in Europe and Asia might be different, but, in terms of U.S. interests, they were best understood as related and had to be considered together in developing policies, responses, and strategies. From this understanding, FDR constructed his arguments and set forth his vision of an internationalist foreign policy. While his efforts from 1937 to 1939 failed to prevent war, the period was nonetheless critical in the development of his foreign policy. As Roosevelt tacked among different courses in his effort to preserve peace, he also began to create closer ties with Great Britain and to build up American preparedness for fighting. In the process, he launched the great strategic debate over America's role in the world as he worked to shift public opinion away from neutrality and toward the internationalist understanding of national security for which he more and more forcefully advocated.

On August 14, 1936, at Chautauqua, New York, Roosevelt delivered the most important foreign policy speech of his first term in office; it was the only one on the topic during his 1936 reelection campaign. The subject was peace. It was a political speech and did not have any policy positions, but in his remarks the president set out much of his internationalist vision, his understanding of American exceptionalism, and various concepts on national security. Roosevelt presciently began by stating that he chose his topic because it was important that Americans not overlook, in their concerns with domestic events, problems "though they lie beyond our borders" that "may, and probably will, have a vital influence on the United States in the future." FDR said that he wanted to remain optimistic, but, that as one who had participated in the decisions of both war and peace in the Great War and "who has spent a goodly portion of every twenty-four hours in the study of foreign relations," he was "more concerned and less cheerful about international world conditions than about our immediate domestic prospects."[1]

Roosevelt recalled that he was convinced well before he became president that the United States "could best serve the cause of a peaceful humanity by setting an example," and that was why his first action in the area of foreign policy was the announcement of the Good Neighbor Policy in his inaugural address. The Good Neighbor Policy, FDR stated, represented his purpose, and now his practice, in foreign policy; and, he said, "the practice has succeeded." The world knows the United States is strong, Roosevelt declared, but smaller nations do not fear it because it has "no predatory ambitions" and stands for peace. The Good Neighbor Policy had produced mutual trust and cooperation with the nations of Latin America.[2]

"But," Roosevelt stated, "peace in the western world is not all we seek" from these actions. "It is our hope that knowledge of the practical application of the good neighbor policy in this hemisphere will be borne home to our neighbors across the seas." The president was "deeply concerned about tendencies of recent years among many of the nations of other continents" and the danger of another general war. The modern world "faces wars between conflicting economic and political fanaticisms in which are intertwined race hatreds." While "we shun political commitments," Roosevelt stated, "which might entangle us in foreign wars," the United States understood that the wars in Europe and Asia presented the danger to the nation "that it also may be drawn into war."[3]

In the most quoted part of his speech, FDR declared: "I hate war." Roosevelt had witnessed the fighting during the Great War and knew the destructive power of modern weapons and the fearful costs of fighting. That was why, the president said, he spent so much time thinking about peace and how to maintain it. From his study Roosevelt concluded that the neutrality laws could not prevent war, "as no laws can be provided to cover every contingency." Washington, he was certain, had to be more active in finding paths to peace and security. One key role for American policy to contribute to peace was the elimination of economic barriers as a means of "discouraging the economic source of war." The reciprocal trade agreements the nation was pursuing were helping to eliminate tariffs, quotas, and embargoes "that place such pressure on nations not possessing great natural resources that to those nations the price of peace sometimes seems less terrible than the price of war." Free trade would not prevent all wars either, Roosevelt acknowledged, but "without more liberal international trade, war is a natural sequence."[4]

International relations, Roosevelt continued, involved "of necessity a vast unchartered area." One had to be ready to tack, recalculate, and avoid unforeseen obstacles or developments in the pursuit of peace. "Safe sailing," FDR declared, "will depend on the knowledge and the experience and the wisdom of those who direct our foreign policy. Peace will depend on their day to day decisions." The United States was "in many ways most singularly blessed" of all nations. Its neighbors knew "that we oppose imperialism" and thus there was peace in the Western Hemisphere. Moreover, Roosevelt asserted, "we believe in democracy; we believe in freedom; and we believe in peace." The blessings the nation had received, its power and its commitment to freedom, placed a unique burden on the United States to lead, both by its example and through action. From this starting point, FDR concluded, Washington offered all nations the handshake of the good neighbor. "Let those who wish our friendship look us in the eye and take our hand."[5]

Earlier that summer when he accepted the nomination to run for reelection, Roosevelt spoke about how at the start of his presidency "we feared fear" in the United States. "That was why we fought fear. And today, my friends, we have won against the most dangerous of our foes. We have conquered fear" at home. He continued by noting that in contrast, there was growing trouble outside of America. "I cannot, with candor, tell you that all is well with the world. Clouds of suspicion, tides of ill-will and intolerance gather darkly in many places." Democracy was under assault due to economic problems, leading many people to abandon democracy for dictatorship. Only the survival and success of democracy in the United States could give hope to others. "They begin to know that here in America we are waging a great and successful war. It is not alone a war against want and destitution and economic demoralization. It is more than that; it is a war for the survival of democracy. We are fighting to save a great and precious form of government for ourselves and for the world."[6]

As he took his first steps to confront the challenges posed by Nazi Germany and Imperial Japan, Roosevelt faced an American public that remained decidedly in support of neutrality and that was wary of any actions by the United States that might involve it in conflicts in Europe or Asia. In January 1937, a Gallup poll showed that almost seventy percent of the American people supported mandatory neutrality legislation, and that ninety-four percent saw keeping the nation out of war as more important than the United States using its influence to prevent an outbreak of war overseas. Against these political winds, Roosevelt set out to redirect the ship of state. His first step was to ask Congress to amend the neutrality laws to provide for a cash-and-carry provision and to give the president discretionary power in implementing the neutrality act.

The idea for cash-and-carry was first proposed by the financier Bernard Baruch, an ardent supporter of Roosevelt and the New Deal. As he explained it in the June 1936 issue of *Current History*, Baruch envisioned a policy that would allow the United States to sell goods to any belligerents, but the terms would be "cash on the barrel-head and come and get it."[7] The appeal of Baruch's proposal was that American producers could sell their goods, while the United States avoided the problems of putting its own ships in harm's way or protecting neutral shipping rights, which allowed the nation to maintain its neutrality. When the Neutrality Act came up for renewal in early 1937, cash-and-carry was at the center of the debate.

Administration officials lobbied hard for the adoption of the cash-and-carry amendment along with the provision that the president be granted the authority to decide when and whether to invoke the neutrality law. Staunch supporters of unconditional neutrality wanted to maintain mandatory restrictions on the sale of arms to any belligerent in order to keep the United States free of any involvement in foreign wars. With proponents of cash-and-carry pointing out the economic benefits that would accrue to the nation while still preserving neutrality, the die-hard noninterventionists yielded on allowing the sale of goods. They still sought, however, to maintain mandatory restrictions whenever a war broke out. Supporters of discretionary power countered that cash-and-carry would work fine in Europe where Great Britain could get to U.S. ports and secure goods, but it was problematic in Asia as it was Japan, and not China, that would be able to purchase supplies. Granting the president the discretionary authority to decide when to impose the law would provide greater flexibility and prevent the sale of goods to nations hostile to American interests. In April, Congress passed the revised Neutrality Act with the cash-and-carry provision and presidential discretionary power in place for the next two years. Roosevelt saw this new law as a means to increase American influence abroad, promote cooperation with Great Britain, and implement a plan of economic appeasement toward Germany while remaining within the parameters dictated by public opinion.

The policy of economic appeasement was designed to maintain the peace in Europe by meeting Germany's economic needs and providing relief from the restrictions of the Versailles Treaty, while opposing Berlin's territorial expansion. It is important to remember that when American officials used the term "appeasement" in the 1930s it was shorthand for calling for negotiations and compromise agreements. The term did not have the negative connotations of a sell-out and the universal opprobrium it received after the start of World War II. Economic arrangements were politically possible, at home and abroad, and were seen as the way to secure greater international trade. By addressing what were seen as legitimate grievances by Berlin, the West could demonstrate to Hitler that he could secure Germany's future prosperity without expansion. This would prevent the feared alternative of a war of aggression that would lead to chaos and concomitant revolutions as it had during the Great War. American officials fully appreciated the threat Germany posed and sought to address that danger and preserve American interests while avoiding any direct political commitments to Europe that would create political opposition at home. This strategy also fit well with the Reciprocal Trade Agreement program. Employing Hull's analysis that economic rivalry was the cause of war and that greater international trade would create interdependence, it was believed that once its trade began to improve, Germany would see that its interests were better served through cooperation with the Western democracies than in combating them.

It was also true that Roosevelt's choices of how to approach Europe were limited. The president could side with the noninterventionists, maintain strict neutrality, and try to steer clear of Europe's problems. Adopting this stance certainly would have been in line with public opinion. Roosevelt, however, saw this as a naïve and shortsighted understanding of the realities of the world and American interests, modern warfare, and what was necessary to defend the nation. Moreover, he believed it was an abdication of America's responsibility as a great nation and an abandonment of America's values that were under constant attack in the world. The question for Roosevelt was how to modify or contain Germany without military confrontation and without relying on the Soviet Union and augmenting the influence of the European left, both of which would bring war. This should not be interpreted as a policy designed to drive Germany to the east to fight the Soviet Union. The United States did not want war anywhere in Europe because the fighting would inevitably spread to the rest of the continent, further destabilizing existing institutions and providing a potential spark for revolution. Rather, it was a policy designed to stop any German territorial expansion, reestablish international cooperation as the best means to peace and prosperity, and prevent a disastrous war in Europe.

The reasoning behind America's appeasement policy was based on three key assumptions. First, it was the accepted view in Washington that Hitler's rise to power was the result of the harsh treatment of Germany under the Treaty of Versailles, which imposed economic sanctions, disarmament, and the war guilt clause while also stripping the nation of its colonies and other lands. The problems that beset Germany after the Great War were exacerbated by the economic problems brought on by the Great Depression. Thus, it was believed that Berlin had legitimate grievances that needed to be redressed to achieve peace, stability, and prosperity in Europe. Second, the unrest and instability caused by the Great Depression increased the influence and appeal of the political left in Europe. In Washington's view, this heightened the danger of revolution and the need for stability and political order to block communism. Liberal democracy was being challenged by both bolshevism and fascism. The issue was how to contain Germany in order to protect the democratic nations without relying on the Soviet Union and the political left. A resolution to Germany's economic problems, therefore, appeared to be the best course of action to solve the political crisis in Europe and avoid war.

Finally, the State Department believed that the Nazi Party was defined by a split between moderate and extreme fascists. Moderates, it was thought, favored international cooperation and the gradual return to liberal policies once the political and economic crises presented by the threat of communism and the unjust agreements of the Versailles Treaty were resolved. Extremists believed in autarchic, nationalistic economic policies and expansion as the solution to their nation's problems. It was, therefore, seen as essential that Washington develop policies that aided the moderates and isolated the extremists. As the American embassy in Berlin reported, "There is no doubt that a very definite struggle is going on between the violent radical wing of the Nazi Party . . . and what might be termed the more moderate section of the party, headed by Hitler himself . . . which appeal[s] to all civilized and reasonable people."[8]

Based on this analysis, the State Department concluded that "economic appeasement should prove to be the surest route to world peace." Finding a solution to Germany's economic problems was essential if war was to be avoided. "If Fascism cannot succeed by persuasion" to solve the crisis in Germany, "it must succeed by force." The United States, therefore, had to assist German economic recovery. A 1937 report bluntly noted that "the problem of European peace . . . may be clearly defined: Can a compromise be found, or a price paid, which will satisfy the economic necessities of the German people, without war . . . ? If so, there will be no war; if not, war is possible, if not probable."[9]

The president knew there were no easy answers and no guarantees. With the nations of Europe rearming themselves, he worried that there might not be enough time for economic arrangements to take hold. Yet, the president wondered what other option he had. To stay neutral was to drift on a stormy sea at a time when the winds were blowing toward war, a conflagration Roosevelt was sure the United States could not avoid. The preferred approach of collective security remained impossible politically. The American public was still not prepared to form an alliance with Great Britain and France. Easing economic tensions seemed the only way. Disarmament, political stability, and peace were tied to economic recovery. "How do we make progress," the president asked in May 1937, "if England and France say we cannot help Germany and Italy to achieve economic security if they continue to arm and threaten, while simultaneously Germany and Italy say we must continue to arm and threaten because they will not give us economic security?"[10] Economic appeasement was, therefore, a temporary and transitional policy until political conditions allowed a full internationalist approach.

The basis for shaping a lasting peace in Europe, Roosevelt and Welles both thought, was already set out in the reciprocal trade program and the model for international cooperation established by the Good Neighbor Policy. The president focused his efforts on finding an overall peace settlement through trade agreements, revisions of the Versailles Treaty, and disarmament. Just as Washington had developed and led the nations of the Western Hemisphere to cooperative peace agreements and beneficial trade arrangements by renouncing intervention and respecting the sovereignty of Latin American nations, FDR believed that a peaceful European order could be established by restoring German economic prosperity and redressing the inequities of the Paris Peace plan. The president explained his thinking in a

January 18, 1937, letter to Virginia Gildersleeve, dean of Barnard College. He stated that he hoped Europe would emulate the system of Pan-American cooperation that the Good Neighbor Policy had created. The recently concluded Inter-American Conference for the Maintenance of Peace in Buenos Aires had demonstrated that "nations may meet in an atmosphere of confidence and good will to seek just solutions to their common problems."[11] What was needed was a European equivalent to the Good Neighbor Policy to create the cooperative process that would allow a solution to the economic and political problems on the continent.

In a series of speeches in 1936 and 1937, Welles set out the Roosevelt administration's understanding of the central problems facing Europe, the main assumptions of the internationalist position, and the case for economic appeasement. At the heart of the problem were the economic dislocations and problems brought about by the Versailles system and the Great Depression, which were driving Germany to change the international status quo and were creating the danger of another war. As Welles stated, peace was the "uppermost question in the minds of every one of us today." In order to secure this, the United States had to acknowledge "that the greater the economic pressure to which a nation is subjected, the more desperate it becomes in its search for markets for its products or goods." The curtailment of trade, lack of raw materials, and unemployment led governments to the "frantic resort . . . without regard for cost, to the rapid increase of armaments through the manufacture of munitions—for the moment as an expedient for reviving industry and to give employment but eventually and infallibly as a means of acquiring, through conquest, that which they failed to obtain through the peaceful channels of normal trade." These conditions called for the leadership of the United States to build on the Reciprocal Trade Agreements program in order to open up all channels of trade and ensure that nations did not resort to force as a road to prosperity.[12]

Welles argued that the current tensions with Germany were the result of the structural problems that beset the international system and were not the result of the ideology of the Nazi government. "The ills from which the world suffers today," Welles stated in July 1937, "revolve primarily about the fundamental fact that the injustices and maladjustments resulting from the Great War have never yet been rectified." Washington understood that a general settlement of Europe's problems necessitated a revision of the Treaty of Versailles, which had left Germany with "intolerable moral and material burdens" imposed upon it by the victors. The lesson to be learned was that "peace of a permanent nature cannot be founded on revenge," and that the international order as currently constructed on this basis was doomed to failure. It was unreasonable to expect the Germans to "face a future without hope" and to toil "in order that they may thus offer reparation for the crimes and mistakes, real or alleged, of an earlier generation." People forced into such a position will always take the first opportunity to free themselves from such an order.[13]

Even though the United States had rejected the Treaty of Versailles and League of Nations, Washington shared some responsibility for the world's economic problems and certainly was not immune from the dangers emanating from Europe. Most notably, the 1930 Hawley–Smoot tariff was a significant factor in the current crisis as it curtailed international trade and "contributed to the creation of all those artificial barriers" to trade "which have become the rule rather than the exception during the past 6 years." The end result, if no changes were made soon, were predictable to Welles. "Surely," he opined, "it must be by now universally accepted that economic warfare is one of the chief contributing causes to warfare by force of arms." Renewed fighting would further the economic problems of the United States and inevitably drag the nation into the conflagration. It was, therefore, incumbent upon Washington to propose a remedy.[14]

Congress, Welles asserted, was on the wrong path to peace. While it sought to minimize the danger of the United States being drawn into war through neutrality legislation, it could neither prevent war nor could it insulate the nation from the impact of war. "War," Welles stated, "must inevitably bring with it economic collapse, social chaos, and hitherto unparalleled human destruction and suffering." As Welles observed in setting out his plan for peace, he saw the conflict in Spain as "a manifestation of the disease from which this world is suffering," which had its roots in the Great War and the failed peace of Versailles, and was now manifested in the challenges to freedom and democracy across the globe. Spain was the "battleground of fundamentally antagonistic dogmas which men have evolved since the outbreak of World War"; these were bolshevism and fascism, "which have had their genesis in want and misery." These conditions and the conflicts provoked by these antidemocratic movements could easily produce a "spark which may light the conflagration of a major international war." It was no secret that the Soviet Union was aiding the Republican forces in Spain and that Nazi Germany and Fascist Italy were supporting the rebels. "It is in that fact," Welles noted, "that the most immediate danger to the peace of the world lies today."[15]

The undersecretary of state proposed a "broad program for world rehabilitation . . . outside of the realm of those political adjustments in which we have no share [to] restore international confidence and lay those foundations of normal and just international relationships which mean peace." The basic principles to be applied were a respect for treaties among nations and the "revitalization of international morals, which means first and foremost the sanctity of the pledged word given between nations." From these would follow a reduction of trade restrictions; the limitation of armaments; and international conferences for the free exchange of ideas and negotiation of agreements to implement these goals. Again, Welles offered the Good Neighbor Policy as an example of the proper approach, and the recent meeting of the representatives of the American republics in Buenos Aires and their declaration of adherence to the principles set out by Welles as the instruments of peace.[16]

Roosevelt, therefore, continued to hold out the Good Neighbor Policy as the model for Europe to follow. In an April 14 speech celebrating Pan American Day, Roosevelt challenged the noninterventionists' assumptions that hemispheric defense was sufficient to protect American interests. He argued that they failed to see the connection between stability and peace in Europe and Asia and the preservation of prosperity, democracy, and reform at home. A close relationship, FDR declared, existed "between international security and the normal development of democratic institutions. Democracy cannot thrive in an atmosphere of international insecurity. Such insecurity breeds militarism, regimentation and the denial of freedom of speech, of peaceful assemblage and of religion." War overseas would threaten American institutions, values, and ideals, even before it reached the nation's shores. National security, he concluded, depended on "a policy based on positive international cooperation, on mutual confidence, and on united effort in the solution of problems of common concern," all the attributes and characteristics of the Good Neighbor Policy.[17]

In Europe, however, there was the problem of rearmament, a problem that the United States did not have to face in forging a closer Pan-American unity. What Roosevelt called the armament "disease" was intrinsically intertwined with any solution to the economic problems of Europe and, Roosevelt believed, presented the greatest obstacle to European cooperation. Writing to

Ambassador Phillips, the president stated in May 1937 that the "more I study the situation, the more I am convinced that an economic approach to peace is a pretty weak reed for Europe to lean on" unless the issue of weapons could also be addressed. Through trade agreements "the progress of the disease is slowed up but the disease remains—and will probably prove fatal in the next few years."[18] In June, Roosevelt expressed the same worry, that spending on armaments diverted too much money from peaceful pursuits and fueled anxiety and fear. He noted that while the "prognosis" for Europe "is better than a few months ago," the "patient will die of the 'armament disease' in a few years unless a major operation is performed."[19]

The problem for Roosevelt was how to move from an analysis of the problem to a solution. He had started to challenge the assumptions of the noninterventionists concerning what was at stake for the United States if war returned to Europe, and now he needed a way to change the course of events. While most Americans wanted to stay out of European affairs, many European leaders were looking to the United States for help. That summer, the president told reporters that he had received a number of proposals from European leaders for some type of peace conference. Europe was, FDR said, "up against a stone wall," but he had no intention of calling for a meeting as he had no plan in mind. The Europeans were looking for someone with "a hat and a rabbit in it," he said. "Well . . . I haven't got a hat and I haven't got a rabbit in it."[20]

That was not quite true. Roosevelt still believed that Europe's problems could be solved short of war, and he had a vision for peace based on disarmament, reciprocal trade, and cooperation modeled after the Good Neighbor Policy. What he lacked was the support of the American people to move forward and take leadership in an effort to find peace in Europe, much less to include the United States as part of any agreement. Having set out to change public opinion, FDR was moving the ship of state cautiously in dangerous waters, ready to tack to another path toward finding a means to help preserve peace.

In July 1937, full-scale fighting erupted in China in the wake of a clash between Japanese and Chinese soldiers at the Marco Polo Bridge outside of Beijing. While the initial encounter on July 7 was only a minor skirmish, it was clear by September that Japan intended to use the incident as a pretext for an all-out assault on China and that the talks to arrange a cease-fire were just a smoke screen to hide Tokyo's intention of establishing the Greater East Asian Co-Prosperity Sphere and its hegemony over East Asia. American sympathies were clearly with China, and Japan was labeled the aggressor in all accounts. Still, the supporters of neutrality insisted that the United States keep clear of the fighting and that the president enact the neutrality law, which led to the first direct clash between Roosevelt and the noninterventionists. Roosevelt's dilemma was how to provide aid to China and resist Japan without getting too far ahead of public opinion. As he told Secretary of the Treasury Henry Morgenthau, it was "a matter of longtime education."[21]

If the president invoked the 1937 Neutrality Act, he would be blocked from helping China, while the cash-and-carry provision would allow Japan to purchase goods in the United States in support of its plans for conquest. Roosevelt worried that, while Japan's actions "immediately threaten our vital interests" and the threat could expand to an attack on European possessions in East Asia, thus setting off a world war, "it might be impossible to persuade either Congress or the American people that it was tantamount to an attack upon our own frontiers and justified military measures of self-defense."[22] Using the discretionary powers granted to him, Roosevelt finessed the situation by refusing to implement the neutrality law on the basis that no official declaration of war existed between Japan and China. To quiet the concerns of the so-called isolationists, Roosevelt did prohibit U.S. merchant ships from transporting any armaments to China or Japan.

The president's action also continued to uphold the Stimson Doctrine of the nonrecognition of Japan's conquests; it also avoided the impression, which Roosevelt believed invoking the Neutrality Act would have created, that the United States would accept any violation of its rights and treaties in China and would never act no matter what Tokyo did. *Time* magazine accurately summarized the predicament the president found himself in, noting that "the scales of public opinion . . . maintained a queasy balance between moral indignation at ruthless international aggression in Spain and China and a feeling that the U.S. must not soil the spirit of peace by taking even a moral stand."[23] That fall, Roosevelt would set out to change this balance.

In early September, in a meeting at his home in Hyde Park, Roosevelt told Assistant Secretary of State Adolf Berle that on his upcoming trip to the West he was going to "preach" about how American national security was impacted by events in Europe and Asia. The public, FDR stated, failed to understand some "important points," especially how Japan's expansion threatened U.S. interests and risked causing a global war.[24] On September 17, prior to heading West, Roosevelt delivered a Constitution Day speech in Washington, DC, in which he addressed the growing international crisis. The president contrasted the relative security of 1787 with the more interdependent world of 1937. "What we do now has enormous immediate effect not only among the nations of Europe but also among those of the Americas and the Far East, and what in any part of the world they do as surely and quickly affects us." In such a world, the ideological challenges from fascism, communism, and militarism, and their "prophesy [of] the early end of democracy throughout the world," threatened the security of the nation as much as the weapons of war. Fear was spreading throughout the world, but the president was confident that "the people of America are rightly determined to keep that growing menace from our shores." The best defense of American values and interests was to confront the danger as far away from the nation's shores as possible. Roosevelt concluded by stating that the Constitution and the democracy it represented was "a common bond . . . for those who see America as Lincoln saw it, 'the last, best hope of earth.'"[25]

Roosevelt, now embarked on his "longtime education" of the American public, charted a course in the direction of internationalism in his Quarantine Speech, delivered in Chicago on October 5, 1937. The speech was designed to provide the American people "a more realistic understanding of the kind of world that was already closing in on the United States."[26] Rather than offering any particular policies, the Quarantine Speech was a statement of Roosevelt's internationalist ideology and understanding of national security. The importance of the location of the speech cannot be overemphasized because the Windy City, through the virulently anti–New Deal *Chicago Tribune*, was seen as the center of isolationist opinion in the country. Visiting Chicago to dedicate the opening of a new bridge, the president surprised his audience by speaking on foreign policy and national security.

Because it was Roosevelt's most significant statement of his internationalist understanding of world events to date, and because it marked the beginning of the great debate over America's role in the world and the president's four-year effort to sway public opinion and confront aggression, it is necessary to quote at length from this speech. Roosevelt began by insisting that the United States must, for its "own future, give thought to the rest of the world." The developments in Europe and Asia threatened both the security of the nation and its values. The hopes of the Great War, the war to end all wars and make the world safe for democracy, the president stated, had given way to the "present reign of terror and international lawlessness" that started with the "unjustified interference in the internal affairs of other nations" and the "invasion of alien territory in violation of treaties." It had "now reached a stage where the very foundations of civilization are seriously threatened. The landmarks and traditions which have marked the progress of civilization towards a condition of law, order and justice are being wiped away."[27]

Turning to Japan's invasion of China, but also capturing the brutality of the war in Spain, Roosevelt noted that without any justification, "civilians, including women and children, are being ruthlessly murdered with bombs from the air. . . . Innocent peoples and nations are being cruelly sacrificed to a greed for power and supremacy which is devoid of all sense of justice and humane consideration." If this was not stopped, and if the aggressors succeeded, it was folly to think that America could remain immune to the consequences. "Let no one imagine," Roosevelt declared, "that America will escape, that it may expect mercy, that this Western Hemisphere will not be attacked and that it will continue tranquilly and peacefully to carry on the ethics and the arts of civilization."[28]

In order to avoid this, the "peace-loving nations must make a concerted effort in opposition to those violations of treaties and those ignoring of humane instincts which today are creating a state of international anarchy and instability from which there is no escape through mere isolation or neutrality." Invoking just war theory, FDR asserted that national security and morality were intertwined. The United States had to work with other nations "for the triumph of law and moral principles in order that peace, justice and confidence may prevail in the world. There must be a return to a belief in the pledged word in the value of a signed treaty." Furthermore, Roosevelt insisted, "there must be recognition of the fact that national morality is as vital as private morality."[29]

Setting out a strategic vision that was global and integrated, the president directly challenged the fundamental assumption that the policy of neutrality would protect the nation from war. "There is a solidarity and interdependence about the modern world," FDR declared, "both technically and morally, which makes it impossible for any nation completely to isolate itself from economic and political upheavals in the rest of the world, especially when such upheavals appear to be spreading and not declining. There can be no stability or peace either within nations or between nations except under laws and moral standards adhered to by all. International anarchy destroys every foundation for peace. It jeopardizes either the immediate or the future security of every nation, large or small. It is, therefore, a matter of vital interest and concern to the people of the United States that the sanctity of international treaties and the maintenance of international morality be restored." Roosevelt contrasted the circumstances in the United States that allowed it to spend money on infrastructure, development, and useful works with the growing militarization of some nations that threatened the rest of the world. This was the threat that had to be stopped.[30]

In his conclusion, the president again employed the disease metaphor that he had used regarding armaments, arguing that war was a contagion that "can engulf states and peoples remote from the original scene of hostilities," and that the "epidemic of world lawlessness is spreading." It was, therefore, necessary for nations to band together to "quarantine" the aggressors to protect the world from the disease's spread. Roosevelt reiterated that he was determined to pursue a policy of peace and keep the nation out of war, but that "we cannot insure ourselves against the disastrous effects of war and the dangers of involvement. We are adopting such measures as will minimize our risk of involvement but we cannot have complete protection in a world of disorder in which confidence and security have broken down." The speech ended with the president stating that "America hates war. America hopes for peace. Therefore, America actively engages in the search for peace."[31]

The initial response to the speech was surprisingly favorable, led by support from the *New York Times*, the *Washington Post*, and numerous other papers across the nation that saw the idea of "quarantine" as a means to stop aggression without war. At a news conference the next day, when asked if he had sanctions in mind, Roosevelt replied that "'sanctions' is a terrible word to use. They are out of the window." The key, he said, was in the last line about the search for peace. "I can't tell you what the methods will be. We are looking for some way to peace."[32] Roosevelt temporized; because the course was not yet clear, and he might have to shift directions in response to events, it was best not to be too specific in choosing the route to the final destination. He was also well aware that there were plenty of criticisms of his speech from those committed to the old policy of hemispheric defense and neutrality. The president correctly understood that the support for his speech did not mean that there was public support for sanctions against Japan or for other steps that might lead to hostilities.

In response to his critics, Roosevelt stated in a fireside chat on October 12, 1937, that the nation cannot "view with indifference the destruction of civilized values throughout the world." He wanted "our great democracy to be wise enough to realize that aloofness from war is not promoted by unawareness of war. In a world of mutual suspicions, peace must be affirmatively reached for. It cannot just be wished for. It cannot just be waited for."[33] As FDR explained his actions to Endicott Peabody four days later, he was "fighting against a public psychology of long standing . . . which comes close to saying 'Peace at any price.'"[34]

As he made clear in an exchange of letters with former Secretary of State Stimson, Roosevelt was tacking, and setting out ideas; but he was not getting too far ahead of his opposition and was always ready to change direction when necessary to reach his goals. In November, Stimson wrote Roosevelt with his support for his speech and asked the president to back up his words with action. Japan, Stimson believed, was run by its military and its goals were "inherently hostile" to the United States and its interests. He suggested that Washington could lead the world in measures short of war by extending the Stimson Doctrine to include an economic boycott. China, he argued, was "fighting our battle for freedom and peace," and to aid it the United States should impose sanctions on Japan to deny it the capacity to wage war.[35]

Roosevelt's response to Stimson set out the continued dilemma he faced: a desire to take action but a caution about how quickly he could move and in what direction because of domestic politics. The president noted that he "wholly" agreed with Stimson, but did not have an answer. Stimson's request that Roosevelt actually quarantine Japan came up against the president's concern that he not get too far out in front of public opinion and his worry that if he took a false step he would set back his effort at education. In his response, FDR told Stimson that his letter stated "considerations which are ever present in my thoughts," but failed to provide him with an acceptable course of action. The Europeans were looking for leadership from the United States, but he was not sure that the "people of this country nor Congress would support any measures of pressure."[36]

On December 12, the U.S. gunboat *Panay*, on patrol in the Yangtze River, was repeatedly bombed and strafed by Japanese planes despite the prominent display of two large American flags, leaving two dead and over thirty wounded. The American naval presence on the Yangtze dated back to a nineteenth-century treaty with China, made to protect American nationals in China. Roosevelt immediately instructed Hull to express to Japan the nation's shock and concern over the indiscriminate bombing of the *Panay*; he should inform them that the United States was assembling all the facts to present to Tokyo, and that Washington expected a full apology and compensation for the attack and assurances against any future incidents.[37] The president ordered the Pacific fleet from San Diego to Pearl Harbor and indicated his willingness to impose sanctions on Japan, while he consulted with the British on the idea of blockade and what further actions might be taken. Finally, he informed Congress that he would seek additional naval appropriations above what had originally been requested for the 1938 fiscal year. "I have used every conceivable effort," FDR wrote the Appropriations Committee, to curtail the production of weapons. "Facts, nevertheless, are facts, and the United States must recognize them."[38]

Rather than becoming another *Maine* or *Lusitania*, the *Panay* was a quickly forgotten episode. Few demanded more action than the president's call for an apology; and many wondered why the *Panay* was in an area of fighting and called for the withdrawal of American ships from China. This climate of opinion deterred Roosevelt from going forward with any punitive measures, and led him to accept the Japanese apology, compensation, and assurances that Americans would be safe in China. So strong was the desire for peace that the incident propelled Representative Louis Ludlow's quixotic quest to transfer the power to declare war from Congress to a national referendum. He introduced a constitutional amendment onto the floor of the House of Representatives for a vote. Polls showed almost seventy-five percent of the public approved such an amendment. Wary of creating a political controversy over a foreign policy issue, Roosevelt, when asked if he thought the amendment was consistent with democratic government, responded: "I suppose the easiest way to answer that is just to say No, and stop there—stop right there."[39] The administration worked hard to block the Ludlow amendment, and it was narrowly defeated in Congress. But the profound fear of war remained a roadblock for the president in his effort to craft a policy to curb aggression short of military conflict.

The problems in Europe kept turning the president's thoughts back to economic solutions and to a proposal from Undersecretary of State Sumner Welles for a European conference on disarmament and trade. Despite his statement in the summer of 1937 that he didn't have a hat with a proposal for peace in it, the president and Welles had been discussing the idea of a meeting to consider the problems of Europe. Roosevelt finally adopted a plan for the United States to call a world conference so that nations would agree on how they could all "obtain the right to have access upon equal and effective terms to raw materials and other elements necessary for their economic life." Arrangements would be based on international cooperation over resources and cooperation on trade with the goal of economic interdependence and shared prosperity that would lead to a reduction of armaments.[40]

Roosevelt was looking for some way to act and change the direction away from the increasing likelihood of conflict in Europe. At the same time, he was not convinced the effort would work. Nonetheless, the president supported the Welles Plan because it stayed within the parameters of acceptable action domestically and was based on the internationalist tenets of foreign policy that he believed in. It also reflected the understanding of his administration, at the time, that the moderate fascists remained in control and could be worked with, and that economic appeasement could succeed without turning to the Soviet Union for assistance against Germany. In addition, the president feared that a policy that only condemned Hitler's actions without offering a solution to what were perceived as Germany's legitimate grievances would drive him into an alliance with Mussolini and bring about war. Some formula was needed to enable Germany to be integrated into the international system short of direct confrontation. Unable to advocate collective security, Roosevelt was searching for an approach to the German problem. At worst, it would demonstrate that FDR was doing all he could to find peace while also serving as a transition to more direct confrontation with the danger posed by the Nazi regime.

Secretary of State Hull agreed with the president's and Welles's analysis and proposal, but insisted that the British first be advised of the plan before Roosevelt took the initiative of extending invitations to the nations of Europe. As presented to London in January 1938, the aim of the conference was to foster an "understanding between this country and the leading powers of Europe to achieve economic co-operation" to create an "international economy based on reduced armaments, a greater common use of world resources, and the improvement and simplification of economic relations" among nations."[41] British Prime Minister Neville Chamberlain had been formulating his own appeasement policy based on bilateral negotiations between London and Berlin, concessions to Germany, and territorial adjustments in

Eastern Europe. Chamberlain, who distrusted the United States and believed that, based on Washington's rejection of the Treaty of Versailles, it could not be counted on to back up any arrangements, rejected Welles's proposal on the grounds that it would interfere with his own negotiations with Berlin. The prime minister informed Roosevelt that any effort by the United States at that time to call for a world conference would "delay consideration of specific points which must be settled if appeasement is to be achieved."[42]

Roosevelt and Welles were upset by Chamberlain's rejection of the U.S. proposal. American leaders believed that a general settlement of Europe's problems had to be reached to avoid war, while Chamberlain was pursuing a piecemeal approach that did not address the central problems. In effect, Chamberlain had excluded the United States from participation in any settlement. In February, British Foreign Minister Anthony Eden persuaded a reluctant Chamberlain to open discussions with the United States based on the Welles plan, but Roosevelt held out little hope that these talks would change the British position. In any event, Hitler's annexation of Austria on March 12, 1938, brought an end to these discussions and to using the Welles plan as a basis for peace.

Having failed to gain the support of London, Roosevelt changed course in 1938. His efforts turned to expanding the zone of American military responsibility, building up American forces, and deterring Japan. The president continued his efforts to get the American people to rethink what it meant to defend the country and to develop a broader conception of national security, and he sought to create a buffer zone around the Western Hemisphere to be better prepared for war.

In a special message to Congress on January 28, 1938, FDR spoke about his efforts at peace, the dangers of modern warfare, and the need for increased budgets for defense. In the process, Roosevelt set out his understanding of the crisis the nation faced, the futility of neutrality, and the need for greater action by the United States. The president began by reminding his audience of the efforts the United States had made to limit and reduce armaments, foster greater international cooperation, and increase trade. Yet, outside of the Western Hemisphere these efforts had been rebuffed. Thus, "we are compelled to think of our own national safety." The Germans and Japanese continued to strengthen their militaries at unprecedented rates, and wars raged in Europe and Asia that threatened to engulf all parts of the world. In light of these circumstances, Roosevelt stated that it was his constitutional duty to inform Congress and the American people that the U.S. military's funding and supplies were "inadequate for the purposes of national security and requires increase for that reason." To redress the problem and insure security, the president requested over $29 million in additional appropriations for improvements and expansion of the navy and army.[43]

In a direct challenge to the idea that neutrality combined with the insulation of two oceans would keep the United States safe, Roosevelt declared that in an age of long-range bombers and modern navies, "adequate defense means that for the protection not only of our coasts but also of our communities far removed from the coasts, we must keep any potential enemy many hundreds of miles away from our continental limits." Roosevelt was arguing that Europe and Asia were the front lines of American national security. "We cannot assume that our defense would be limited to one ocean and one coast and that the other ocean and the other coast would with certainty be safe." It was the president's duty to promote peace, but also to "protect our Nation."[44]

Certainly, Franklin Roosevelt knew it was going to take a great effort. He believed it would be a long struggle to change American public opinion, as well as gain support for his interpretation of world affairs and the correct direction of American foreign policy. As Roosevelt again noted in a letter to his friend Arthur Murray in London in February 1938, he was now "in the midst of a long process of education—and the process seems to be working slowly but surely." Part of this was dissuading people "who saw in Nazi-ism ideals of peace and good-will."[45] In a fireside chat of April 14, 1938, on economic conditions, FDR told the American people that "you and I agree that security is our greatest need." The president was thinking about peoples' "economic needs" and "their personal liberties—the most precious possession of all Americans. I am thinking of our democracy and of the recent trend in other parts of the world away from the democratic ideal." The "only sure bulwark of continuing liberty is a government strong enough to protect the interests of the people" at home and abroad. The president concluded by noting that he was "right in the course we have charted." He would "sail ahead," for to reach the port of real security "we must sail—sail not tie at anchor—sail not drift."[46]

Gerald Nye led the Congressional opposition to Roosevelt's proposal for additional funding for the military. He argued that the proper defense of the nation was based on the distance the two oceans provided from hostile nations, neutrality, and protecting American interests in the Western Hemisphere.

Increased spending would move the United States closer to war, Nye argued, as it was designed to allow the nation to fight thousands of miles away from home and would entangle it in foreign wars. Yet, Japan's attack on China and Germany's increasing belligerence had raised concerns about national defense, and the need for military preparedness had eroded the support for neutrality. Congress passed a munitions bill in May that provided a twenty percent increase in naval spending and funds to fortify bases in the Pacific Ocean. This was not enough to deter Japan, but it indicated that Roosevelt was gaining in the battle over how to define national security and in public support of his preparedness policies.

In the wake of the *Anschluss*, Berlin's absorption of Austria into the German state, the United Kingdom continued its piecemeal approach to appeasement. Prime Minister Chamberlain returned to his negotiations with Berlin over territory, seeking a means to satisfy Hitler. In addition, London reached a series of accords with Rome relating to the Mediterranean and recognition of Italy's possession of Ethiopia. With no other avenues open to him, Roosevelt backed the prime minister's efforts. In a presidential statement released on April 19, Roosevelt noted that the United States had consistently sought the maintenance of law and order, and the promotion of peace "through the friendly solution by peaceful negotiations between nations." While it did not pass judgment on the substance of the arrangements, it "urged the promotion of peace through the finding of means for economic appeasement."[47]

Events, however, were moving too quickly as Hitler escalated his demands to now include the absorption of the Sudetenland in Czechoslovakia into the Third Reich. The basis of the German claim was that the majority of the people in this part of Czechoslovakia spoke German and, therefore, should be part of the German nation. Prague initially resisted Berlin's pressure and sought assistance from other nations against Germany. As German troops gathered near the Czechoslovakian border, Roosevelt contacted the British, French, Germans, Italians, and Czechs, urging them all to continue negotiations and bring a peaceful resolution to the crisis. France and Great Britain were opposed to any actions that would bring war. While the Soviet Union indicated it would use force, Poland and Romania refused to allow its forces to cross their borders. Isolated, in late September, Czechoslovakia yielded to pressure from London and announced it would surrender the territory to Germany. After Chamberlain's announcement that he would meet Hitler and Mussolini in Munich to work out an agreement around the transfer of territory, Roosevelt sent him a two-word cable: "Good Man."[48] The president was hoping against hope, but really thought that Chamberlain, at best, could bring a temporary postponement to "what looks to me like an inevitable conflict within the next few years." Voicing his frustration with the course of events and his lack of influence, the president noted that "perhaps when it comes the United States will be in the position to pick up the pieces of European civilization and help them save what remains of the wreck—not a cheerful prospect."[49]

Any optimism over Munich was short-lived in the face of Germany's renewed repression of German Jews and continued belligerence. The State Department began what Berle called its "death watch" on Europe. By late October, it was indisputably clear to Roosevelt that appeasement had failed and war was coming. As FDR told Treasury Secretary Morgenthau, "These trade treaties are just too god-damned slow, the world is marching too fast. They're just too slow."[50] The only option now, the president believed, was to accelerate military spending. He announced that month he intended to spend an additional $300 million. Munich also prompted FDR to further his efforts to shift American public opinion away from neutrality and toward support of internationalism.

Speaking at the *New York Herald Tribune* Forum on October 26, 1938, Roosevelt fully rejected any further notions that relations with Nazi Germany could be handled in the same manner as relations with other nations or that reasonable, moderate fascists were in control. He emphasized the danger Germany presented to the United States, declaring that "you cannot organize civilization around the core of militarism and at the same time expect reason to control human destinies." Modern weapons had eliminated the security formerly provided by the two oceans, meaning that the "world today has become our neighbor." Increasing the size of the military was "a step we do not like to take, and do not wish to take," but America could not "accept disarmament while neighbor nations arm to the teeth." In a challenge to his critics, Roosevelt stated that the "way of democracy is free discussion" but added that the exchange of ideas is "useful when it is restrained and relates to facts." Portraying the stance of the noninterventionists as irresponsible and a danger to national security, the president called for a common effort to defend the United States "so that we may, if the test ever comes, have the unity of will with which alone a democracy can successfully meet its enemies."[51]

On November 9, 1938, the Nazis attacked Jews across Germany in the night of broken glass, *Kristallnacht*. Almost one hundred were killed, tens of thousands arrested, and thousands of homes, businesses, and synagogues destroyed. Roosevelt stated at a press conference on November 15 that he "could scarcely believe that such things could occur in a twentieth century civilization."[52] The American ambassador to Berlin, Hugh Wilson, was called home for consultations, and he never returned. Roosevelt called Hitler a fanatic, "a pure unadulterated devil," who could not recognize Germany's real interests or be reached by rational appeals.[53] The president had concluded that Germany would have to be stopped by force.

The threat, however, extended beyond Central Europe. It was global. Roosevelt believed that for the first time since the War of 1812 and the Latin American wars of independence in the early nineteenth century, there was the "possibility of an attack on the Atlantic side in both the Northern and Southern Hemispheres." The best deterrent was a larger air force to provide range and defense in depth of the American republics. It would also assist other nations resisting Germany and provide credibility to Roosevelt's diplomatic moves. He told his advisors on November 14 that "when I write to foreign countries I must have something to back up my words. Had we had this summer 5,000 planes and the capacity immediately to produce 10,000 per year . . . Hitler would not have dared to take the stand he did."[54]

At the same time that the crisis in Europe deepened, the Roosevelt administration was divided on the course of action to take in the Pacific. Even without the restraints placed on policymaking by public opinion and Congress it was not clear what direction to take. Many held that American interests were best served by resistance to Japan, the imposition of sanctions, and taking a tough line toward Tokyo. They were opposed by those who sought to adjust to Japan's actions and find ways of accommodating it in East Asia. These positions were best represented by the two longtime stalwarts of U.S. policy toward Japan, Stanley K. Hornbeck, now the State Department's Senior Advisor on Political Relations, and U.S. Ambassador to Japan Joseph Grew.

For Hornbeck, the key issue was "that Japan not gain control of China." If that were to happen, the United States and the West would be driven out of East Asia. He, therefore, urged the use of economic sanctions as the only viable method, short of war, to stop Japanese expansion, protect China, and uphold American interests and the Open Door policy. Japan, Hornbeck believed, had "embarked upon a program of predatory imperialism" that was in direct conflict with the values and legitimate interests of the United States, and unless that march was halted soon "the time will come when Japan and the United States will be face to face and definitely opposed to each other." If Tokyo's policy of expansion continued, it would mean war. The only way to prevent that was to adopt a policy aimed at stopping Japan and averting war. For Hornbeck, the course of necessary action was clear. "The march," Hornbeck argued, "will be halted only by the power of resistance of material obstacles and material pressures." The problem, of course, was that if the United States took this course of action, it would have to be prepared "to use, if it prove necessary, armed force."[55]

Given this, it was essential, Hornbeck wrote, that the United States provide assistance to China while "withholding those things which are of assistance to the Japanese" in order to strengthen Chinese resistance, prolong the fighting, and weaken Japan. The first step would be to abrogate the 1911 U.S.–Japan Commercial Treaty, followed by a repeal of the Neutrality Act, retaliatory tariff measures, an embargo on trade, and a deployment of the United States Navy to demonstrate Washington's resolve to protect its interests.[56]

Grew disagreed with these recommendations and warned Washington against imposing economic sanctions. Similar to Hornbeck, Grew was searching for a policy that would protect American interests and prevent war. He, however, started from the premise that Japan was in China to stay, that the Open Door could no longer be the basis of American policy, and that the United States would have to accommodate itself to the new realities in East Asia. No American action, including a complete embargo on all trade, "would cause the Japanese to relinquish their program in China." They were "inured to hardships" and determined to establish the Greater East Asian Co-Prosperity Sphere. "The so-called 'new order in East Asia' has come to stay," Grew concluded, and he saw no chance to create domestic discontent in Japan with the military leaders or deter them from their goals.[57]

Facing these realities, as Grew understood them, the ambassador recommended that the United States work with Japan to protect American interests in the new order as much as possible. This was the only way to protect American commercial and cultural interests in the region and bring future improvement. The worst abuses, Grew believed, such as bombings of properties and "violations of our commercial rights can be stemmed, but unless we are prepared to fight for it, the Open Door, as we conceive it, is not going to be kept open." The choice, therefore, was "losing everything or saving something from the wreckage, while opening the way to a potential building up of our relations with Japan." Tokyo, he believed, still wanted good relations with Washington, and the United States had a great deal still to lose if a permanent break occurred between the two nations.[58]

Roosevelt's views were in line with Hornbeck's, but he did not believe he could take those steps in 1939. Instead, he chose a middle path, seeking to put some pressure on Japan through increased military spending and aid to China, but refusing to follow Hornbeck's advice for tariff restrictions, an embargo, and confrontation with Tokyo. Most importantly, the president served notice to Tokyo in July 1939 that Washington would not renew the 1911 commercial treaty between Japan and the United States, which officially expired in January 1940. This opened the door to further economic restrictions and an embargo. While Grew and others argued that sanctions would not deter Tokyo, Japan did rely heavily on American oil and scrap metal for its military machine; it was vulnerable to decisions made in Washington as the United States supplied fifty percent of Japan's petroleum, iron, and copper, all essential for military operations. The ending of the treaty would make it legally possible for the administration to impose sanctions or an embargo on Japan without Congressional approval.

In his State of the Union speech in January 1939, Roosevelt focused on the growing international crisis and the need to revise America's neutrality laws to allow aid to nations facing aggression abroad. He began by noting that while "a war which threatened to envelop the world in flames has been averted" due to the Munich deal, "it has become increasingly clear that world peace is not assured." What was at stake, Roosevelt declared, was both the physical security of the nation and its values. In addition to the material danger to the United States that the dictators presented, the "storms from abroad directly challenge three institutions indispensable to Americans": religion, democracy, and international goodwill. "There comes a time in the affairs of men," Roosevelt told Congress, "when they must prepare to defend, not their homes alone, but the tenets of faith and humanity on which their churches, their governments and their very civilization are founded. The defense of religion, of democracy, and of good faith among nations is all the same fight. To save one we must now make up our minds to save all."[59]

While the Western Hemisphere was united due to the Good Neighbor Policy, the world "has grown so small and weapons of attack so swift that no nation can be safe in its will to peace as long as any other single powerful nation refuses to settle its grievances at the council table." In his most direct attack on the logic of neutrality, the president declared that "we have learned that when we deliberately try to legislate neutrality, our neutrality laws may operate unevenly and unfairly—may actually give aid to an aggressor and deny it to the victim." But the nation had learned something else since 1931, that the "probability of attack is mightily decreased by the assurance of an ever ready defense," preparedness, and cooperation with like-minded countries. "We have learned that God-fearing democracies of the world which observe the sanctity of treaties and good faith in their dealings with other nations cannot safely be indifferent to international lawlessness anywhere. They cannot forever let pass, without effective protest, acts of aggression against sister nations—acts which automatically undermine all of us."[60]

Even if the United States was not under direct attack, institutions and values that were essential to the defense of the nation and to the promotion of peace were being undermined overseas. The dictatorships of Germany, Japan, and Italy sought to destroy these and in doing so were seeking to create a world that was hostile to the United States and that would eventually cause it harm. Continuing his efforts to establish a new strategic vision of defense, the president stated that national security necessitated armed forces strong enough to defend the nation and "ensure sustained resistance and ultimate victory." But, FDR noted, there was another key element to national security: freedom at home. "Our nation's program of social and economic reform is therefore a part of defense, as basic as armaments themselves." Just as the tools of government that were in place in 1933 were now outmoded, so were the concepts of neutrality and nonintervention. It was up to the United States to protect democracy and freedom. "Once I prophesied that this generation of Americans had a rendezvous with destiny," Roosevelt stated. "That prophecy comes true. To us much is given; more is expected."[61]

With German and Japanese aggression mounting, public opinion in the United States began to shift in 1939. In March, Germany, breaking the agreement made at Munich, annexed the rest of Czechoslovakia. Great Britain finally abandoned appeasement and, along with France, provided assurances to Poland that they would come to its aid if it was attacked by Germany. After the German annexation of Czechoslovakia, the president requested an additional $525 million for preparedness, which Congress passed in April. In addition, for the first time a majority of the American people favored providing Great Britain and France with weapons, planes, and other war supplies.

The administration fought with the proponents of neutrality throughout the summer of 1939 to persuade Congress to amend the Neutrality Act to end the arms embargo provision in order to assist Germany's enemies and defend the United States. Roosevelt told the members of the Senate Military Affairs Committee in a closed session that he did not "belong to the school of thought that says we can draw a line of defense around this country and live completely and solely to ourselves." In the face of German aggression, "the first line of defense of the United States" was the survival of Great Britain and France. If they fell, and the president saw the odds of defeating Germany as "fifty-fifty," Hitler would then turn to Africa and South America, seeking "the gradual encirclement of the United States by removal of the first lines of defense." Japan would join and attack the European possessions in East Asia, leaving the Western Hemisphere "surrounded by hostile states." The only way to prevent this was to see the threat in global terms and enact reform so that the scenario the president outlined did not happen. When it was leaked that the president had placed America's frontier at the Rhine, FDR denied it and called it a "deliberate lie."[62]

When the Senate Foreign Relations Committee voted in July to defer any action until January, Roosevelt sent a direct message written by Hull to be read in Congress, calling for immediate action. The key point for the president was that the only way for the United States to stay out of war now was to allow it to send arms to the democracies threatened by Germany and Japan. A continuation of the arms embargo "plays into the hands of those nations which have taken the lead in building up their fighting power. It works directly against the interests of the peace-loving nations."[63] Four days later, Roosevelt met with Senate leaders to encourage them to reconsider the bill. Holding to their position that arms sales would drag the nation into war and that neutrality was the best means to preserve peace, the senators remained opposed to any repeal of the arms embargo. Senator William Borah went so far as to claim that he had "private information," from better sources than the State Department had, that there would be no war in Europe in the near future, and he argued that any changes would foster war rather than prevent it.[64]

The headlong rush to war in Europe did not hinge on the decisions made by the Senate regarding neutrality. In August, Germany and the Soviet

Union shocked the world with the announcement of the Nazi–Soviet nonaggression pact, which assured Germany it would not have to fight a two-front war when it attacked Poland. The German invasion came on September 1, 1939. In a press conference that day, when Roosevelt was asked if the United States could stay out of the war, he responded: "I not only sincerely hope so, but I believe we can; and that every effort will be made by the Administration so to do." Speaking to the nation on September 3, the day Great Britain and France declared war on Germany, Roosevelt noted that "for four long years a succession of actual wars and constant crises have shaken the entire world and have threatened in each case to bring on the gigantic conflict which is today unhappily a fact." While Americans desired peace, "we are forced to realize that . . . every ship that sails the sea, every battle that is fought, does affect the American future." While the United States would be officially neutral and FDR called for national unity, he could not ask people to be neutral in their thoughts. "Even a neutral has a right to take account of facts. Even a neutral cannot be asked to close his mind or his conscience." He did promise "that the influence of America should be consistent in seeking for humanity a final peace which will eliminate, as far as it is possible to do so, the continued use of force between nations."[65]

Still facing stiff political headwinds, FDR was now less willing to trim his internationalist sails than in the past. The outbreak of war in Europe in September 1939 led FDR to call for a special session of Congress to amend the neutrality laws and repeal the arms embargo. In his September 21 message to Congress, Roosevelt declared that the existing legislation "so alters the historic foreign policy of the United States that it impairs the peaceful relations of the United States with foreign nations." He told the nation that he regretted that Congress had passed the Neutrality Act and that "I regret equally that I signed that Act." The president declared that it would be unwise to think that the crisis would pass by quickly. Rather, he thought that the worst had not yet come from "the forces that assault the foundations of civilization." Although supporters of the existing law mounted an all-out campaign to defeat any revisions, they were no longer strong enough to prevent the change the president requested. Roosevelt's argument, that Great Britain and France were fighting America's battle and that assisting them was both the moral and materially correct course of action, had won. In November, FDR signed the new law that repealed the arms embargo and allowed him to provide aid to the opponents of fascism.[66]

With general war in Europe and Asia, Roosevelt now faced a new set of problems that would test all of his political skills and require more tactical changes of course. In an evaluation of events since 1933, FDR stated that "peace was the very keystone of our entire foreign policy" because of "a realistic appreciation that any European war would be a definite danger to our own peace and security, and to the welfare of the entire western hemisphere and the rest of the world." The three pillars of that effort were the Good Neighbor Policy, disarmament, and free trade through reciprocal trade treaties. These had been successful in establishing "the solidarity of the western hemisphere on a permanently peaceful basis"; however, the hope that the example set by the cooperation of the American republics and their reliance on collective security for peace would have "influence upon the rest of the world" had, "unfortunately, . . . proved to be in vain."[67]

While Roosevelt had often warned the American people of the growing danger, it was difficult for most, including policymakers, to fully understand the malevolence and ambitions that drove the dictators. Peace was destroyed "by a handful of relentless men who sought selfish power for themselves." Reasonable efforts at negotiation and compromises "to bring about peaceful settlement of disputes among nations" had been pursued throughout the decade "were quite apparently not going to prevail in the world." Thus, it became necessary in FDR's second term for the United States to "embark on a program of increasing its own national defense" as it was becoming apparent that the nation would have to "rearm against this increasing threat of aggression."[68]

Franklin Roosevelt knew that the triumph over the restrictive neutrality laws did not mean the nation was ready to join the war, nor that it should. Still, it was imperative, from his perspective, that the public understand that the war "was not merely a European conflict which meant nothing to them." Rather, the American people had to understand "that the Nazis had embarked on a definite program of world domination which was an immediate and serious threat to the United States and the western hemisphere"; the conquest Germany sought "was not merely a domination of military might but a domination of ideas, in which the whole world was to be bent to the Nazi philosophy of force, of slavery, of anti-religion."[69] The president's campaign to educate the American people had begun to undermine the position held by the advocates of neutrality. As he continued to cast the struggle with Germany and Japan in moral terms and as a threat to American values and institutions, and as he highlighted Berlin's and Tokyo's clear responsibility for the existence of war in Europe and Asia, Roosevelt was able to define the noninterventionist position in negative terms as naïve, callous, irresponsible, and, most of all, dangerous to the nation. The great debate was far from over, but FDR was gaining the upper hand.

FDR sailing the *Amberjack II* from Marion, MA, to Campobello Island, N.B., Canada, June 16–29, 1933. His sons James, Franklin Jr., and John are closest to him.

Unless otherwise noted, photos appear courtesy of the Franklin D. Roosevelt Presidential Library archives.

FDR sailing the *Sewanna* from Rockport, ME, to Campobello Island, N.B., Canada, July 14–28, 1936. His sons John, Franklin Jr., and James are with him.

FDR in Montevideo, Uruguay, December 3, 1936, with Uruguay president Gabriel Terra after the Inter-American Conference for the Maintenance of Peace.

Secretary of War Henry L. Stimson draws the first date in the national lottery for Selective Service registrants, October 29, 1940.

FDR and Prime Minister Winston Churchill on *HMS Prince of Wales* at the Atlantic Charter meeting, August 10, 1941.

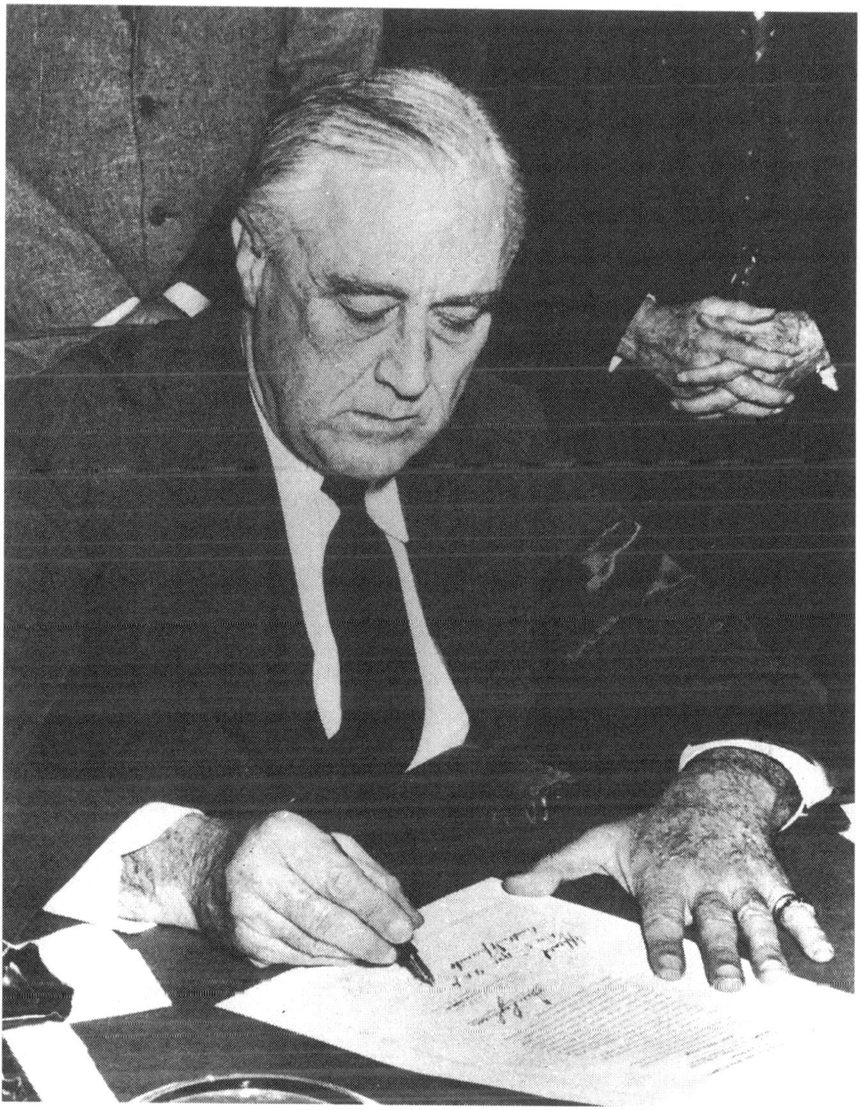

FDR signing declaration of war, December 8, 1941.

FDR and Harry Hopkins in the president's White House study, June 1942. (Courtesy of Margaret Suckley and the Franklin D. Roosevelt Presidential Library archives.)

FDR, Soviet premier Joseph Stalin, and Churchill at Tehran Conference, January 29, 1943.

FDR reviewing the troops in Rabat at the Casablanca Conference, January 1943.

FDR's address to Congress after the Yalta Conference, March 1, 1945.

4

The Fulcrum of Roosevelt's Foreign Policy

The outbreak of war in Europe brought the final revisions of the Neutrality Act that President Roosevelt sought, but this success did not solve the larger problems that confronted the nation abroad. The questions facing the president were how to increase aid to Great Britain and France without getting too far ahead of public support, and how to increase American preparedness without causing alarm that he planned to take the nation to war. Despite having picked sides in terms of their willingness to aid the Western democracies, the American public remained overwhelmingly opposed to U.S. participation in the war and feared being dragged into the fighting through direct support to London. Roosevelt knew he still had to convince the American people about the last part of his internationalist vision, that the United States should take on the role of world leader and be a direct participant in the global struggle against fascism. The great debate was far from over, and his decision to run in 1940 for an unprecedented third term as president called for continued caution on Roosevelt's part. Nevertheless, FDR was determined to win both reelection and his battle against the noninterventionists in his effort to redefine American national security.

The war in Europe was the top priority of the administration as it believed that Germany posed the greatest threat to American interests. Still, the potential of a Japanese attack on the Western colonies in Southeast Asia directly linked the war in Europe with East Asia and made the conflicts, in Roosevelt's view, part of a singular world war with many fronts that demanded a global strategy to defend the nation. Given this, in 1940 the issue in making policy toward East Asia was how much pressure to place on Japan after the termination of the commercial treaty without provoking Tokyo to expand the scope of the war. Roosevelt did not want to imperil the Europeans' access to the wealth and resources of their colonies and, thus, their ability to resist Germany, but he also could not allow Japan to grow stronger and increase its threat to the United States.

Events in Europe in 1940 and the formation of the Axis alliance resolved parts of these problems. Beginning in the summer of 1940, Roosevelt began taking a series of steps that would provide essential aid to Great Britain, prepare the United States for war, and increase pressure on Japan. From June 1940 to March 1941, the president put into place his war cabinet, obtained direct aid for Great Britain, and imposed a partial embargo on Japan. In the wake of the fall of France in June 1940, FDR pushed for even greater expansion of American military and armaments production, arguing that, in the modern era, preparedness was vital for national defense. All of these efforts were connected to a global strategic vision, and much of Roosevelt's thinking about the state of the world, the war, and the role the United States would have to play proved prescient.

FDR believed that American democracy and values could not survive in a world where Nazism controlled Europe; in his statements on the international crisis he continued to declare that World War II was a battle for the survival of freedom. In December 1940 and January 1941, Roosevelt set out the ideological justifications for war, calling on the United States to be the "arsenal of democracy" in defense of the four freedoms: freedom from want and fear, and freedom of belief and speech. In conjunction with the proposal for lend-lease, this proved to be the fulcrum of the president's policy, in which Roosevelt set out what the country was fighting for. His efforts to persuade the American public to follow his internationalist policy succeeded; the nation abandoned neutrality and isolationism and looked to collective security and world leadership as the only means to defend the nation and its interests. For FDR, the four freedoms were not mere rhetoric; they represented the central purpose, values, and meaning of the war. While direct American involvement was still six months off after the passage of the Lend-Lease Act on March 11, 1941, Roosevelt had established the concepts of the just war and the fight to defend the nation and its values as the basis for American involvement in the conflict.

After Germany's quick defeat of Poland and its dismemberment by the Third Reich and the Soviet Union, fighting stopped on the ground in Europe for the winter of 1939–1940. The Allies used this time of the so-called phony war to mobilize, plan, and prepare their defenses in the West. By the end of the year, with no battles in over three months, many hoped that a negotiated end might be found that would spare the continent further warfare. Roosevelt thought otherwise, believing that any agreement would only be a temporary respite akin to another Munich. As he wrote in December 1939, "I do not want to take part in a patched up temporizing peace which would blow up in our faces in a year or two." Whether Germany won the war or just achieved a peace favorable to it, the security of the United States would remain "in peril." Moreover, many Americans still did not fully comprehend the threat Germany posed and the consequences that a fascist victory would have on the nation's security and the future of Western civilization. "What worries me, especially," FDR wrote, "is that public opinion over here is patting itself on the back every morning and thanking God for the Atlantic Ocean (and the Pacific Ocean)." Events, however, moved with "such terrific speed" that it was essential to take a global perspective and "to warn the American people that they, too, should think of possible ultimate results in Europe and the Far East." The problem was to "get the American people to think of conceivable consequences without scaring the American people into thinking that they are going to be dragged into this war."[1] That is, Roosevelt wanted them to enter the war on their own terms and for their own reasons to ensure support.

This dilemma was a central theme of the president's State of the Union Address on January 3, 1940. Roosevelt noted that in many previous messages to Congress he had warned that the United States would not be immune to the "shock of events on other continents." Given the events of September 1939, the threat was "no longer mere theory." As FDR noted, "There is a vast difference between keeping out of war and pretending that this war is none of our business." The danger was so acute that the nation had to look ahead and envision the lives its children would lead if most of the rest of the world "were compelled to worship a god imposed by a military ruler, or were forbidden to worship God at all; if the rest of the world were forbidden to read and hear the facts . . . if they were deprived of the truth that makes men free." In addition to issues of morality, it was also imperative that Americans "recognize the practical fact that with modern weapons and modern conditions, modern man can no longer lead a civilized life if we are to go back to the practice of wars and conquests of the seventeenth and eighteenth centuries."[2]

Conversely, unilateral, nationalist policies such as the "blind economic selfishness in most countries" after the Great War, "including our own, resulted in a destructive mine-field of trade restrictions which blocked the channels of commerce among nations . . ." and "was one of the contributing causes of the existing wars." Peace, prosperity, and security, as demonstrated by the Good Neighbor Policy, would only come through cooperation, mutual respect, and freedom in all nations, the values that Americans cherished. While the nation hoped to remain at peace, it would work with other like-minded countries "to encourage the kind of peace that will lighten the troubles of the world, and by so doing, help our own nation as well."[3] To back up his position, in his budget request submitted to Congress the same day, FDR requested further increases in American defense spending.[4]

In this context, Roosevelt authorized Undersecretary of State Sumner Welles's mission to Europe in February and March 1940 to evaluate the prospects for a peace consistent with American values and interests. While skeptical that there was a real chance for peace with Hitler, FDR nonetheless was willing to explore any avenue that might prevent the massive destruction of a European war. If nothing else, it would again demonstrate to the American people that he had gone to great lengths for peace and would show the intractability of the Axis powers and their responsibility for the war.

Welles's trip did serve other purposes for the president. The undersecretary of state would provide Roosevelt a firsthand account of the situation in Europe, and his talks in Rome, Berlin, London, and Paris might help prolong the lull in the fighting, to the advantage of the Allies. Most significantly, Roosevelt and Welles hoped to take advantage of Italy's nonbelligerent status to split the Axis. Roosevelt believed the Allies would win, but only after a long and bitter contest that would bring economic and social collapse to Europe. If Mussolini could be persuaded at least to keep Italy neutral, if not to switch sides as Rome had done in 1915, it would aid Great Britain and France by containing the fighting to northern Europe.[5]

Welles made Italy the first and last stop on his European mission. He told the Italian dictator that Roosevelt was pleased that he had maintained the peace in the Mediterranean and Balkan regions, and that the president was sympathetic to Italy's needs and hoped to meet with Il Duce some day. Although Welles's mission officially called for him to evaluate only the prospects of a just and durable negotiated peace, he was determined to find a way to break Rome away from Berlin by persuading Mussolini that Italy's interests would be better served by cooperation with the United States and support of the Allies. If Mussolini cooperated, Washington would be sure to help Italy obtain the concessions it sought in any peace agreement. No deal, however, was reached. After his visit to Berlin and discussions with Nazi leaders, Welles abandoned any notion that a negotiated settlement could be found to prevent further fighting. When he returned home in March, Welles reported to Roosevelt that a negotiated peace was "a forlorn hope" and that he "did not believe there is the slightest chance of any successful negotiation at this time." It was clear that Hitler was determined to seek German control over all of Europe. Still, despite the failure to get any commitment, Welles was guardedly optimistic that Italy's influence would work to limit the spread of the war, but he knew that the situation remained fluid.[6]

Germany's invasion of Denmark and Norway on April 9, 1940, shocked the West; the quick and brutal strike showed the apparent vulnerability of all nations to Hitler's forces. The renewed fighting in Europe made the matter of keeping Italy out of the war more urgent in Washington. In April and May, Roosevelt sent Mussolini four messages asking him to remain neutral. In each, the president praised Italy's restraint up to that point. Hoping to force Mussolini to look beyond Germany's early victories, the president made it clear that he believed Germany would ultimately lose the war; he indicated that any further spread of the war would harm significant American interests and lead to American intervention through increased aid to the Allies, and possibly more. "No man," Roosevelt wrote, "can today predict with assurances, should further extension take place . . . what nations, however determined they may be today to remain at peace, might yet eventually find it imperative in their own defense to enter the war."[7] The threat could not have been made clearer.

Germany's lightning attack on May 10, 1940, into the Low Countries and France brought an end to the so called phony war. In just six weeks, Belgium, Holland, Luxembourg, and France fell, leaving Great Britain to fight the Axis alone. These stunning events made it clear that Rome was going to join Berlin in the war, and led President Roosevelt to take a series of steps in response to the German victories. Speaking to Congress on May 16, Roosevelt delivered his most impassioned plea yet for the American public to recognize the threat fascism posed to the nation and the world. "These are ominous days," Roosevelt declared. "The brutal force of modern offensive war has been loosed in all its horror. New powers of destruction, incredibly swift and deadly, have been developed; and those who wield them are ruthless and daring." The developments of the past few days had exposed "the clear fact that the American people must recast their thinking about national protection." In the past, "the Atlantic and Pacific oceans were reasonably adequate defensive barriers when fleets under sail could move at an average speed of five miles an hour. . . . Later, the oceans still gave strength to our defense when fleets and convoys propelled by steam could sail the oceans at fifteen or twenty miles an hour. But the new element—air navigation—steps up the speed of possible attack to two hundred, to three hundred miles an hour." Not only coastal cities but also places such as St. Louis and Kansas City would be endangered if the Axis secured bases close to the United States.[8]

The nation had to take stock of this new situation and be prepared for the consequences. "This means military implements," Roosevelt instructed Congress, "which are ready and available to meet any lighting offensive against our American interest." The lessons should be clear; nations that were unprepared had found themselves conquered. "So-called impregnable fortifications no longer exist. A defense that allows an enemy to consolidate his approach without hindrance will lose." Roosevelt called on Congress to provide the necessary funds, an additional $1.1 billion, to provide "ready-at-hand weapons capable of great mobility because of the potential speed of modern attack." Specifically, FDR wanted the United States to increase its production of airplanes from the current 12,000 a year to at least 50,000, and for the American army and navy to have at least 50,000 planes each for the defense of the United States, along with more supplies, modernization of production facilities, and essential equipment for war. He also asked Congress not to impede the delivery of planes to Great Britain as that, "from the point of view of our national defense, would be extremely short-sighted."[9]

The objective of the nation was still to keep the peace, the president insisted, but not at any cost. Roosevelt pulled together the two threads of national security, the protection of territory and values, when he concluded that while the United States hoped to stay out of the war, "nevertheless, we stand ready not only to spend millions for defense but to give our service and even our lives for the maintenance of our American liberties. Our security is not a matter of weapons alone. The arm that wields them must be strong, the eye that guides them clear, the will that directs them indomitable. These are the characteristics of a free people, a people devoted to the institutions they themselves have built, a people willing to defend a way of life that is precious to them all, a people who put their faith in God."[10]

The public response was overwhelmingly positive, with eighty-six percent approving the plan for defense spending. The president followed up his message to Congress with a fireside chat on national security on May 26. Roosevelt declared that the greatest strength of the United States came from the American people. The military might be the first line of defense, the president told his audience, but he knew that "underlying them all, giving them their strength, sustenance and power, are the spirit and morale of a free people." Because of this, the gains made by the New Deal would be maintained and the democratic process respected, no matter what turmoil lay ahead. At a time when the entire world "is threatened by forces of destruction, it is my resolve and yours to build up our armed defenses." The task was to defend "the blessings of a free society. . . . This is the promise of America. . . . But we build and defend not for our generation alone. We defend the foundations laid down by our fathers. We build a life for generations yet unborn. We defend and build a way of life, not for America alone, but for all mankind. Ours is a high duty, a noble task."[11]

When Italy declared war on June 10 and attacked France that day, the rest of Europe was plunged into the fighting. With the fall of Paris, Europe was controlled by Nazi Germany and its allies, from the Russian border in the east to the Atlantic coast. Only the British Navy and Air Force stood between the United States and the Nazi juggernaut. Roosevelt was now prepared to act on the position he had been trying to convince the American people was necessary: a policy of collective security, aid to Great Britain, and taking up the role of world leader. To back up his words, FDR asked Congress for further dramatic increases in defense funding totaling over $12 billion by the end of 1940. The shock of France's quick fall had a significant impact on the American public's views of the danger Nazi Germany posed and opened the door for Roosevelt to take bolder moves to aid Great Britain. Roosevelt and Winston Churchill had by this time established their secret correspondence, and the British Prime Minister was pushing hard for more supplies and greater American support, requests that Roosevelt was sympathetic to and would seek to meet as much as possible.

As Congress passed the appropriations bills to finance a larger military and more weapons, Roosevelt tacked in a more political direction to build support for his policies through military preparedness and by linking security to national unity, American exceptionalism, sacrifice, and the protection of the American way of life. On June 19, FDR established a war cabinet to help him create bipartisan support for his policies. He asked former Secretary of War and Secretary of State Henry L. Stimson to be secretary of war and Frank Knox to be secretary of the navy. Both men were leading Republicans who supported the president's policies. Stimson, the more notable of the two, was known as a leading internationalist and advocate of mobilization and aid to Great Britain. Indeed, Stimson was well ahead of the president in terms of publicly calling for greater American involvement in the war against Hitler and for institution of a peacetime draft. He was a long-standing critic of the Neutrality Act and a proponent of an economic embargo on arms, munitions, and raw materials against Japan.

Being so far ahead of Roosevelt's positions, Stimson was surprised when the president called him to request that he take the position of secretary of war and informed him that he was appointing Knox as secretary of the navy. It was no secret in Washington that FDR was displeased with the lack of leadership being shown by the current secretary of war, Harry Woodring, at a time when military spending was rapidly growing. When they talked, Stimson made it clear that he would not participate in domestic politics and that he needed to be free to appoint his own staff. He also wanted to be sure that Roosevelt knew his positions, particularly on the draft, and that they would not be a problem for FDR. The president responded that he was in "full accord" with Stimson's views.[12] Thus, the president added a widely respected elder statesman, whose worldview was compatible with his own, to run the most critical wartime executive department beside the White House. It also aided FDR politically that Stimson was a Republican whose advocacy of aid to London, naval convoys of supplies, and the draft would help him move the country in the direction FDR believed it had to take. Having already promoted General George C. Marshall to Chief of Staff, Roosevelt had in place his national security team that would oversee the victory in World War II.

That team faced a myriad array of challenges in the summer of 1940. The rearmament program had started but the United States was not yet able to provide the amount of supplies a desperate Great Britain needed to ensure its defense. At the same time, Japan sought to take advantage of Germany's victories in Europe by moving into the French colony of Indochina in order to strengthen its ability to fight in southern China, gain more raw materials, and improve its position in Southeast Asia, thus creating a threat to all Western colonies in the region. Finally, there remained the domestic political battles and the upcoming election in which FDR sought a third term. Roosevelt was well aware that while the public now supported his defense spending, it remained opposed to direct American military involvement in Europe.

To meet these problems, Roosevelt acted to increase the nation's defense. Throughout the summer, the administration sought more Congressional appropriations for national security and worked to gain passage of the Selective Service Bill. As he requested more money for supplies, weapons, and the expansion of production facilities, Roosevelt continued to pair military needs with the defense of American values. Speaking again to Congress on July 10, FDR reiterated his desire to keep the United States out of the war, but emphatically stated that the nation "would repel aggression against the United States or the Western Hemisphere." He cautioned America's adversaries not to misread his position. No one should "believe that because we in America still cherish freedom of religion, of speech, of assembly, of the press; because we maintain our free democratic political institutions . . . that we are weak." Rather, America was "the greatest industrial nation in the world" and it would not fail. Referring to the recent fall of France, the president stated that "the principal lesson of the war up to the present time is that partial defense is inadequate defense." Roosevelt warned against trying to prepare for defense in a piecemeal manner. "We must be able to defend ourselves wholly and at any time. Our plans for national security, therefore, should cover total defense." Congress continued to provide what the president requested and authorized an additional $5.1 billion for the War and Navy Departments.[13]

There had never been a peacetime draft in American history, and the administration had to overcome this legacy along with opponents' arguments that it was a step that would increase the risk of war. Speaking for the administration, Secretary of War Stimson argued that because voluntary enlistment left the army well below its authorized strength, the draft was the only fair and democratic means to raise a modern army and meet the security needs of the nation. The administration's efforts succeeded, and on September 16, 1940, President Roosevelt signed the Selective Service Act, which required all men from 21 to 36 to register for the draft. With the president looking on, Stimson drew the first numbers in the draft lottery on October 29.

As it sought the adoption of the draft, the administration continued its efforts to find the best means to get desperately needed military equipment to Great Britain. Winston Churchill had been asking since May for more American supplies, and, in particular, for destroyers to help protect the British Isles. Roosevelt had resisted these efforts, in part because American military leaders did not consider the two hundred old destroyers from World War I superfluous, and in part because he believed he would have to get Congressional approval for any transfer. In August, Knox suggested to Roosevelt that he trade fifty of the destroyers for eight British bases in Greenland, the West Indies, and on the Atlantic Coast of Canada. With the support of Attorney General Robert Jackson, the president made the deal to lease naval and air bases in the Bahamas, Jamaica, St. Lucia, Trinidad, Antigua, and British Guiana in exchange for the destroyers by executive authority. Two other bases, in Newfoundland and Bermuda, were gifts to the United States. The president presented the "Destroyers for Bases" deal, announced on September 3, as part of the nation's defense preparations. Linking it to another famous executive action, he proclaimed the deal the "most important action in the reinforcement of our national defense that has been taken since the Louisiana Purchase. Then as now, considerations of safety from overseas attack were fundamental."[14]

The arrangement marked a turning point for the administration in its efforts to support England. The American public, its sympathy for Great Britain bolstered by the British people's heroic resistance to the German bombings of its cities, broadly supported this first direct military aid to Great Britain; and the swapping of destroyers for British bases served as a precursor for the logic and appeal of the president's lend-lease policy. The German air attacks on British cities highlighted the threat the president claimed faced the nation and confirmed the picture of an aggressive, brutal state determined to destroy democratic institutions and values. With the Germans, Italians, and Japanese on the offensive around the globe, and daily reports of the suffering inflicted at their hands, Americans in larger and larger numbers came to see the actions of Berlin, Rome, and Tokyo as a threat. The protests of the so-called isolationists and those who demanded neutrality were muted compared to what they had been in the mid-1930s.

Japan's official announcement of its intention to create the Greater East Asian Co-Prosperity Sphere, and the movement of its forces into the French colony of Indochina in June 1940, served to cement the view that there was no difference between the totalitarian and aggressive natures of Tokyo and Berlin. Japan was clearly taking advantage of the German victories in Europe to bring its dream of dominating East Asia to fruition, and its attack on Southeast Asia demanded an American response. Hornbeck set out the issue facing the United States on July 19, calling for action from the administration in response to Japan's move to the south. "If Japan gets possession of huge new supplies . . . her embarkation upon carrying out of new acts of aggression will be greatly facilitated. If action is taken on our part which results in failure on Japan's part to receive these new supplies," Hornbeck continued, "such action and the resultant failure might retard or prevent such new adventuring and would certainly make it . . . more difficult."[15] It was clear to all senior administration officials that continued patience and restraint would just encourage more expansion, and that it was time to move beyond just providing aid to China and to directly oppose Japan. The question was, how to do so? What measures could be taken to deter Tokyo, short of war?

Following Hornbeck's recommendation, on September 26, Roosevelt approved an embargo on trading iron, scrap metal, and other materials that could be used in war with Japan. Omitted from the list of goods was oil. Japan imported nearly fifty percent of its supply from the United States, and its war machine could not function without it. The president, however, feared that cutting off oil at that time would drive Japan to attack the Dutch East Indies (Indonesia) to secure its supply, a move the president wanted to delay or prevent if possible in order to keep the wealth of this area available to Great Britain. The next day, Tokyo announced the formation of the Axis, as it formally aligned with Berlin and Rome through the Tripartite Pact, aimed explicitly at the United States. In response, Roosevelt discussed with Stimson a complete embargo and military maneuvers in Hawaii and Alaska to demonstrate the United States' "refusal to be bullied by Japan in regard to our mission in the Pacific," but ultimately he decided to wait on any stronger measures.[16]

The administration's goal to increase support for Great Britain and Roosevelt's positions in the great debate were bolstered by groups such as the Committee to Defend America by Aiding the Allies (CDAAA), a nonpartisan organization founded in May 1940 by the Kansas editor William Allen White to mobilize support for Roosevelt's foreign policy and counter neutrality. Through hundreds of chapters in all states, the CDAAA took up the main themes of the president's internationalist arguments: the need to aid Great Britain, increase America's strength, control the Atlantic Ocean, prevent subversive actions by America's enemies in the Western Hemisphere, and protect democracy and American values in the world. Coordinating its efforts with the administration, the CDAAA followed the president in linking their arguments about national defense to the necessity of protecting democracy and freedom of religion.[17]

The 1940 election showed that the president's speeches and actions and the CDAAA had had an impact on public opinion and increased support for the president's new policies. Roosevelt's Republican challenger, Wendell Willkie, supported most of Roosevelt's defense measures and initiatives taken that summer and fall. This left it to the newly created America First Committee (AFC) to provide the main opposition to Roosevelt's policies. Arguing that the oceans provided the protection America needed, the America First Committee supported preparedness but not aid to Great Britain. Peace and American freedoms, the AFC argued, could only be preserved by keeping out of any involvement in the war in Europe. Aid would just drag the nation into another European war and would repeat the mistakes made during World War I. Rather than wasting resources by sending them abroad, the United States should build itself up so that no nation would dare try to attack it. There was little new in this position, but the arguments that had been so persuasive throughout most of the 1930s were now, in the face of Axis aggression, no longer convincing to most Americans.

Toward the end of the campaign, Willkie did try to distance himself from Roosevelt by claiming that he supported measures necessary for defense, but that the president, if reelected, intended to take the nation into the war. The Republican candidate promised that he would not send American boys to fight foreign wars. Roosevelt responded to this in a series of speeches at the end of the campaign. On October 16, the day millions of men registered for the draft, Roosevelt stated that this measure, "the keystone in the arch of our national defense," was obviously for "defensive preparation only" and had been "imposed upon us from without" by nations "who have dared to threaten the whole world with war." Speaking in Madison Square Garden on October 28, Roosevelt accused Willkie of "playing politics with national security" and said that if the nation had followed the Republican Party's plans, it would be weaker and be forced to make concessions to the dictators. Finally, speaking in Boston on October 30, the president directly refuted

Willkie's charge by declaring that "I have said this before, but I shall say it again and again. Your boys are not going to be sent into any foreign wars." So close to the election, the president dropped the qualifying phrase "except in the case of attack" that he usually added so as to not raise fears that Willkie's charges were correct.[18]

Aid to Great Britain and preparedness, the central themes of the campaign for a third term in office, would have been unthinkable back in October 1937 when FDR began his campaign to educate the American public about the threats the nation faced from abroad. Now, after three years of tacking in different directions to navigate the political winds, Roosevelt had the support of Congress and the majority of the American people for a peacetime draft, massive appropriations for defense, and a commitment to provide aid to Great Britain. Certainly the shocking events in Europe and Asia played an important role, but Roosevelt was able to explain and respond to the growing international crisis in a manner that produced this dramatic shift in public opinion toward internationalist foreign policy and a redefinition of American national security.

With the election won and the danger of a British defeat ever present, the Roosevelt administration began to take more active steps to prepare the public for what many now saw as the inevitability of American participation in the war. The appropriations secured throughout 1940 were beginning to show dividends as large amounts of war materials were being produced by the end of the year. But as supplies became available in December, two new problems confronted the Roosevelt administration. American laws restricted the ability of the president to transfer weapons to another nation, and Great Britain was going broke and was unable to pay, as cash-and-carry required, for the materials and munitions it needed to hold off the Germans. In a lengthy letter sent on December 8, British Prime Minister Winston Churchill set out the British shortages in weapons, ships, and planes, the devastating losses being suffered at sea from German attacks, and the fast approaching exhaustion of British financial ability to purchase goods from the United States. American officials had been aware of British needs, but not of the full extent of the coming crisis if no new action was taken.

Roosevelt broke the logjam with his call for the policy of lend-lease. Speaking to reporters on December 17, the president stated the key point of his developing national security policy, that the "best immediate defense of the United States is the success of Great Britain in defending itself." FDR was acutely aware of the problems with loans and credits. The issue caused difficulties during and after World War I, and it was a touchstone of the neutrality laws. So, FDR presented a novel approach. "Now, what I am trying to do," he said, is to "get rid of the silly, foolish old dollar sign." To explain what he meant, Roosevelt used his since famous garden hose analogy, noting that if your neighbor's house is on fire, and they lack a hose to put it out, you would not ask them to buy your hose from you prior to letting them use it. You would lend your hose to them and they would either return it when done or replace it if it was damaged. Similarly, the United States would supply Great Britain with the necessary supplies for winning the war "with the understanding that when the show was over, we would get repaid something in kind, thereby leaving out the dollar mark in the form of a dollar debt and substituting for it a gentleman's obligation to repay in kind."[19]

On December 29, in his first fireside chat since the election, Roosevelt told the nation that this was "not a fireside chat on war. It is a talk on national security." Roosevelt pulled together all of the key themes of the internationalist position as he made the case that American security only could be secured through alliances with others, by providing global leadership, and through a willingness to fight just wars that would defend and spread American values and institutions. The president compared the world crisis facing the nation with the domestic crisis it faced eight years earlier when he first took office, and he called upon the American people to meet this new crisis with the same courage and forthright manner it demonstrated in 1933. "Never before since Jamestown and Plymouth Rock," Roosevelt declared, "has our American civilization been in such danger as now." The threat posed by the Axis nations was clear: Germany intended to "enslave the whole of Europe, and then to use the resources of Europe to dominate the rest of the world." Hitler, Roosevelt stated, not only admits "but *proclaims* that there can be no ultimate peace between their philosophy of government and our philosophy of government." With such a nation and its use of force there could be no peace until the aggressor nations were defeated in their quest to conquer the world.[20]

The only thing currently keeping the dictators away from America, Roosevelt pointed out, was the heroic fighting of the British in the Atlantic and of China, along with the American fleet, in the Pacific. "Does anyone seriously believe," Roosevelt asked, " . . . that we could rest easy if the Axis powers were our neighbor" in the Atlantic Ocean? If Great Britain fell, "the Axis powers will control the continents of Europe, Asia, Africa, and Australasia, and the high seas—and they will be in a position to bring enormous military and naval resources against this hemisphere." The United States would be living at the point of a gun, in a world where in order to survive "we would have to convert ourselves permanently into a militaristic power on the basis of a war economy."[21]

This was not a war, Roosevelt argued, of America and Great Britain against the Axis, but of democracy against world tyranny. Only the productive capacity of the United States to build more ships, guns, planes, and munitions, and the will of the American people to meet the world crisis and threat to its security, would turn the tide and assure victory over the dictators. The only way to keep war away from the United States was to "build more ships, more guns, more planes—more of everything" as quickly as possible. "We have," the President proclaimed confidently, "the men—the skill—the wealth—and above all, the will" to succeed. The United States, he declared in conclusion, "must be the great arsenal of democracy" to ensure victory. "For us this is an emergency as serious as war itself. We must apply ourselves to our task with the same resolution, the same sense of urgency, the same spirit of patriotism and sacrifice as we would show were we at war." If this was done, the president was sure "that the Axis powers are not going to win this war."[22]

The final piece of the president's effort to define the meaning of the war for the United States came in his State of the Union message to Congress on January 6, 1941. Devoted completely to the international crisis, Roosevelt's speech started with his now familiar theme that the moment in time was "unprecedented" in the history of the United States as the nation's security was for the first time threatened from without. "The democratic way of life," Roosevelt warned, "is at this moment being directly assailed in every part of the world," including the United States, and it was incumbent upon the nation to act with resolve and speed in meeting this attack. Given this, the most urgent needs were "a swift and driving increase in our armament production" and the passage by Congress of the lend-lease bill. "We cannot" tell the Allies, FDR proclaimed, "and we will not, tell them that they must surrender, merely because of a present inability to pay for the weapons which we know they must have." Instead, "let us say to the democracies: 'We Americans are vitally concerned in your defense of freedom. We are putting forth our energies, our resources and our organizing powers to give you the strength to regain and maintain a free world. We shall send you, in ever-increasing numbers, ships, planes, tanks, guns. This is our purpose and our pledge.'"[23]

In calling for sacrifice from the nation, Roosevelt told his audience that the goal was both victory over the Axis and the creation of a better world. He concluded his remarks by setting out what the nation was sacrificing for and what it should seek in the postwar world. In Roosevelt's vision, the values being protected and the world that emerged from the aftermath of the fighting would be a

> world founded upon four essential human freedoms. The first is freedom of speech and expression—everywhere in the world. The second is freedom of every person to worship God in their own way—everywhere in the world. The third is freedom from want—which, translated into world terms, means economic understandings which will secure to every nation a healthy peacetime life for its inhabitants—everywhere in the world. The fourth is freedom from fear—which, translated into world terms, means a world-wide reduction of armaments to such a point and in such a thorough fashion that no nation will be in a position to commit an act of physical aggression against any neighbor—anywhere in the world.[24]

These concepts were a concise statement of the president's values, of the need to defeat the Axis, and of what the United States was protecting in order to create a postwar order that would bring peace and prosperity. For FDR, this was not a distant dream, but a goal to attain "in our own time and generation." It was the antithesis of the world the Axis sought to impose on other countries, but it was the international order that could be brought forth through American leadership. Roosevelt concluded by declaring that "there can be no end save victory."[25] The American public agreed. At the end of January 1941, the president's approval rating was seventy-one percent.[26]

The lend-lease bill was introduced on January 10, 1941. For the next two months it was at the center of an intense national debate about the specific request, but more importantly about U.S. foreign policy and the best means to provide for the nation's security. By the time the legislation was introduced, Roosevelt's arguments over the past four years to promote the internationalist position gave lend-lease the support of a large majority of the American public and members of Congress. Still, the president wanted a full debate to further build support, to allow certain amendments to allay the fears of those who had reservations, and to show that the administration was listening to its critics. In the process, Roosevelt hoped to cement a broad consensus among the American people in favor of his understanding of America's role in the war.

The administration and its allies framed the debate as one about national security, defense, and responsibility for upholding American values, protecting civilization, and preserving a viable world order. They repeated the key points the president had made in his recent talks to the nation, emphasizing Axis aggression and the crucial need to sustain Great Britain so as to contain the German threat; they highlighted the infeasibility of dependence on hemispheric defense, given modern air power, the danger of subversion, and the economic dislocation that would come from an Axis-dominated world. Lend-lease was, therefore, vital to the nation's security; it was a defensive action and was a crucial component in the struggle to protect democracy in the world. If Germany defeated England, it would only be a matter of time before Hitler attacked the United States.[27]

A number of groups and individuals fervently opposed the measure, including leading Senators such as Bennett Clark, Gerald Nye, Robert Taft, Arthur Vandenburg, and Burton Wheeler, the America First Committee, and the aviator Charles Lindbergh. They claimed that the bill gave the president too much power, bordering on dictatorial control over the economy, that it would pull the United States into the war, not keep it out, and that it would harm America's ability to defend itself by sending vital goods and equipment overseas. Central to all of these arguments was World War I, which they held as an example of why the United States should avoid all European wars. Opponents noted that those debts had yet to be repaid. More importantly, there was the question of how the goods would get to England without naval escorts, given the presence of German submarines. Finally, they asserted that no vital American interests had been secured or protected in the First World War and that there was no reason to think the outcome of the current war would be any different. Great Britain, it was said, still had plenty of assets that it could use to buy supplies. London was just trying to get the American taxpayer to subsidize the fighting and American boys to do the fighting because it knew it could never defeat Germany. The America First Committee and its allies argued that, given this, lend-lease was not a matter of aiding England or a defensive action, but was a means of getting the United States directly involved in the war.

Senator Nye, the president's longtime nemesis, led the opposition once again. He believed that Roosevelt was lying to the American people about his intentions and that the bill was aimed at taking the nation to war. If the president was honest, he declared, he would call it "a bill to put the United States fully into the bloody business of licking Adolf Hitler."[28] Taft agreed, noting that the bill was a virtual declaration of war that would allow Roosevelt to become the "great protagonist of the forces opposing Hitler." "There is here no question of appeasement," Taft continued. "Appeasement means the yielding to demands with the hope that such yielding will prevent further aggression." Yet, "Germany has made no demands on the United States; has made no attack on the United States."[29]

Lindbergh, speaking on behalf of the America First Committee, attacked the logic of Roosevelt's position that lend-lease would aid the nation's defense. He claimed, on the one hand, that Germany would defeat Great Britain no matter what the United States did. There was, therefore, no use in trying to prevent it as all the aid sent would just go to waste. On the other hand, Lindbergh questioned the president's claims that the nation would be in danger from long-range bombers, arguing that any air attacks would be futile and that Germany could not conquer the United States that way. He insisted that a hemispheric defense remained viable and was the best protection for the nation as it would deter any Axis attack.

Secretary of War Stimson took the lead in presenting the administration's case. Testifying five separate times before Congress, Stimson argued that passage of the Lend-Lease Act was vital to America's defense. It would provide order to the current chaotic system of procuring weapons for the Allies, permit the government to exercise centralized control over weapons production, and allow the president the full authority he needed in the time of national emergency. Preparedness, planning, defense, support of Great Britain, and maximized production were the main issues, the secretary of war told the legislature, not the fear of presidential power or antagonizing Germany.

Sumner Welles linked lend-lease back to the Good Neighbor Policy. In a major speech, "The United States and the World Crisis," he noted how Roosevelt's Latin American policy proved "that democracy works in the realm of foreign policy as well as in the realm of domestic policy." Reiterating the president's point that the nation was confronting "the most critical moment it has had to face" in its history, the undersecretary of state reminded his listeners that the administration had proactively prepared for the defense of the nation, as demonstrated by the Pan-American agreements signed in Buenos Aires, which embodied the self-defense principles of the Monroe Doctrine. Due to this, the hemisphere was united against the aggressor states to protect freedom and was prepared to act should the dictators gain control of the Atlantic or Pacific Oceans.[30]

Prior to the final vote, opponents were able to secure some important amendments, including a time limit on the bill, periodic reports to Congress by the administration on the amount of spending, type of goods, and shipment records, and a statement that the act did not authorize U.S. naval escorts to protect shipping. None of these, however, changed the main components of the bill or the direction in which the president's policy was taking the nation. In the end, on March 11 the Lend-Lease Act easily passed in both houses of Congress, 60–31 in the Senate and 260–165 in the House. The law allowed the president to "sell, transfer title to, exchange, lease, lend, or otherwise dispose of" any defense article to any government deemed vital to the defense of the United States, providing Roosevelt with the legal authority over all military supplies. In all but name, the United States had now formed an alliance with Great Britain against Germany. The next day, the president submitted a request to Congress for seven billion dollars as the initial amount to accomplish the objectives of the legislation.[31] The War Department was well prepared for the bill's passage and the first supplies were shipped out right after Roosevelt signed the legislation.

Speaking on March 15 to the Annual Dinner of the White House Correspondents' Association, Roosevelt declared that Americans just now had "engaged in a great debate. It was not limited to the halls of Congress. It was argued in every newspaper, on every wave length, over every cracker barrel in all the land." The outcome was clear. "The democracies of the world will be able to prove that dictatorships cannot win."[32] It was a war to save civilization, the president believed, and the majority of the American people now supported him when he insisted that the United States, as a great power, had to take up the role of world leadership to preserve democracy, freedom, and American interests at home and abroad.

5

Internationalism and War

President Roosevelt's critics were right on one point in the debate over lend-lease; its passage was a turning point. The massive shipment of goods across the Atlantic required naval escorts and set the nation on the road to war. This, however, was in line with the public's understanding of the crisis. Opinion polls showed the full extent of the president's political achievement in building support for his internationalist position: two-thirds of the public favored the bill. Moreover, seventy-nine percent of the American people thought the president's policies were "about right" or had not gone far enough to help Great Britain. While a year earlier, a large majority had said it was more important to stay out of the war than to aid Great Britain, by the spring of 1941 nearly sixty percent said sending aid to England, even if it meant the United States might be drawn into the war, was essential and should be American policy. Reflecting the support for his handling of foreign policy, Roosevelt's personal approval rate stood at seventy-six percent at the end of June 1941. Support for the policy of helping England continued to grow right up to the attack on Pearl Harbor.[1]

Throughout the summer and fall of 1941, Roosevelt moved the country toward war, as world events showed the American public that his analysis of the international crisis and the policies he was pursuing were correct. In the process, Roosevelt implemented his more expansive vision of the Monroe Doctrine, pushing the parameters of the Western Hemisphere and America's defensive frontiers out into the Atlantic and Pacific Oceans to better meet the threats posed by the dictators. The German invasion of the Soviet Union in June and Japan's taking of all of Indochina in July further widened the war and made clear the global threat posed by the Axis. In response, Roosevelt extended American aid to the Soviet Union, thus creating the Grand

Alliance of the United States, Great Britain, and the Soviet Union against Germany, and solidified Washington's relations with London through the Atlantic Charter. In East Asia, the president concluded that American interests, in both Europe and the Pacific, could only be protected by opposing Japanese actions in China and Southeast Asia. He, therefore, extended the economic embargo to include oil and maneuvered with Japan so that it would be clear who the aggressor was when America entered World War II.

President Roosevelt was well aware that it was the actions of the Nazis that brought about most of the change. As he wrote in 1941, it was "with the realization and with full appreciation of the true nature of the Nazi design upon the world, that the feeling of strict neutrality and aloofness which influenced the American people in September of 1939 and during the beginning of 1940 has completely disappeared." German brutality, attacks on small and neutral nations, and violations of treaties "all showed clearly that the Nazis had embarked on a definite program of world domination which was an immediate and serious threat to the United States and to the western hemisphere." Moreover, fascist aggression "was not merely a domination of military might but a domination of ideas, in which the whole world was to be bent to the Nazi philosophy of force, of slavery, of anti-religion." Thus, the American people came to agree with the president that the war was not just a problem for the people of Europe and Asia. The Axis victories, their tactics, and modern weapons had "brought the area of conflict physically so close to us, that we now realize that we are the subject of potential armed attack as soon as the Axis powers come within striking distance."[2]

Still it was necessary for someone to set the context for understanding these developments, provide a narrative to explain them, and develop a coherent and effective set of responses to shape public opinion to support the specific actions and policies. It was not preordained that Roosevelt would win the great debate or that the nation would rally to his definition of national security and vision of just war. For this, FDR deserves the most credit. His keen political sense of the temper of the American public; his ability to link his internationalist concepts to American exceptionalism and nationalism; and his confidence in the nation, in its values and institutions, and in himself as he tacked to and fro in his education campaign led to a complete change in American strategic thinking.

In 1941, Roosevelt shifted his thoughts from mobilizing public opinion and preparedness to directly meeting the Axis threat. American policy was guided by the "grand strategy" developed by the administration in early 1941. As defined by Kent Roberts Greenfield, grand strategy was policymaking "at the highest level of outlook and decision," not campaign or field strategy in battles. Just as he had shaped the direction of American foreign policy prior to the war, President Roosevelt oversaw and determined U.S. strategy throughout the period prior to and during World War II. To do so, he had, in 1939, moved the Joint Board of the Army and Navy into the newly created Executive Office of the President, thus placing the Joint Chiefs of Staff directly under the president. This does not mean that Stimson, Marshall, Hopkins, and others did not play significant roles or influence policy. They certainly did in countless ways. Still, in the end, World War II strategy and policy was established and directed by Franklin D. Roosevelt and reflected his priorities and vision.

Roosevelt established the survival of Great Britain as the first component of the American grand strategy when he ordered full military assistance for England, doing so over the objections of his military commanders, who did not share Roosevelt's confidence that Britain would withstand a German attack. They had wanted to preserve American war materials in case the United States had to fight the Axis alone.[3] To further facilitate this effort in conjunction with lend-lease, Roosevelt announced on January 3, 1941, that he was sending Harry Hopkins to London as his "personal representative" to establish "personal contact between me and the British Government."[4] This was a role Hopkins would fill many times for the rest of the war. Upon Hopkins's return from this first visit, Stimson, in an assessment that would be widely shared by many throughout the war, remarked that "the more I think of it, the more I think it is a godsend that he should be at the White House."[5] The British found Hopkins equally effective in this capacity, with Churchill dubbing him "Lord Root of the Matter."[6]

American, British, and Canadian military officials had secret meetings from January to March 1941 to coordinate efforts and discuss strategy. Roosevelt instructed the American planners that the deliberations had to be guided by the understanding that "our military course must be very conservative until our strength [has] developed," and that the United States had to be "ready to act with what is available." The second element of the grand strategy that emerged from the meetings was the agreement with Great Britain that Germany presented the greatest danger to the West and its defeat had to be the priority in military planning. Japanese actions were a concern, but even if war came in the Pacific, victory over the Nazis would still take precedence.[7]

Roosevelt expanded the scope of territory covered by the Monroe Doctrine and the definition of what constituted the Western Hemisphere as part of his effort to protect lend-lease shipments and redefine national security. As noted in chapter one, as early as January 1915, Roosevelt had outlined a strategic vision of the area covered by the Monroe Doctrine; it ran from the North Pole through the middle of the Atlantic Ocean, around Cape Horn and out to America Samoa, the Philippines, and Guam, and back up to the Aleutian Islands. He reiterated this understanding during the 1940 campaign, stating in September that he had "a map mind" that he used to conceptualize the threats to the United States and its security needs.[8] In a speech on October 12, FDR declared that defense of the Western Hemisphere included more than just the territory of the two continents and their adjacent islands; it was also "the right to the peaceful use of the Atlantic and Pacific Oceans. That has been our traditional policy." Thus, for Roosevelt, the conception of "a defense strong enough and wide enough to cover this half of the world" had its origins in 1823.[9] All of the key decisions of 1940–1941 showed Roosevelt employing his map mind as he prepared the nation for war.

In a press conference on February 25, 1941, that was "*really* off the record," the president stated that the borders of the Western Hemisphere "would be a line drawn in the Atlantic about halfway between the most westerly part" of the Americas, "which is the sticky-out point of Brazil, and the same relative point on the other side, which happens to be the sticky-out point of Africa." This definition placed Greenland well within the Americas and, as the State Department had stated in 1940, "within the provisions of the Monroe Doctrine."[10] On April 10, Roosevelt announced that the United States had signed an agreement with the Danish Minister in Washington that placed Greenland within "our system of cooperative hemispheric defense." The move was justified under the Monroe Doctrine to protect Greenland against a German attack, to ensure access to valuable minerals, and to secure the air and naval routes of the northern Atlantic. To protect Greenland's safety, the U.S. would establish a series of bases on the large island to deter the Germans and demonstrate American resolve to protect its hemisphere.[11]

The president had also already taken action to establish the Manhattan Project, which would develop the atomic bomb. On August 2, 1939, Albert Einstein signed the so-called Nassau Point letter, written by physicist Leo

Szilard, designed to alert Roosevelt to the potential of "a nuclear chain reaction in a large mass of uranium" that could produce "vast amounts of power." It was "almost certain" that this could be done "in the immediate future," and that it could lead to the production of a bomb powerful enough, if carried by boat into a city harbor, to "very well destroy the whole port together with some of the surrounding territory." Delivered to FDR by the economist Alexander Sachs on October 11, 1939, the letter also warned that Germany was at work on this research and that it had control over the uranium ore in the former Czechoslovakia while the United States "has only very poor ores of uranium in moderate quantities." Roosevelt instructed his military advisor General Edwin M. Watson that "this requires action," leading to the establishment of the Advisory Committee on Uranium and the first funds to support the research being conducted by Szilard and other physicists at Columbia University. In 1941, the president appointed Stimson, along with Vice President Henry Wallace, General Marshall, Dr. Vannevar Bush, and Dr. James B. Conant, to a committee to oversee the development of the weapon and advise him on questions of policy and potential use. From that point forward, Stimson would be the senior official responsible for the Manhattan Project.[12]

The immediate concern in the spring of 1941 was the movement of lend-lease supplies to Great Britain. For lend-lease to be effective, it was necessary to ensure the British lifeline in the North Atlantic. Noting the staggering losses in shipping—over four million tons of Allied and neutral shipping in 1940—due to German submarines, Stimson had urged Roosevelt to forcibly stop the Germans, to "plug the leaky bathtub," by using the navy to escort all supplies to English ports to ensure Great Britain's survival. With the passage of the Lend-Lease Act, Stimson again pressed the case for convoys to protect shipping and asked the president to face the fact directly that only "naval action and vigorous action at that" would suffice to make the policy a success. The president, however, was not yet ready to take such a bold step. He was well aware that the decisions he was making could lead to an incident on the seas and lead to war just as it had in 1917. Roosevelt feared Congress would refuse to grant him the power to convoy ships and that the debate would revitalize the neutralist position and, at the same time, harm British morale. As the president noted in a cabinet meeting on April 25, the patrols were another "step forward" in meeting the German danger; Stimson rejoined: "Well, I hope you keep on walking, Mr. President. Keep on walking." Roosevelt, unlike Stimson, was still willing to wait on circumstances to develop before he asked for bolder steps from Congress.[13]

When FDR announced in April that the United States would patrol the western half of the Atlantic Ocean, out to the 25° longitude line, thus freeing the British navy to concentrate on the waters closer to home, he made sure to elaborate on the difference between a patrol and a convoy, stating they were as different as a horse and a cow. Roosevelt stated that patrols were not new and had begun in September 1939 to keep watch and provide warning. "A patrol is a reconnaissance . . . of certain areas of ocean to find out whether there is any possible aggressive ship within that area . . . which might be coming toward the Western Hemisphere, or into the Western Hemisphere." All that was being done was extending the area of patrol for the safety of the hemisphere. There was no active involvement with or protection of shipping, the purpose of a convoy. When asked how far the zone for patrols might go, Roosevelt responded: "That is exactly the question I hoped you would ask. As far on the waters of the seven seas as may be necessary for the defense of the American hemisphere." The measure was accepted as patrols were portrayed as a defensive move to keep watch for hostile actions close to home. What most people missed was that Roosevelt had moved away from the Monroe Doctrine and was now employing the concept of national security to explain his strategic actions and the geographical extension of America's defensive frontier.[14]

No matter what actions the United States took, the news from Europe continued to worsen. In April and May, Germany gained almost complete control over the Balkans while the destruction of shipping continued to rise, with over 680,000 tons lost in April alone. So desperate was the situation becoming that in May, British Prime Minister Churchill telegraphed Roosevelt asking for the first time that the United States declare war on Germany. Stimson urged the president to take the lead, make the case for war, and rally the nation to the necessity of defeating Germany.[15] As reported by Secretary of the Interior Harold Ickes, FDR told his cabinet: "I am not willing to fire the first shot."[16] While Stimson was sure the nation would support Roosevelt if he sought a declaration of war, the president was not and remained committed to taking gradual steps. Still, FDR told Adolf Berle that in his upcoming speech he would try to "scare the daylights out of everyone" to get the public to understand the full magnitude of the crisis and threat to the United States.[17]

On May 27, Roosevelt declared an unlimited national emergency, placing all military forces on readiness to defend the nation and the Western Hemisphere.[18] That evening, he explained his action to the nation and set out an expanded vision of America's proper defense sphere and national security requirements. "The pressing problems that confront us are military and naval problems," Roosevelt declared. "What we face is cold, hard fact. The first and fundamental fact is that what started as a European war has developed, as the Nazis always intended it should, into a war for world domination." He recalled for the American people the constant path of aggression that Nazi Germany had followed and declared that unless Germany was stopped, the Western Hemisphere would soon "be within range of the Nazi weapons of destruction" and the target of Hitler's aggression. He also reviewed the measures he had taken up to then to defend the nation, from concluding agreements with the other American republics for hemispheric defense, to the rearmament program, naval buildup, the draft, and lend-lease policies of the past year.[19]

Yet not enough had been done as the danger posed by Nazi Germany to Great Britain, the Western Hemisphere, and the United States was greater than ever. "The blunt truth is this," Roosevelt warned. "The present rate of Nazi sinkings of merchant ships is more than three times as high as the capacity of British shipyards to replace them; it is more than twice the combined British and American output of merchant ships today." With the recent German victories in the Mediterranean, the fascists threatened to control all Northern Africa to Dakar and the "island outposts of the New World—the Azores and Cape Verde Islands." The war was "approaching the brink of the Western Hemisphere itself. It is coming very close to home." What the president termed the "Battle of the Atlantic" extended from the "icy waters of the North Pole to the frozen continent of the Antarctic." A German "occupation of Iceland or bases in Greenland would bring the war close to our own continental shores, because those places are stepping-stones to Labrador and Newfoundland, to Nova Scotia, yes, to the northern United States itself." A similar danger from a southern direction existed if the Nazis occupied the Azores or Cape Verde Islands.[20]

A loss of the islands of the Atlantic, or a German occupation of Iceland and Greenland, "would directly endanger the freedom of the Atlantic and our own American physical safety." Anyone with an atlas could see the problem. "When the enemy comes at you in a tank or a bombing plane, if you hold your fire until you see the whites of his eyes, you will never know what hit you. Our Bunker Hill of tomorrow may be several thousand miles from Boston." The United States, Roosevelt pledged, would never submit to Nazi tyranny or the fear Germany created. It would only accept a world where the four freedoms held fast, where they were valued and protected. "Magna Carta, the Declaration of Independence, the Constitution of the United States, the Emancipation Proclamation, and every other milestone in human progress—all were ideals which seemed impossible of attainment—and yet they were attained." In closing, Roosevelt quoted the words of the signers of the Declaration of Independence, "that little band of patriots, fighting long ago against overwhelming odds, but certain, as we are now, of ultimate victory: 'With a firm reliance on the protection of Divine Providence, we mutually pledge to each other our lives, our fortunes, and our sacred honor.'"[21]

Following up on his speech, in early June Roosevelt secretly decided that the United States had to occupy Iceland as part of its effort to protect the Western Hemisphere and aid Great Britain. After American forces landed on July 7, 1941, the president told the nation that the United States "cannot permit the occupation by Germany of strategic outposts in the Atlantic to be used as air or naval bases for the eventual attack against the Western Hemisphere. . . . Assurance that such outposts in our defense frontier remain in friendly hands is the very foundation of our national security." Acting as Commander in Chief, Roosevelt ordered the Navy "that all necessary steps be taken to insure the safety of communications in the approaches between Iceland and the United States, as well as on the seas between the United States and all other strategic outposts."[22]

On July 11, FDR tore a map of the North Atlantic out of *National Geographic*, entitled "Iceland, Between Two Worlds, Holds a Strategic Place in the Battle of Britain and the Battle of the Atlantic," and used a pencil to draw a line demarcating the Western Hemisphere's security zone. It mostly ran on the longitude line at 25°, his previously stated boundary for patrols, but when it got north of the 80th parallel, the line moved east and curved around Iceland and then up to the Arctic Ocean. This marked the new, expanded patrol zone for the U.S. Navy, and reduced the size of the area the British navy had to protect. When Harry Hopkins left for London a few days later, he took the map with him to show it to Churchill.[23]

Germany's strike into Russia on June 22 dramatically changed the calculus of the war and presented Franklin Roosevelt with many difficult decisions.

German forces rapidly advanced hundreds of miles into the Soviet Union, forcing the Red Army into a disorganized retreat. Most senior American military officials thought the Russians would collapse and that the Nazis would be victorious by the end of the summer, at the latest. Secretary of War Stimson wrote Roosevelt the next day after consulting with Marshall and the General Staff. They unanimously agreed that "Germany will be thoroughly occupied in beating Russia for a minimum of one month and a possible maximum of three months." This would force Germany to delay any planned invasion of Great Britain or any effort to block the United States' occupation of Iceland, much less any effort to put further pressure on Africa and South America, or threaten Egypt from the east.[24]

Given their prediction of a German victory, they saw little reason to send aid to the Soviet Union as it would only be wasted or fall into German hands. Instead, they proposed that this "precious and unforeseen period of respite should be used to push with the utmost vigor our movements in the Atlantic theater of operations." This was the best means to aid England, warn Germany, and "strengthen our own position of defense against our most imminent danger." It was imperative, Stimson wrote FDR, to act while German resources were deployed elsewhere. "By this final demonstration of Nazi ambition and perfidy, the door is opened wide for you to lead directly towards winning of the battle of the North Atlantic and the protection of our hemisphere in the South Atlantic."[25]

Roosevelt certainly understood that Hitler's drive to the east provided relief for Britain and an opportunity to further strengthen America's position in the Atlantic; he was not so sure this was the only approach to the new development in the war. Unlike others, the president thought the Soviet Union would withstand the Wehrmacht's onslaught. He believed that knowledge of Russian history alone should caution against reaching the conclusion that Germany would win, and do so quickly. Moreover, for FDR, the Soviet Union's ability to survive and fight the Germans would be decisive not only in relieving the pressure on Great Britain but also in ultimately defeating Germany. As he wrote Admiral William Leahy four days after the start of the war on the eastern front: "Now comes this Russian diversion. If it is more than just that, it will mean the liberation of Europe from Nazi domination." He continued by stating that "at the same time I do not think we need worry about any possibility of Russian domination."[26] For FDR, nationalism, not ideology, explained Soviet foreign policy, and this distinction provided a basis for cooperation. From this insight, the Grand Alliance was formed.[27]

Roosevelt held no illusions about the nature of the Soviet regime. The year before the president had noted that "the Soviet Union . . . is run by a dictatorship as absolute as any other dictatorship in the world."[28] The primary concern at the moment, however, was defeating Germany. Roosevelt worried that if aid was not sent to the Soviet Union and the Germans were victorious, one would always wonder if support might have made a difference. While the president was painfully aware of the shortages of key supplies, had no desire to waste them, and knew that no significant amount of supplies could soon reach Russia, he believed that a statement of support from Washington would help Soviet morale. The president announced on June 24 that any request for material assistance by the Soviet Union "would be given immediate attention," that Russian accounts in the United States would be unfrozen, and that Washington would not "issue a proclamation of neutrality under the terms of the so-called Neutrality Act."[29] The grand strategy of the United States now included aid to Russia to ensure the survival of the Soviet Union.

While he was already in Great Britain in July for meetings with Churchill, Hopkins suggested to Roosevelt that he visit Moscow to meet with Stalin and assess the Soviets' needs. "I have a feeling that everything possible should be done to make certain the Russians maintain a permanent front," he cabled the president, "even though they be defeated in this immediate battle." He thought if Stalin could be influenced at this critical time it should be done "by a direct communication from you through a personal envoy. I think the stakes are so great that it should be done. Stalin would then know in an unmistakable way that we mean business on a long term supply job."[30] Having promised support, these questions remained: what was the state of the fighting on the eastern front, what was needed, and what would be possible?

Roosevelt concurred with Hopkins. The president instructed Hopkins to "concentrate on the materiel which can reach Russia within the next three months" in order to help it survive. At the same time, the president was taking the long view and wanted the meeting to help establish relations between Washington and Moscow. Hopkins, therefore, was also told to discuss the mechanics of delivery so the United States could begin to send "a great amount" of supplies starting in the winter.[31]

In his quick summary of his meetings, sent from Moscow on August 1, Hopkins reported to FDR that he had had "two long and satisfactory talks with Stalin and will communicate personally to you the messages he is sending." He wanted Roosevelt to know right away "that I feel ever so confident about this front. The morale of the population is exceptionally good. There is unbounded determination to win." He also noted that Stalin was anxious that discussions on loans "be agreed upon at the earliest possible moment."[32] Based on this report and his own strategic calculations, Roosevelt demanded immediate action on the sending of aid, particularly airplanes, insisting to his advisors that it was the time to "take some risks."[33] On August 2, he wrote Wayne Coy, his special assistant on defense matters and liaison officer with the Office of Emergency Management, that he was upset "that nearly six weeks have elapsed since the Russian War began and that we have done practically nothing to get any of the materials they asked for on their actual way to delivery in Siberia. Frankly, if I were a Russian I would feel that I had been given the run-around in the United States." He told Coy to get out the list and "with my full authority, use a heavy hand—act as a burr under the saddle and get things moving!" The president wanted Coy to concentrate on supplies that could be delivered "in time to take part in battle between September first and October first," the date the president expected active fighting to end due to the weather. "If Germany can be held until then, Russia is safe until the Spring. Step on it!"[34]

In Hopkins's longer reports of his meetings with Stalin on July 30 and 31, he noted that he began the first meeting by assuring Stalin that Roosevelt "considered Hitler the enemy of mankind and that he therefore wished to aid the Soviet Union in its fight against Germany." Notably, he specified that the question of supplies had two parts, "what would Russia most require that the United States could deliver immediately, and what would be Russia's requirements on the basis of a long war?"[35] At their second and more substantive meeting, Hopkins received from Stalin a long analysis of the war with Germany. Hopkins then reiterated that FDR wanted to send aid that could be used in the next few weeks, but that "plans should be made for a long war." Along those lines, the president's emissary noted that Washington would be unwilling to send any heavy munitions such as tanks and airplanes until after a conference was held to discuss strategy, needs, and available equipment. While Hopkins noted that he lacked the authority to make his suggestion of a meeting an official offer, Stalin agreed that such a meeting would be valuable and that he would receive an official proposal positively. In the course of their talk, Stalin handed Hopkins a note in his own handwriting that set out, in Hopkins's words, the supplies he wanted in "the order of importance": light anti-aircraft guns, aluminum for airplanes, 50-caliber machine guns, and 30-caliber rifles.[36] The most important conclusions Hopkins drew from his meetings in Moscow were that the Russians believed they would survive the initial battles now being waged and that, despite recognizing that it would be a long and bitter war, they were determined to fight and defeat Germany.

There were, of course, concerns about relations with the Soviet Union. Hopkins quickly learned that he could not elicit any useful information from any Soviet official other than the Soviet dictator. "There is literally no one in the whole Government who is willing to give any important information other than Mr. Stalin himself." For this reason, Hopkins insisted that the meeting he proposed had to be held after October 1 and in Moscow. It had to be conducted with Stalin personally, and by then the question of where the front was when fighting began again in the spring would be settled.[37] He later wrote that from this trip, and the fear he saw that subordinates had of their superiors, "the difference between democracy and dictatorship were clearer to me than any philosopher, historian or journalist could make it." While he respected the Russian contribution to the war and was sympathetic to its needs, Hopkins was frustrated, as were so many American officials, with the difficulties that existed in conducting business with Moscow.[38]

Nonetheless, Roosevelt and Hopkins knew that the survival of the Soviet Union was a matter of national security and was necessary for the defeat of Germany. The American strategy depended on Russia providing the main force on the ground while the United States provided the naval and air power, supplies, and ultimately its own ground troops. Without the Red Army, victory would be much more costly and difficult. Hopkins's talks in Russia confirmed the belief he expressed while in London: that supplies should be sent even if the Red Army could not stop the German advance to Moscow. The president wrote Stimson that he saw the fall meeting in Moscow and the ability to send aid to the Soviet Union immediately and throughout the course of the war "to be of paramount importance for the safety and security of America." Roosevelt, therefore, requested a recommendation of what supplies could be provided from the present until June 30, 1942.[39] The War Department's "Joint Board Estimate of United States Over-all Production Requirements" of September 11, 1941, provided the requested comprehensive estimate of needs and set out a global military strategy for the war. Prepared by General

Marshall, Admiral Stark, and the Chiefs of Staff, the major national objectives listed were in line with the grand strategy already determined by the president: the preservation of the United States and the Western Hemisphere, the survival of Great Britain, the containment of Japanese power, and the postwar establishment of political stability in Europe and Asia to ensure "the future security of the United States." The "first major objective" of the United States had to be "the complete military defeat of Germany," which could only happen "through military victories outside this hemisphere." This could not be done "by the European Powers now fighting against her. . . . Therefore if our European enemies are to be defeated, it will be necessary for the United States to enter the war, and to employ a part of its armed forces offensively in the Eastern Atlantic and in Europe or Africa" while also fighting Japan.[40]

"It is out of the question," the report concluded, "to expect the United States and its Associates to undertake in the near future a sustained and successful land offensive against the center of German power"; this left mainly defensive operations on the sea and in the air for the present time. These actions "may prevent wars from being lost, and by weakening enemy strength may greatly contribute to victory," but alone could not win the war with Germany. The exception to this situation was in Russia where "*the maintenance of an active front* . . . offers by far the best opportunity for a successful land offensive against Germany, because only Russia possesses adequate manpower, situated in favorable proximity to the center of German military power." Although it was difficult to predict the outcome of the present fighting, "were the Soviet forces to be driven even beyond the Ural Mountains, and were they there to continue an organized resistance, there would always remain the hope of a final and complete defeat of Germany by land operations. The effective arming of Russian forces . . . would be one of the most important moves that could be made by the Associated Powers."[41] All calculations going forward would be made based on these conclusions.

Right after emphatically ordering the movement of supplies to the Soviet Union, Roosevelt slipped away from Washington, DC, for a secret meeting with Winston Churchill in Placentia Bay off the coast of Newfoundland. The conference from August 9 to 12 would be the first of many meetings between the two men during the war. Besides British pressure for the United States to enter the war immediately, there was little disagreement over strategy in the Atlantic. The main areas of discussion were how to contain Japan, London's worries about access to supplies from Asia and control of shipping lanes, and the joint declaration of war aims. Roosevelt told Churchill that he believed "very strongly that every effort should be made to *prevent* the outbreak of *war with Japan*." Still, he would maintain the sanctions that the United States had imposed on Japan, and when he met with the Japanese ambassador upon his return to Washington, FDR informed him that "any further move by Japan would produce a situation in which U.S. Government would be compelled to take certain measures even though this might lead to war between U.S. and Japan."[42] If war came in the Pacific, the president assured the prime minister that the defeat of Germany would remain the first strategic aim of the United States. To further that end, Roosevelt and Churchill agreed with Hopkins's proposal for a high-level conference in Moscow in the fall to determine the needs of the Soviet Union and what equipment to supply the Red Army.

The culmination of the meeting was the release of the "Atlantic Charter" on August 14, designed to set forth the "principles relating to the civilization of the world as a whole."[43] The eight points that made up the statement of war aims reflected the essential elements of Roosevelt's internationalism: no territorial aggrandizement from war, self-determination for all nations, the Open Door policy for international trade, disarmament, and a permanent peace built upon international cooperation and adherence to these values.[44] There were, however, disagreements between the two leaders prior to the approval of the statement. For the Americans, the inclusion of the Open Door, which challenged the British imperial preference system, was, in Sumner Welles's words, a "*vital principle*." If the restoration of free trade was not included, "they might as well throw in the sponge and realize that one of the greatest factors in creating the present tragic situation in the world was going to be permitted to continue unchecked in the post-war world." On the other side, Roosevelt refused to include the wording that peace would be maintained by an "*effective international organization*," as the British wanted, because he feared domestic opposition and the problems that had beset Woodrow Wilson. Introducing the concept that would become the "Four Policemen," Roosevelt suggested they might have to wait on the creation of a new international organization until stability returned at the end of the war, after a time "during which an international police force composed of the United States and Great Britain had had an opportunity of functioning." In the end, he would only agree that point eight include the phrase "the establishment of a wider and permanent system of general security."[45]

Opponents of the president quickly criticized the Atlantic Charter for its failure to include explicit statements on freedom of religion and speech, claiming incorrectly that these represented concessions to the Soviet Union. However, there had been no discussions with Moscow concerning the statement, or about Russia and its response to the principles set forth. Despite the oversight of not including freedom of religion and speech in the Atlantic Charter (an omission that would be officially rectified by their inclusion as part of the Proclamation of the United Nations on January 1, 1942), Roosevelt had expanded the four freedoms to be the joint principles of the Anglo–American war effort, which he saw as essential to a new, peaceful, postwar international order and to American national security.

On August 15, Roosevelt and Churchill released an often overlooked joint message to Stalin. They praised the Soviets for their "splendid defense" against the Nazi attack and noted that shiploads of supplies had already been sent, with more to follow, to aid Russia in its fight. The key point of the message was the formal request for a meeting in Moscow of senior officials to ascertain the Soviet Union's needs for manufactured goods, weapons, and raw materials in order to maximize the effectiveness of production planning and their use. The two leaders informed Stalin that if he approved the idea, the West would continue to send supplies as rapidly as possible until such a meeting. In conclusion, they set out their hope for wartime cooperation, noting "how vitally important to the defeat of Hitlerism is the brave and steadfast resistance of the Soviet Union" and the necessity for "planning the program for the future allocation of our joint resources."[46] As the president noted in a press conference on August 16, all of this was based on the assumption that Russian resistance would continue into the winter.[47]

The conference in Moscow was held on September 28–30, with W. Averell Harriman representing the United States. In his letter of introduction for Harriman, Roosevelt wrote Stalin that he was "thrilled" to have learned from Hopkins about his "encouraging and satisfactory visits with you," and of the "gallant defense of the Soviet armies." Harriman was "well aware of the strategic importance of your front" and was ready to bring the negotiations to "a successful conclusion." The president concluded by noting his "great confidence" that Soviet forces "will ultimately prevail over Hitler and to assure you of our great determination to be of every possible material assistance." On October 30, FDR approved the agreements reached to send everything from tanks to boots, over 150 different categories of items, to Russia and pushed to have delivery made as quickly as possible.[48]

From this point forward, Roosevelt spoke as if the nation was already an active participant in the fighting. He publicly urged the American people to make more sacrifices, to speed up production, and to recognize the threat Germany posed and the necessity of using the American military in the conflict, even if he was still waiting on an incident and was unwilling to ask Congress for a declaration of war. At an August 19 press conference, FDR quoted something Lincoln said in 1862, one year after the Civil War had begun: that some people still thought they could get out of the conflict through strategy rather than fighting, and that some people had not "yet made up their minds that we are at war with the South." In Lincoln's observation that the "country hadn't yet waked up to the fact they had a war to win," Roosevelt found an "interesting parallel" to the present.[49]

Roosevelt's decision to expand America's defense perimeter and institute naval patrols culminated in his September 11 speech, in which the president took his final steps toward war with Germany. On September 4, a German submarine attacked the American destroyer *Greer* off the coast of Greenland. With the decision to occupy Iceland, FDR had decided that all ships, not just American, would be protected in the shipping lanes from North America to 200 miles around the island. He had told Churchill at their meeting that he was going to speak on his new policy in September, and the torpedo strike against the *Greer* provided him the perfect opportunity. In a fireside chat, Roosevelt told the American public that the attack was an unprovoked action against a ship that was carrying mail and that had the American flag clearly displayed, inside the zone in the Atlantic that the United States claimed as its waters of self-defense. "This was piracy—piracy legally and morally," Roosevelt declared. "The important truth is that these acts of international lawlessness are a manifestation of a . . . Nazi design to abolish the freedom of the seas, and to acquire absolute control and domination of these seas for themselves," all with the ultimate aim of the domination of the United States and the Western Hemisphere. The president pledged that "no matter what it takes, no matter what it costs, we will keep open the line of legitimate commerce in these defensive waters."[50]

Roosevelt did not tell the public that the *Greer,* along with British air craft, had been following the sub for hours in hopes that the British could sink it. Rather, he compared the German submarine to a rattlesnake and noted that when it is "poised to strike, you do not wait until he has struck before you crush him." Given that, he announced what came to be called the policy of "shoot-on-sight." American naval vessels and planes would no longer wait for German subs to strike first, but would attack if they found German ships inside the Atlantic defense sphere. "From now on, if German or Italian vessels of war enter the waters, the protection of which is necessary for American defense, they do so at their own peril."[51]

In early October, Roosevelt asked Congress to again amend the Neutrality Act to allow American merchant ships to be armed and to deliver goods into the war zone of Europe. The president stated that the change was another necessary step in the defense of the nation to help ensure that lend-lease supplies arrived in England and Russia.[52] While Congress debated the president's proposal, Germany attacked the American destroyer *Kearney* on October 16. Declaring that "the shooting has started," Roosevelt noted that "history has recorded who fired the first shot. In the long run, however, all that will matter is who fired the last shot." America had been attacked. The *Kearney* was not just a Navy ship, FDR stated. "She belongs to every man, woman, and child in this Nation." The purpose of these attacks was to frighten the American people and get the United States to retreat. In doing so, Hitler had badly "misjudged the American spirit." To drive home the immediacy of the German threat and design for world domination, FDR cited two documents in his possession: a secret map that divided South America "into five vassal states" that included the Panama Canal, and "a plan to abolish all existing religions" and establish an "International Nazi Church," with the "god of Blood and Iron" replacing "the God of Love and Mercy." The stakes, Roosevelt had made clear, could not be higher. Having faced and overcome numerous challenges before, the nation now confronted "the newest and greatest challenge of them all."[53]

The president still did not seek a formal declaration of war. His current policies had broad support, but the difficult battle in Congress over the amendment that would allow for the arming of merchant ships, and the close electoral victory in November 1940, indicated that this support fell short of sending American forces into battle. All senior officials agreed that Germany could not be defeated unless the United States entered the fighting, but FDR still worried about a split in public opinion if he were to take that final step without provocation. Moreover, with Japan's renewed aggression in Southeast

Asia, Roosevelt worried about a two-front war, particularly before the nation had fully mobilized its productive power. The president had to be sure that his actions maintained public support and that his policies worked in conjunction with the Allies toward the defeat of the Axis and not at cross-purposes. Roosevelt continued tacking; he let the American people get accommodated to each new course and direction, but always kept his sights on where he wanted to take the nation.

Throughout 1940 and 1941, American efforts were concentrated primarily on Europe and the threat of Nazi Germany. The survival of Great Britain was still not certain; if Germany defeated the Soviet Union, its military and industry would be greatly strengthened and it could again turn its full attention to the British Isles. Moreover, up to the middle of 1941, senior officials did not believe that Japan would be bold or foolish enough to provoke the United States, much less attack it. They were confident that the United States had much greater power than Japan, that Japanese leaders knew this, and that any such action would be suicide for Tokyo. This did not mean that Japan was ignored. The Roosevelt administration had taken steps to deter further Japanese aggression and set out its determination to protect American and Western interests in Southeast Asia. When Japan took advantage of Germany's victory over France in 1940 to move into northern Indochina, the American embargo of scrap metal and iron was felt by Japan's military, and the lack of any further moves was interpreted by many American officials as proof that the sanctions served as a sufficient deterrent. Tokyo, having to deplete its reserves to sustain the fighting, renewed efforts to open up negotiations with Washington. As Stimson noted, summarizing American policy at the end of 1940, "when the United States indicates by clear language and bold actions that she intends to carry out a clear and affirmative policy in the Far East, Japan will yield to that policy even though it conflicts with her own Asiatic policy and conceived interests."[54]

Indeed, so sure were many American officials that Japan would not strike against the United States that they discussed the removal of the American fleet from Hawaii and the West Coast to the Atlantic in 1941, and believed that time was an ally in East Asia. In part, this confidence stemmed from the development of the B-17 bomber. The newest version of the Flying Fortress had a range great enough to strike Japan from the Philippines and, so thought many strategists, would provide an additional deterrent to any further Japanese expansion. Thus, policy was designed to preserve the status quo in the Pacific. Keeping Japan from further attacks on the European colonies in Southeast Asia was seen as the best course of action in support of the Allied war efforts in Europe. To that end, American policy focused on providing aid to China in the hope that a strong Chinese resistance would tie down Tokyo's forces and discourage any further acts of aggression that would further stretch Japan's military capacity.

Yet the status quo was hardly ideal; it was not a situation that the United States wanted to see become permanent, and no one could confidently predict Japanese actions. Conflict at some point appeared inevitable. If Japan renewed its expansion and pushed toward the south, the question was whether it would be to the advantage of the United States to have, in the words of Ambassador Grew, a "showdown sooner or to have it later." The answer to that question depended on whether war with Japan would harm U.S. ability to aid Britain in Europe and, thus, make the difference between victory and defeat for England. It was also contingent on when the United States would be prepared to take on commitments in two oceans. In any event, it was clear to everyone, including Grew, who had previously led the faction that urged a negotiated settlement, that there was no peaceful solution to the problem. Japan, the ambassador now acknowledged in a letter to Roosevelt, was "openly and unashamedly one of the predatory nations and part of a system which aims to wreck about everything that the United States stands for." The remaining question was, how much pressure should be applied? A full American embargo would "seriously handicap Japan in the long run," but it could "push the Japanese onward in a forlorn hope of making themselves economically self-sufficient." As Grew concluded, it was "not whether we must call a halt to the Japanese program, but when."[55]

The president responded in January 1941 that he was in complete agreement with Grew. In deciding on a course of action, it was imperative to understand "that the hostilities in Europe, in Africa, and in Asia are all parts of a single world conflict" that had forced the United States into "defending our way of life and our vital interests wherever they are seriously endangered." This demanded a "global strategy which takes account of every front and takes advantage of every opportunity to contribute to our total security." Thus, it was not just a question of whether war with Japan would divert American resources away from helping Great Britain. It was also necessary to "consider whether, if Japan should gain possession of the region of the

Netherlands East Indies and the Malay Peninsula, the chances of England's winning in her struggle with Germany would not be decreased thereby." The resources of the area and British access to them were also vital to the war effort. "Our strategy of giving them assistance toward ensuring our own security must envisage both sending of supplies to England and helping to prevent a closing of the channels of communication to and from various parts of the world, so that other important sources of supply will not be denied to the British and added to the assets of the other side." The problems posed by Japan were so interrelated with the war in Europe, Roosevelt concluded, that "any attempt to state them compels one to think in terms of five continents and seven seas."[56]

Starting in February 1941, Japan's new ambassador to the United States, Admiral Nomura Kichisaburō, engaged in a series of talks with Secretary of State Hull, seeking to find some ground for an American accommodation to Japan's domination of China and Tokyo's imperial project. Kichisaburō represented the moderate faction in the Japanese government that still sought a modus vivendi with the United States in the hope that Japan could secure its goals without war. The Japanese position that the U.S. should accept the status quo in East Asia, however, was untenable to the Roosevelt administration, and the talks went nowhere that winter and spring. The United States was content at this time to drag the talks out, buying time for its mobilization and allowing it to focus on getting aid to Great Britain.

The events of June and July 1941 would change these views. On the one hand, the German invasion of the Soviet Union had changed the strategic equation in Europe and confirmed for President Roosevelt his view that the fighting was all one world war, albeit with multiple fronts, that demanded a coordinated American response to the international crisis. On the other hand, Japan's taking of all of Indochina in July indicated that there might not be any way of stopping its effort to establish the Greater East Asian Co-Prosperity Sphere, short of war. In particular, Roosevelt worried that a Japanese attack against the Soviet Union might tilt the balance and lead to the defeat of Moscow. The question was whether a hard line or some other approach was the best means to deter Tokyo from any further action; but, if war was to come with Japan, Washington preferred it to be in Southeast Asia, where the United States was stronger and where the battles would not so dramatically change the fortunes of the Russian war against Hitler. Thus, after Japan moved to take over southern Indochina on July 24, Roosevelt announced that he was freezing Japanese assets in the United States, imposing, in effect, an oil embargo against Japan. The need to ensure the survival of the Soviet Union necessitated taking a firmer position and incurring greater risks in the policy toward Japan. If Tokyo was to expand the war in East Asia, the administration wanted to influence its direction. Without specifically saying so, the president's action indicated that his thinking had changed. If Japan was to attack anywhere, it should be to the south. Thus, he took the step he had resisted the previous year.[57]

The freezing of Japan's assets and the oil embargo led Kichisaburō to start another round of talks in mid-August, again designed to seek American acceptance of Japan's position in China. The Japanese promised to guarantee the integrity of the Philippines and to withdraw their forces from Southeast Asia and the Southwestern Pacific, pending an agreement by the United States to cease sending aid to China. In return the United States would lift its embargo and normalize relations with Japan. Not surprisingly, this was rejected by the State Department. In a meeting on August 17, FDR warned the ambassador that further Japanese aggression would force the United States to take "whatever steps might be necessary toward safeguarding its legitimate interests and rights . . . and toward insuring the security and safety of the United States."[58] Roosevelt was willing to have the State Department continue talks with Tokyo, but turned down a proposal for a meeting between himself and Japanese Prime Minister Fumimaro Konoe. The administration's position was that relations would improve only when Japan agreed to respect the sovereignty and territorial integrity of China and the Open Door policy, and agreed to stop its aggression.[59]

The implications for the United States of these decisions were set out in the September "Joint Board Estimate of United States Over-all Production Requirements." It noted that Japan's goal of establishing an "East Asia Co-Prosperity Sphere" was "a heavy task for Japan's strength, a fact well realized by the Japanese." Given that, it was "unlikely that Japan will simultaneously attempt a major effort to the Northward and to the Southward, because of her lack of equipment and raw materials." The "*retention of Eastern Siberia by Russia*" was seen as "necessary if Japan is to be checked." At the same time, if Japan struck to the south "against the British in Malaya and against the Dutch in the Netherlands East Indies, the British and Dutch forces probably could not successfully withstand such an advance in the absence of active military assistance from the United States."[60]

As talks with Japan went nowhere that fall, the War Department began preparations for the defense of the Philippines and the coming of war. Stimson told Hull he would need three months to secure American defenses in the region and that, therefore, he favored a continuation of the efforts at "stringing out negotiations during that time." In mid-October, he noted that it was important to conduct American "diplomatic fencing" in such a way "as to be sure that Japan was put into the wrong and made the first bad move—overt move." Hull asked Stimson if he favored an immediate declaration of war. The secretary of war, who had sought a declaration of war against Germany for months, emphatically responded no. The United States needed "to take advantage of this wonderful opportunity of strengthening our position in the Philippines by air." Hull, because he thought the Japanese emperor favored a peaceful settlement, still believed negotiations could succeed. He was alone among the senior administration officials in thinking this. Nonetheless, Stimson, while convinced that war was now a foregone conclusion, agreed with and reflected Roosevelt's views as he encouraged Hull to continue the talks as long as possible because to delay the start of war could only help with the buildup of American supplies and forces. Stimson summed up his position by quoting Theodore Roosevelt: the United States' policy was to "speak softly and carry a big stick." What was needed was just a little more time to get the stick prepared.[61]

By late November, it was clear that time was running out. The final Japanese offer on November 20 of a withdrawal from southern Indochina in return for a lifting of U.S. sanctions was rejected. This modus vivendi, if accepted, would force the United States to abandon China. The U.S. counteroffer, that Japan would agree to leave China in exchange for renewed trade, was dismissed by the Japanese representatives. Because the United States had broken the Japanese diplomatic code, Washington knew that this final breakdown of talks meant war. It was just a matter now of when and where. Two days later a dispatch from Tokyo was intercepted that indicated that November 29 was the final deadline for negotiations to reach a successful agreement. After that, the plans for war would go into effect. Roosevelt notified Churchill on November 24 that "we must all be prepared for real trouble, possibly soon."[62] On December 1, the Japanese Imperial Conference concluded that there was no turning back and gave the green light for the attack on Pearl Harbor.

It was believed that Japan would strike to the south, at the Dutch East Indies, Malaysia, and possibly the Philippines, in order to remove the American and British navies from the area and gain access to the riches of the region, particularly oil. Washington was shocked when on December 7 the attack came on Pearl Harbor in Hawaii. Upon hearing the news while having lunch with the president, Hopkins expressed his view that the report must be a mistake, "that surely Japan would not attack in Honolulu."[63] Although the initial reports from the islands were troubling, there was a sense of relief in the nation's capital. The indecision and anticipation of war was over. As Stimson put it, due to the Japanese attack, the war "had come in a way which would unite all our people."[64] When Roosevelt met with Hopkins, Stimson, Hull, Knox, Marshall, and Stark that afternoon, they were all prepared for a long and difficult struggle, and were convinced, in Hopkins's words, "that in the last analysis the enemy was Hitler and that he could never be defeated without force of arms."[65] This was not to discount the concern over the failure at Pearl Harbor or the damage inflicted. It was an acknowledgment of what the president had concluded that fall; in order to protect American interests and national security, the United States had to do more than provide aid to its allies and prepare its defenses. It had to become a belligerent itself so as to ensure victory during the war and to seize the second chance at establishing a peaceful postwar world conducive to American interests, institutions, and defense.

Almost immediately, charges began to be made that there was a conspiracy by the Roosevelt administration to set up the attack on Pearl Harbor as a way to overcome the noninterventionist sentiment in the nation and provide a back door to the war in Europe that the people would not support otherwise. These charges were serious and wrong. It was true that the president and his senior advisors knew that the rejection of Japan's final negotiation proposal meant war, that they had long been frustrated by political opposition at home and the desire of so many to stay out of the fighting, seemingly at any cost, and that they had decided the United States had to enter the war to be sure the Axis would be defeated and America protected. Moreover, they wanted Japan and/or Germany to make the first overt attack so as to make clear who the aggressor was and to unite the nation in combat.

However, no evidence exists in the records to support the claim that the Roosevelt administration manipulated Japan into war and that the president left the Pacific fleet open to the devastating attack on Pearl Harbor on purpose, in the process hampering the American ability to defend against the Japanese strikes in the southern Pacific. Officials in Washington were genuinely surprised by the attack. The United States had broken Japan's diplomatic code, not its military code, and it did not have prior knowledge of the specifics of Japan's war plan. As already noted, it was assumed that Japan would strike to the south, which it did in addition to the attack on Hawaii. Washington's failure was in underestimating the capabilities of the Japanese military. Local commanders shared that perception and failed to act fully on the alert that had been sent out from Washington to all officers and bases in the Pacific to be prepared for war. Furthermore, despite Stimson's urging, Roosevelt did not ask for a declaration of war on Germany after the attack on Pearl Harbor, even though all senior officials agreed that the Nazis posed the greater threat to the United States. The attack on Pearl Harbor had overcome all resistance to war at home, but the public wanted to fight Japan, not Germany. The president wanted Hitler to act and declare war. He knew, through an intercepted November 29 cable, that Berlin had informed the Japanese that if they "became engaged in a war against the United States, Germany would of course join in the war immediately," which Hitler, and Mussolini, did on December 11.[66] Roosevelt had always made much of the Axis alliance, as he saw the fighting as one world war, with the events and consequences for the United States linked. The German and Italian declarations of war confirmed Roosevelt's claims that the Axis was a global threat to democracy and that American national security had to be defended beyond the Western Hemisphere.

There is no need to provide any further refutation of these claims. As early as 1948, Robert Sherwood, in his book *Roosevelt and Hopkins*, effectively debunked the back door thesis. No subsequent declassified records have challenged his main findings, and no secondary works have discredited his interpretation. Sherwood's explanation for the surprise attack on Pearl Harbor remains convincing based on the documentary evidence. "It may well be said," he wrote, "that those in high authority in both the United States and Britain made two original errors of calculation: they greatly underrated Japanese military strength and daring, and they greatly overrated Japanese political astuteness."[67] The cause of the war was the aggression of the Axis powers.

Speaking to Congress the day after Pearl Harbor was attacked, Roosevelt declared that December 7, 1941, was "a date which will live in infamy." The United States "was suddenly and deliberately attacked by naval and air forces of the Empire of Japan." The bombing of Hawaii caused extensive damage and loss of life. It was also part of a broader offensive as Japanese forces had also struck Malaysia, Hong Kong, Guam, the Philippines, Wake Island, and Midway Island. The president pledged that "no matter how long it may take us to overcome this premeditated invasion, the American people in their righteous might will win through to absolute victory" and will make sure "that this form of treachery shall never again endanger us. Hostilities exist. There is no blinking at the fact that our people, our territory, and our interests are in grave danger." He concluded his brief address asking for a declaration of war by stating: "With confidence in our armed forces—with the unbounding determination of our people—we will gain the inevitable triumph—so help us God."[68]

The following evening FDR delivered a fireside chat to the American public in which he set out Pearl Harbor as the culmination of a decade of aggression by the Axis nations; he recalled for his listeners all the attacks made on nations by Japan, Germany, and Italy, starting with Japan's invasion of Manchuria in 1931 to Germany's attack against Russia the past June. The task ahead would be difficult, the president warned. The Axis was powerful and determined. "It will not only be a long war," Roosevelt stated. "It will be a hard war." It was necessary to acknowledge the difficult situation in the world and the trials ahead, both at home in terms of production and sacrifice, and in the fighting abroad. "We don't like it—we didn't want to get in it—but we are in it and we're going to fight it with everything we've got." The Axis had to be defeated. Roosevelt ended his address by looking to the future. "The true goal we seek," FDR stated, "is far above and beyond the ugly field of battle. When we resort to force . . . we are determined that this force shall be directed toward ultimate good as well as against immediate evil. We Americans are not destroyers—we are builders."[69]

There would be forty-four months of difficult, bloody, and costly war ahead. As the nation turned to that effort, FDR was also focused on how the fighting would influence the peace. In the past five years, Roosevelt had redefined the concept of American foreign policy, which had been based on neutrality, hemispheric defense, and freedom of the seas, to an internationalist view of the United States as a world leader that based its defense on preparedness and collective security in order to protect its interests—as defined by the four freedoms—and that worked with multilateral, international organizations to promote American values and institutions. This understanding of national security was the basis for wartime mobilization and would guide the administration in its strategy and planning throughout the war. As Roosevelt declared to the American people at the end of his December 9, 1941, fireside chat: "We are going to win the war and we are going to win the peace that follows."[70]

6

Forging the Grand Alliance

World War II was the bloodiest and most destructive conflict ever. Over 60 million people lost their lives—including 465,000 Americans—tens of millions were displaced, and cities, towns, and farms were destroyed across the world. It brought upheaval, revolution, and dislocation to people in Africa, Asia, and Europe and led to changes of governments, borders, and social structures. If the nearly 3,000 killed at Pearl Harbor was a searing experience for the people of the United States, it is not difficult to imagine the impact that invading armies, aerial bombardment, and occupation had on others. It was truly a world war, and no one understood that better than Franklin Roosevelt.

President Roosevelt alone among the world leaders grappled with the issues of multiple fronts and the varied problems presented by the effort to defeat Germany, Japan, and Italy. The United States faced the task of mobilizing its own military while continuing to provide supplies to Great Britain, the Soviet Union, and China, and coordinating its efforts with allies who did not share all of Washington's goals. In addition, it was Roosevelt more than anyone who provided a unifying purpose to the fighting for the American people as, throughout the war, he consistently invoked the four freedoms and the idea of the United Nations. The war entrenched the new concepts about foreign policy that the president had articulated prior to Pearl Harbor. In meeting the challenges of war, liberal internationalism and national security provided the guideposts for decision making and efforts to create an international system that protected American interests and values.

Roosevelt became the leader of the Grand Alliance, and the United States the ultimate arbiter of the various disputes. His vision for a postwar peace was based on the United Nations—what Roosevelt originally termed the coalition of twenty-six nations fighting against the Axis—and collective security. The grand strategy of ensuring the survival of Great Britain and then the Soviet Union, and expanding the Western Hemisphere through the protection of shipping and cargo, had been built on the understanding that Germany was the most powerful and dangerous enemy, and that American security, and the protection of democracy and freedom, could not be achieved without the defeat of Berlin first. Pearl Harbor did not change that. While the American public's anger at Japan and desire for revenge and victory over Tokyo was understandable, Roosevelt knew that Hitler presented the greatest danger. The Grand Alliance had been formed mainly in response to the actions of Germany. Yet, even with the common purpose of defeating Germany, there were many disagreements among the Big Three, Roosevelt, Churchill, and Stalin; none was larger than the question of the second front in Europe, which was the central subject of Allied strategic discussions and disagreements from 1942 until D-Day on June 6, 1944.

In matters of the grand strategy, FDR set his destination and did not waver from the goal. Although the president sought input from his advisors and the military, and could be flexible on the course taken, he stuck to his main objectives and key strategies. In pursuit of victory and a permanent peace, Roosevelt was willing to accept compromises of principles, tacking when and where he thought necessary, but always moving forward. The main contribution of the United States to victory in the early years of the war would be serving as the arsenal of the Allies. Additionally, the president always pursued strategies designed to keep American casualties to a minimum. This led Roosevelt to adopt a policy of delay on the big decisions about the postwar world, waiting until American power could be fully felt on the battlefields and its influence was at its peak, and to pursue policies that at times appeared to be in conflict if not altogether contradictory. The difficulties Roosevelt would face tested all of his abilities as a leader, and rarely did he fail.

President Roosevelt's thinking was shaped by the concept that World War II provided the United States with a second chance for world leadership, and that only American leadership could bring postwar peace, prosperity, and stability. It was a central tenet for the supporters of internationalism that the dual crises of the Great Depression and the Second World War stemmed in large part from the failure of the United States to take up its proper role in the world after the Great War. Hence, when FDR declared on December 9, 1941, that the nation was going to win both the war and the peace afterward, he was expressing a vision and an understanding of the recent past that emerged from his victory over the noninterventionists and isolationist sentiment.

In February 1941, Henry Luce, the publisher of *Fortune*, *Life*, and *Time* magazines, captured the logic behind much of the internationalist position on foreign policy, its proponents' highest aspirations, and the emerging, confident mood of the nation that joined the new conceptions of national security with American Exceptionalism in his essay "The American Century." Luce argued that the failure of the United States to accept its responsibility as a great power and take up the position of world leader during the interwar period "had disastrous consequences" for the nation "and for all mankind." A permanent peace and continuous prosperity could only be secured in a world where the United States took up its rightful role and responsibilities. Luce asserted that in 1919 the United States had missed "a golden opportunity . . . to assume the leadership of the world. . . . We did not understand the opportunity. [President Woodrow] Wilson mishandled it. We rejected it." The result was the Great Depression and a second world war. To avoid repeating the same mistake with the same consequences this time, the United States had to seize the second chance presented to it to lead the world.[1]

If the United States did not establish a new international system, economic disruption and political chaos would return. Stating the central ideas held by all leading American internationalists, Luce argued that it was essential that the United States promote American ideals of freedom, justice, and opportunity to make sure they spread throughout the world. "America as the dynamic center of ever-widening spheres of enterprise," Luce declared, "America as the training center of the skilled servants of mankind, America as the Good Samaritan, really believing again that it is more blessed to give than to receive, and America as the powerhouse of the ideals of Freedom and Justice—out of these elements surely can be fashioned a vision of the 20th Century to which we can and will devote ourselves." It was in this spirit, Luce concluded, that the United States was called to "create the first great American Century."[2]

Roosevelt himself set out the concept of a second chance succinctly and clearly in his January 6, 1942, State of the Union address, declaring that it was the "will of the American people to make very certain that the world will never so suffer again" from the threats that brought about the war. "Our own objectives are clear," Roosevelt declared: the defeat of militarism with the "objective of establishing and securing freedom of speech, freedom of religion, freedom from want, and freedom from fear everywhere in the world." Thus, the United States had to win the war but also "maintain the security of the peace that will follow." The sacrifices that would be required for victory were not made "to return to the kind of world we had after the last world war. We are fighting today for security, for progress, and for peace . . . not only for one generation but for all generations."[3]

As the nation embarked on the arduous task of fighting World War II, President Roosevelt assured the American people that they would win but that it would be a long struggle and would take sacrifices from all citizens whether they were among the over 16 million who joined the military or were working on the home front. Just as he had declared in 1933 that the country had "nothing to fear but fear itself," FDR again called upon the nation to face the challenge with confidence and resoluteness. Speaking on December 9, 1941, the president told the public that "we must share together the bad news and the good news, the defeats and the victories—the changing fortunes of war." The initial news was bad, from Hawaii to the Philippines, to Guam, Midway, and Wake Island; yet, Roosevelt declared, the United States "can accept no result save victory, final and complete."[4]

The most pressing tasks in the first two months of the war were the full mobilization of the economy for military production and the coordination of military strategy with Great Britain. The time devoted to increased military preparedness during the prior year and a half quickly paid off. Industrial production was already reaching full capacity by Pearl Harbor, and the building of new plants, or the expansion of existing ones, was well under way. Munitions manufacturers, too, were meeting the demands of lend-lease and the American military. Early increases in production from both factories and farms was going so well that Secretary of War Stimson confidently declared in April 1942 that, although the Axis had mobilized earlier and moved ahead of the United States in the first stage of the war, the United States would now start demonstrating its greater strength and "would pull down its enemy by sheer endurance and unbreakable morale."[5] Sacrifice was called for and rationing of many goods imposed as the president asked for unprecedented levels of output. The American people met this challenge. From 1942 to

1944, production increased from $1.5 billion to $37.5 billion, making the American military the best equipped and most powerful force in history. At the same time, billions of dollars' worth of military equipment and other necessities in lend-lease aid continued to reach the Soviet Union, Great Britain, and, to a lesser extent, China. From July 1, 1940, to July 31, 1945, the United States produced 296,601 military airplanes, 71,060 naval ships with a displacement tonnage of 8,250,000, and 86,388 tanks, along with millions of rifles, munitions, cargo ships, and all other necessary equipment for war. It was a stunning achievement that more than met Roosevelt's desire to be the arsenal of democracy and to have an "overwhelming superiority of armament" over the Axis.[6] It was for this reason that Joseph Stalin, at the Tehran Conference in November 1943, proposed a toast to the "productive capacity of the United States." Without it, "the war would have been lost."[7]

British Prime Minister Winston Churchill arrived in Washington, DC, on December 22, 1941, for what became known as the Arcadia Conference. In preparing for the meetings with the British, and throughout the war, FDR received advice, strategic suggestions, and invaluable support from the superb team he had assembled to lead the war effort. In addition to his special assistant Harry Hopkins, Secretary of War Stimson, Chief of Staff Marshall, Admiral King, General Eisenhower, and Admiral Nimitz worked closely together to advise the president and, once Roosevelt had made his decisions, to carry out his goals on the battlefields of Africa, the Atlantic, Europe, and the Pacific.

Prior to Churchill's arrival, Stimson, concerned about pressure that might shift the primary attention to the Pacific, reminded the president that "our joint war plans have recognized the North Atlantic as our principal theatre of operations should America become involved in the war" and that area should "now be given primary consideration" as "its safety must underlie all our other efforts in the war." Roosevelt agreed, and approved the completion of the American garrison in Iceland and the dispatching of "at least two divisions" to Northern Ireland to help defend Great Britain.[8] The British also feared that the attack on Pearl Harbor might shift the Americans' focus away from Europe and indicated that their top priority for the meetings was an agreement on joint strategy. In preparation, the Joint Army and Navy Board sent a report to the president to reaffirm that "the broad strategic objective of the Associated Powers is the defeat of Germany and her allies." It would begin with defensive measures and local offensives, as appropriate to theater conditions, followed ultimately by "an all-out offensive," first against Germany and her European allies, and second against Japan.[9]

Thus, Roosevelt's meeting with Churchill reaffirmed the "Germany first" strategy. The Nazis presented the gravest threat, were the primary enemy to defeat, and had to be attacked as early as possible. General George Marshall and Admiral Harold Stark assured their British counterparts that for the United States "Germany was the predominant member of the Axis Powers, and consequently the Atlantic and European area was considered to be the decisive theatre." While much had changed since the ABC-1 meetings, most notably the attack on Pearl Harbor, "our view remains that Germany is still the prime enemy and her defeat is the key to victory. Once Germany is defeated, the collapse of Italy and the defeat of Japan must follow."[10]

As Roosevelt, Churchill, and their advisors began the planning for global war and the strategy for fighting in 1942, discussions focused on ways to weaken Germany and provide support for Soviet resistance by all possible means. Most notably, planning for an attack in North Africa, as early as March 1942 if Hitler attacked Spain, was begun as well as discussions on how soon an assault could take place on the continent to open up a second front, most likely in 1943. Second, it was agreed, after some resistance from Churchill and his aides, that there would be a unified command of the American and British militaries, the Combined Joint Chiefs of Staff, that would operate out of Washington, just as all joint boards that managed shipping, raw materials, and munitions did.[11] It was clear that the United States would be the senior partner in the Anglo–American alliance.

Finally, Roosevelt and Churchill agreed to a "Joint Declaration of the United Nations Pledging Cooperation for Victory," which was announced on January 1, 1942; it was signed by twenty-six countries, including the Soviet Union and China. Roosevelt substituted the phrase "United Nations" for the previously used descriptions of the Allies and Associated Powers to avoid any reminders of World War I and to frame his vision of the future. The signatory nations pledged their agreement with the principles of the Atlantic Charter and promised that, to "defend life, liberty, independence, and religious freedom," they sought "complete victory" over the Axis Powers "in a common struggle against savage and brutal forces seeking to subjugate the world." Furthermore, the nations pledged "not to make a separate armistice or peace with the enemies."[12] The coalition that defeated Germany, Japan, and Italy was established and the creation of the postwar United Nations begun, both committed to a statement of principles based on the Atlantic Charter and FDR's four freedoms.

The Joint Declaration also served to uplift the people of the United States at the beginning of the New Year, in the face of the defeats in the Pacific by Japan and the increasing toll that German submarines were taking on shipping in the North Atlantic. After Pearl Harbor, Japan had taken Guam, Wake Island, and Hong Kong, and was on the attack in Malaysia, the Dutch East Indies, and the Philippines. In the Battle of the Atlantic, German U-boats were sinking ships on both sides of the ocean, including 132 ships in the Western Atlantic along the nation's coast in the first two months of the year, and an even greater number in the shipping lanes to Great Britain and the Soviet Union. As Roosevelt told the American public in his State of the Union message five days later, the nation was not alone and would soon be on the attack. "Powerful and offensive actions must and will be taken in proper time. The consolidation of the United Nations' total war effort against our common enemies is being achieved." The Axis "now face the fact that superior forces are assembling against them. . . . We of the United Nations will so dispose our forces that we can strike at the common enemy wherever the greatest damage can be done him." Germany and Japan started the war, "but the massed, angered forces of common humanity will finish it."[13]

The president's optimistic words could do nothing to change the fact that the early months of 1942 saw continued Japanese victories in Southeast Asia and German success in Europe and North Africa. It was in this context that Secretary of War Stimson received on February 3 a request from General John DeWitt, the commander of the West Coast, to evacuate all the Japanese in California, Oregon, and Washington. Long-standing racism and unsubstantiated claims of spying and sabotage, such as those made by Secretary of the Navy Knox concerning Pearl Harbor just days after the attack, along with an uncritical acceptance of charges of disloyalty, led to suspicion and hostility toward all people of Japanese descent, two-thirds of them American citizens, and to the military's request for the removal of over 120,000 persons. General DeWitt's request was also, in part, a response to pressure from local officials who, in the words of the *Los Angeles Times*, called upon the federal government to "remove Japanese from vital military areas." It was time, the paper editorialized, to recognize "public feeling on the subject" and "to realize that the rigors of war demand proper detention of Japanese and their immediate removal."[14] As Assistant Attorney General James Rowe recalled, the request came in during the "early three months of the war when the United States was beaten all over; we were all frightened, we were all scared, particularly in California," and that led to a hysteria that created a problem that did not exist.[15]

Attorney General Biddle, while acknowledging the president's power to take steps against enemy aliens, objected to any actions that amounted to the arrest of American citizens. He told Roosevelt on February 7 that he "believed mass evacuation at this time inadvisable."[16] Even though Stimson understood that such an action "will make a tremendous hole in our constitutional system," he thought the nation had "made an enormous mistake in underestimating the Japanese" and that, in wartime, national security concerns had to outweigh civil liberties. "Where the safety of the Nation is involved," Stimson wrote in his diary, "consideration of the rights of individuals must be subordinated to the common security."[17] In this view, he represented the attitude of the president.

Bypassing the objections from the Department of Justice, the secretary of war, on February 11, called Roosevelt and asked for permission to begin removing Japanese Americans, including citizens. The president approved the request, although the full scope of the action was not defined until February 19, when Roosevelt issued Executive Order 9066. It declared that because "the successful prosecution of the war requires every possible protection against espionage and against sabotage," the secretary of war was authorized "to proscribe military areas in such places and of such extent" as deemed necessary "from which any or all persons may be excluded."[18] The rights of a small group of citizens were sacrificed in the name of security despite no evidence of any danger. Roosevelt's greatest failure during the war came early and at home.

As the bad news from the war continued, Roosevelt delivered on February 23 what Samuel Rosenman accurately called "one of the most important and effective" of his fireside chats.[19] The president had asked newspapers to print world maps so that people could follow him as he set out to explain the global extent of the fighting and the military strategy for the war. In the process, FDR sought to boost the nation's morale while preparing it for a long and costly war. Speaking on George Washington's birthday, Roosevelt recalled how General Washington and his forces had faced difficult odds and early defeats, but had demonstrated the "moral stamina" necessary to secure victory because they knew "that no man's life of fortune was secure, without freedom and free institutions." The effort to maintain the freedom originally declared in 1776 and gained through the struggle of the American Revolution now depended "upon the security of the rights and obligations of liberty and justice everywhere in the world."[20]

The president explained that the current conflict was a war that was different than any other, "not only in its methods and weapons but also in its geography," being fought on every continent and in every sea. In particular, the "broad oceans which have been heralded in the past as our protection have become endless battlefields on which we are constantly challenged by our enemies." Directing his audience to their maps, Roosevelt asked that they look at China, Russia, the British Isles, Australia, New Zealand, the Dutch Indies, India, the Near East, and Africa, and the vast armies and resources they all represented. The people in these places were just as determined as those in the United States and the Western Hemisphere to resist and defeat the Axis. The key at this stage of the war was to keep these territories connected. "It is obvious," Roosevelt stated, "what would happen if all of these great reservoirs of power were cut off from each other." It was up to the United States to ensure that this did not happen and that all of the allied nations continued to receive American supplies. The United States was the arsenal of democracy, and increased production meant greater allied strength. To those who argued that these places were far away, who "wanted the American eagle to imitate the tactics of the ostrich," Roosevelt rejoined, "we prefer to retain the eagle as it is—flying high and striking hard."[21]

All of this would require tacking by the president to meet the shifting dangers presented by the many fronts of the war. Roosevelt was reiterating a key strategic policy, defense in depth, that had guided his expansion of the concept of the Western Hemisphere and that he had noted in his State of the Union message; it was vital to keep the enemy "far from our shores, for we intend to bring this war to him on his own home grounds."[22] The United States, however, would provide more than just armaments to the battle. Its forces would chase the Axis across the globe and unify the Allied coalition. While the United States had certainly suffered losses from German U-boats in the Atlantic and to Japanese advances in the Pacific, "we and the other United Nations are committed to the destruction of the militarism of Japan and Germany. We are daily increasing our strength. Soon, we and not our enemies will have the offensive; we, not they, will win the final battles; and we, not they, will make the final peace." To that end, the president reminded the American people that the "United Nations had agreed on certain broad principles in the kind of peace we seek. The Atlantic Charter applies not only to the parts of the world that border the Atlantic but to the whole world; disarmament of aggressors, self-determination of Nations and peoples, and the four freedoms—freedom of speech, freedom of religion, freedom from want, and freedom from fear." The nation, in facing its greatest test, needed to draw on the meaning of the American Revolution as set out in the words of Thomas Paine: "Tyranny, like hell, is not easily conquered; yet we have this consolation with us, that the harder the sacrifice, the more glorious the triumph." Roosevelt concluded, "So spoke Americans in the year 1776. So speak Americans today!"[23]

In March, senior military officials turned their attention to an overall plan to defeat Germany that placed an attack across the British Channel into France as the top priority. Stimson and others worried about decisions that would lead to a series of diversions of troops and supplies, most notably the plan proposed by the British for fighting in North Africa. At a March 5 meeting of senior officials with FDR, Stimson took the lead in presenting the military commanders' understanding of the different theaters of fighting and strategy. The secretary of war noted that the war with Japan would mainly be a naval affair with limited opportunity to take the offensive until the fleet was rebuilt and strengthened, most likely in 1943. Both Chief of Staff Marshall and General Eisenhower agreed that the Pacific had to be the "secondary theatre" and that a second front in Europe was the highest priority. "If we win over Japan there," Stimson stated, "we still might not win the war; but if we lost there, we would surely lose the war." Direct aid to the Soviet Union and keeping it fighting were the most crucial concerns. The means available to do this, however, were limited by the difficulties of getting materials there. The convoys from the North Atlantic faced the problems of weather, German submarines, and limited escort and supply ships. Sending forces through the Persian Gulf was infeasible, although limited supplies could be moved that way, and both Marshall and Eisenhower believed that activity in the Mediterranean should not even be discussed. This meant the only strategy that would hurt Germany and aid the Soviet Union "was sending an overwhelming force to the British Isles and threatening an attack on the Germans in France." It would "have the effect of giving Hitler two fronts to fight on if it could be done in time while the Russians were still in."[24] Marshall argued that an assault on France was the "only place in which a powerful offensive can be prepared and executed" and "will afford the maximum of support to the Russian front."[25] As Eisenhower put it the following day, the crucial point "was to keep Russia in the war which was of primary importance for, if she went out of the war" the best he could see was "nothing better than a stalemate for us." That demanded "a powerful attack through Great Britain into France."[26]

London, however, sought a different strategy, one that focused on an attack into North Africa to support its forces in Egypt and help secure contact with vital parts of its empire. It wanted to avoid a direct assault on Germany's main forces, and instead sought to begin the process of taking control of the Mediterranean Sea. The key premise for the British was that there should be a slow encircling of Nazi forces, to defeat Hitler by a series of smaller engagements in North Africa, Italy, Greece, and the Balkans, the so-called soft underbelly of Germany's military position. The benefits, the British claimed, were ensuring an early victory against the Germans and alleviating some of the pressure on the Russian front. This strategy was one that Churchill continuously returned to for the next two years and was exactly what Stimson, Marshall, and Eisenhower feared.

On March 25, Roosevelt met with Hopkins, Stimson, Marshall, and Knox to further discuss strategy. Marshall made the case for a cross-channel invasion and argued strenuously against the British position, insisting that it represented an improper dispersion of American forces and supplies to a secondary area of concern. The military leaders worried about the long immobilization of American forces, and saw the need to take risks and start fighting Germany directly to help relieve the Russian front. Aid to the Soviet Union was a military necessity to ensure victory. In the end, Roosevelt gave his support to develop the plan for a second front. Code-named Bolero, it called for a full-scale invasion of France in the spring of 1943. If, however, the Russians faced a serious defeat and a collapse of their defenses, the United States had a contingent plan for a smaller attack in the fall of 1942, called Sledgehammer, to provide an early attack on France in order to give relief to the Soviets by drawing away German forces.

Stimson, Marshall, and Eisenhower were well aware that such an effort in 1942 could fail but believed it was worth the risk to keep the Red Army in the war. Without Russia fighting in the east, it would be extremely difficult to dislodge Germany from the rest of Europe. Stimson advised the president to send his most trusted advisors to London to press the British for approval. The lack of sufficient landing barges was the only substantive point the British had in objecting to the attack on France. Once an agreement was reached, every effort needed to be made to rearrange production schedules and supplies to ensure the necessary ships were ready. Stimson wrote Roosevelt that "so long as we remain without our own plan of offensive, our forces will inevitably be dispersed and wasted."[27] The president approved the plan on April 1 and sent Hopkins and Marshall to London to inform the British. Churchill, after lengthy discussions with the Americans, reluctantly agreed with the principle of a second front, but continued to raise objections and potential problems.

A related concern regarding the Grand Alliance was the question of relations with the Soviet Union and the issue of postwar borders. Roosevelt opposed any early agreement on this point, and set out to thwart London's and Moscow's 1942 negotiations of a treaty whereby Great Britain would recognize Russia's 1941 borders, including the Baltic States as part of the Soviet Union. The president thought it was vital to delay such decisions until late in the war to make sure all nations continued fighting until Germany was defeated. The promise of a second front, FDR and Hopkins agreed, would help take the political pressure off of Moscow's demands by placing attention back on fighting the war. To this end, Roosevelt cabled Stalin on April 11 asking him to send Soviet Foreign Minister Vyacheslav Molotov to Washington to discuss "a very important military proposal involving the utilization of our armed forces in a manner to relieve your critical western front."[28]

With productivity increasing and war planning moving forward, Roosevelt spoke to the country on April 28 about the status of the war. As always, he sought to provide as much information about the fighting as he could without revealing anything that would be of value to America's enemies. The president acknowledged the defeats suffered in Asia, in the Philippines, the Dutch East Indies, Burma, and the Malaysian Peninsula, and the long, hard road ahead for the nation in both the Atlantic and the Pacific. Yet, not all of the news was bleak. The biggest news was "without question the crushing counter-offensive of the great armies of Russia" against Germany where they "have destroyed and are destroying more armed power of our enemies . . . than all the other United Nations put together." In East Asia, "we have passed through a phase of serious losses," but the Japanese "had to pay a very heavy toll . . . and were feeling the effects of those losses." It was even reported by Japan, Roosevelt noted in reference to the then still secret Doolittle raid, "that somebody has dropped bombs on Tokyo." The daring raid, which was the president's idea, had occurred ten days earlier. When the information was made public the next month it lifted the nation's morale, as FDR hoped it would. Most significantly for the American people, Roosevelt told them, their armed forces were now being dispatched by the hundreds of thousands to bases far from home, their naval ships were engaged in combat in the Arctic, Atlantic, Indian, and Pacific Oceans, and American war planes were fighting over all continents and seas.[29]

The president emphasized that the war was being fought on another key front that included the efforts of all Americans, and that was the home front. World War II was "total war," and whether one worked in a munitions plant, in a shipyard, or on a farm, producing raw materials or weapons, everyone was called upon to help win the war. Roosevelt rejected the use of the term and concept of sacrifice to describe the necessity to accept taxes, rationing, and other economic restrictions. Rather, he argued that all citizens would have "the privilege of making whatever self-denial is necessary" to supply the military and "keep the economic structure of our country fortified and secure during the war and after the war." It was not a sacrifice to save civilization. "When, at the end of this great struggle, we shall have saved our free way of life, we shall have made no 'sacrifice.' The price for civilization must be paid in hard work and sorrow and blood. The price is not too high. If you doubt it, ask those millions who live today under the tyranny of Hitlerism." The war would be won "by the indomitable will and determination of the people as one great whole."[30] The American people agreed with the president's vision and requests, and overwhelmingly supported FDR's leadership. A Gallup poll the next month showed a seventy-eight percent approval for the president's leadership and conduct of the war.[31] Roosevelt's rating would stay above seventy percent throughout the war.[32]

Although not announced publicly until the end of the summer, the first positive news regarding American forces in the Pacific was received in Washington in May. While not a victory, the American Navy, in the Battle of the Coral Sea, for the first time stopped a Japanese effort to expand its reach. More good news arrived in the beginning of June. Admiral Nimitz's smaller force out-dueled Admiral Yamamoto's fleet in the Battle of Midway, sinking all of his aircraft carriers in the process and delivering a decisive first defeat to Japan. Ironically, this major victory allowed the focus of the American military buildup to remain on Europe rather than Japan by guaranteeing the safety of Hawaii and the eastern Pacific, ending any worries about Japan's ability to directly threaten the United States, and beginning the process of driving Japan back in the Pacific.

It was in this context that two crucial meetings took place in Washington regarding the second front in May and June, the first the visit by Soviet Foreign Minister Molotov, the second by British Prime Minister Churchill. American efforts to aid the Soviet Union continued to be hampered by German attacks along the northern Atlantic–Arctic Oceans route to Murmansk. For example, from April to June 1942, just over half of the eighty-four supply ships from the United States that set out for the Soviet Union along this sea lane reached their destination. Twenty-three were sunk and seventeen were forced to unload in Scotland due to the lack of escort ships. The other routes, via Siberia and the Persian Gulf, presented their own problems of access, distance, and lack of transports. All of this made relations tense and the Soviet need for help urgent. Molotov told the Americans that Moscow was confident they could hold out even though the Germans had more men and equipment. Yet this optimistic picture could be changed if the Nazis sought to deliver a final, crushing blow. A second front that drew off some forty German divisions would "insure beyond question [Hitler's] ultimate defeat." If the second front materialized, 1942 would be the year the war was decided. "If you postpone your decision," Molotov concluded, "you will have eventually to bear the brunt of the war, and if Hitler becomes the undisputed master of the continent, next year will unquestionably be tougher than this one." Roosevelt asked Marshall if the United States was ready to say to Stalin that it was preparing a second front. "Yes," he said. The president then told Molotov he could let Stalin know "that we expect the formation of a second front this year."[33]

Roosevelt informed Churchill that "Molotov's visit has been a real success," and that they had agreed to increase the shipment of goods for the second front by reducing materials sent to the Soviet Union without diminishing the supplies that the Russians needed in order to fight that summer. All this made the president "more anxious than ever that bolero shall begin in August and continue as long as the weather permits."[34] The decision was publicly announced on June 11 with a statement that a "full understanding was reached with regard to the urgent task of creating a second front in Europe in 1942."[35] Expressing his own as well as FDR's views, Hopkins wrote to the American ambassador to Great Britain, John Winant, that the meeting with Molotov "at least bridged one more gap between ourselves and Russia. There is a long way to go but it must be done if there is ever to be any real peace in the world."[36]

As the American military leaders feared, Churchill came to Washington on June 21 and wasted little time before he criticized the American plan, seeking to revisit the decisions on the second front and revive the North African operation, Gymnast. At first FDR held firm against Churchill's arguments. The British leader remained adamant, expressing the legitimate concern about the lack of landing craft and lobbying for London's preference for action in the Mediterranean. Out of this, a compromise was reached. Planning for the attack on France would continue until September 1 and then would be evaluated "to see if a real attack could be made without the danger of disaster."[37]

However, the British did not wait that long to reopen the debate. Marshall informed Stimson in early July that Churchill was again raising objections and seeking discussions on gymnast. This set off a contentious dispute over a second front. While Roosevelt assured Stimson and Marshall that he supported the existing plans, the secretary of war had his doubts, believing that the North Africa campaign was "the President's secret baby."[38] Seeking a final resolution, the president sent Hopkins, Marshall, and King to London later that month to meet with the British.

Stimson sought to get the president to stick to the June agreement, including Sledgehammer, the small-scale attack on France in 1942. The planning had to go ahead to be ready for an operation in the fall and to ensure the full-scale cross-channel assault in 1943. The president, however, was in a bind. While he agreed with his advisors on strategy, and the goal of opening a second front to aid Russia, he also knew that a cross-channel invasion could not be executed without British cooperation and participation, and that the odds of any success in 1942 were long. The longer the argument lasted, the less chance there was of any significant operation in 1942, and FDR was determined that American forces would engage in combat by the end of the year. Roosevelt expressed his disappointment with the British, but he finally acceded to their opposition and approved the attack on North Africa that fall. As he told Hopkins on July 15, even if Sledgehammer was impossible, he wanted to plan for a cross-channel invasion in 1943. "But my main point is that I do not believe we can wait until 1943 to strike at Germany," and if a small-scale attack on France in 1942 was out, "then we must take the second best." And there were great advantages to the North African operation: it was "a purely American enterprise, it would secure Western Africa and deny the ports to the enemy, it would offer the beginning of what should be the ultimate control of the Mediterranean."[39]

In the instructions for their talks in London, the president stated that it was his highest priority "that U.S. ground troops be brought into action against the enemy in 1942." Roosevelt asked his representatives to remember "three cardinal principles—speed of decision on plans, unity of plans, attack combined with defense but not defense alone. This affects the immediate objective of U.S. ground forces fight against Germans in 1942."[40] In other words, FDR did not want more than a year to pass without American troops engaged in combat against Germany.

A week of arguments by Hopkins, Marshall, and King brought no consensus with the British. At this point, Roosevelt agreed to go forward with Gymnast, now renamed Operation Torch. The president and his advisors shared the same objective; they wanted to get American forces on the offensive to provide relief to the Soviet forces. Stimson and Marshall could even see the merits of the North African operation, but they understood that once engaged it would divert massive amounts of shipping, supplies, and forces to the Mediterranean that would cripple the Bolero plan. Yet, having pushed their arguments as hard as they could, and still concerned that the president's support of Torch would derail the cross-channel invasion in 1943, Marshall, Stimson, and Eisenhower turned their attention to the North Africa campaign and how to make it succeed. Faced with British opposition to an attack on France, and no assurances that such an attack could succeed, and committed to having U.S. forces in action on the ground in 1942 where they could engage German forces and secure a victory, FDR accepted Torch and tacked to the south.

In the spring of 1942, Franklin Roosevelt began to set out his vision for the postwar world. It was axiomatic that the mistakes of World War I and 1919 had to be avoided, most importantly the United States' rejection of world leadership. Just as lend-lease was informed by the problems of war loans, the president sought to create an international order and multilateral institutions that did not replicate the weaknesses of the League of Nations, which gave too much influence to small nations and depended on a world organization for security. The Big Four—the United States, Great Britain, the Soviet Union, and China—and not the United Nations, would ensure the peace. For FDR, the Good Neighbor Policy provided the model for how to organize the postwar world and replace empire with collective security. It was built on cooperation, nonaggression, and multilateral exchange. Unlike the League of Nations, results were achieved without any binding conditions on members; through discussion about concerns and possible actions, procedures or policies would finally emerge that were conducive to settling an issue and in line with keeping peace for all nations. While the United States held overwhelming power and influence in the region, peace was maintained because it actively led the Pan-American system, consulted with other nations, and provided protection. There was no balance of power in the Western Hemisphere, yet there was no imperial empire either. The substitute for balance of power and empire, FDR believed, was restraint, collective security, free trade, and multinational institutions led by the great powers. In other words, the Good Neighbor Policy, expanded to the whole world. As Roosevelt stated in May 1942, the goals of his policy toward Latin America were to "first, remove from their minds all fear of American aggression—territorial or financial—and, second, to take them into a kind of hemispheric partnership in which no Republic would obtain an undue advantage."[41]

The great powers of the Grand Alliance would act as the four policemen, the guarantors of peace and order. Roosevelt explained his idea to Grace Tully and Samuel Rosenman, saying that "the central idea involves a situation where there should be four policemen in the world—the United States, Great Britain, Russia, and China—charged with the responsibility of keeping peace. The rest of the world would have to disarm." He said that there would be inspections to make sure that nations "did not begin to arm secretly as Germany did after the last war." Reviving his concept from 1937 about isolating aggressors, FDR noted that "as soon as any of the other nations was caught arming they would be threatened first with a quarantine and if the quarantine did not work they would be bombed." All of this would be coordinated through a new international organization established to provide collective security and keep the peace.[42]

Moreover, colonial empires would be gradually ended through trusteeships and independence. Multilateral institutions would be set up for recovery, reconstruction, and the restoration of trade, while Germany, Japan, and the smaller powers would be disarmed to the point where they could not threaten others. In Roosevelt's vision of it, the organization that would become the United Nations would acknowledge the realities of the war by accepting spheres of influence for the victors and the necessity of their leadership, but would do so through cooperation and without traditional balance of power or imperial conflict. A regional system led by one power, as exemplified by the Good Neighbor Policy, was necessary in order to avoid the problems of traditional power politics. Thus, the road to peace lay in the continuation of the Grand Alliance and the cooperation of the Big Four.

In his meeting with Molotov on May 29, the president sketched his views for the foreign minister so they could begin discussions and so that he could share them with Stalin. He also raised these first with Molotov because FDR believed that if there was to be peace in the postwar world it depended on U.S.–Soviet relations. These thoughts, the president explained, were to remain confidential until Germany was defeated, but he wanted Washington, Moscow, and London to have a "meeting of the minds" to be prepared when victory came. Roosevelt told him that "he visualized the enforced disarmament of our enemies and, indeed, some of our friends after the war; that he thought that the United States, England, Russia and perhaps China should police the world and enforce disarmament by inspection." Other nations would not be allowed to have military forces, although that could change if "experience proved they could be trusted." Regarding the Chinese, FDR understood their inclusion "would depend on whether they could organize and maintain a strong central government."[43]

The question that was foremost on the president's mind was, he noted, the one he had "put to Churchill when the Atlantic Charter was being drawn up": "How do we implement it?" This pertained to the four freedoms as well. Roosevelt "could not visualize another League of Nations with 100 different signatories; there were simply too many nations to satisfy, hence it was a failure and would be a failure." Thus, "he could see no alternative to some type of police force and, hence, compulsory disarmament, followed by inspection to see that the nations stayed disarmed." The president was sure that England would agree "if the Soviet Union and the United States insisted upon it." When Molotov asked if this was Roosevelt's final judgment, he replied yes. He again noted that China had not been consulted and that its inclusion would depend on the events of the war. Concerning France, FDR stated that, although he did not think at this time it should be included, it was a nation that "might at a later date join the four powers he has mentioned"; but he also noted that there was a "great danger if there were too many 'policemen.'" Molotov replied that he found the president's proposal "extremely important" and "quite realistic on the basis of our present experience." In conclusion, Roosevelt said that "we must have a brand new approach to world peace; that the old balance of power theory did not work."[44] In the late summer, the president added the intention of the United States, in conjunction with the United Nations, to conduct war crime trials for the "barbaric crimes" committed by the Axis nations as part of the way to secure a permanent peace, enact the four freedoms, and hold the aggressors accountable.[45]

These war aims reflected FDR's view of history and the United States; he believed that the nation and the world had to move beyond the structures of the nineteenth century and into a new era. He thought America was destined to be a world leader and would play a central role in creating a better future at home and abroad. The approach Roosevelt set out to Molotov served U.S. national security by consolidating the strategic and diplomatic gains made during the 1930s in terms of defense in depth, collective security, and organized association with other countries. Now that his approach had triumphed over the idea of hemispheric security, positive measures had to be taken to ensure an international order conducive to the four freedoms, free trade, and collective security. This new approach also recognized that the era of European empires was ending; to bring stability in East Asia, it sought to promote in China a pro-Western Third Way, between colonialism and revolution. FDR's plan also served as a guide to successfully protect the peace by making the defeat of Germany, Japan, and Italy definitive and avoiding the mistakes of Versailles.

Moreover, it acknowledged the power of the Soviet Union and the contribution it had made to the war, and it took into account Soviet interests. Roosevelt had no illusions about the Soviet Union or the difficulties ahead in maintaining U.S.–Soviet relations in the postwar period once the common goal of defeating Hitler was accomplished. As Hopkins put it in October 1943, given the nature of the Soviet regime, relations with Moscow could always "blow up at the last minute."[46] Yet, FDR firmly believed that just as victory over Germany depended on the Grand Alliance, a long-standing peace after the war was only possible through cooperation among the United States, the Soviet Union, and Great Britain. For this cooperation to be possible, it would be necessary to recognize the sacrifice made by the Russians and their central role in defeating Germany. The West must acknowledge

Moscow's postwar needs and be willing to compromise in negotiations and must demonstrate respect for the Soviet Union as a great power. Communism, Roosevelt and his closest advisors believed, was a flawed system doomed to fail. If Washington could build on the wartime collaboration and establish a working relationship with Moscow, it could see a gradual decline in distrust and a change in Soviet behavior. Disagreements, misunderstandings, and tensions over certain points were going to occur, but conflict was not inevitable. To think otherwise, to see the Soviet Union only through an ideological lens, was to abandon much of what was achieved in the war, the hopes and promises of the four freedoms, and to accept a course of action that would lead to conflict and potential disaster.

The biggest problem was to gain agreement from the Soviets and British, given the tensions within the Grand Alliance. The disagreements between Washington and London paled in comparison to Moscow's displeasure when Churchill informed Stalin in August of the delay of the attack on France. The Soviet dictator disapproved of the decision and veered from enthusiasm for the North African campaign to complete indifference. He accused the West of being afraid of Germany and unwilling to take risks while, at the same time, the Red Army faced 280 German divisions and made tremendous sacrifices as they fought to defeat Germany. Furthermore, he criticized the failure of the delivery of supplies and questioned how difficult it was to send six to eight Allied divisions across the English Channel. Before the British prime minister left, more cordial personal relations had been restored. Stalin, without giving up on a true second front, again expressed an understanding of the benefits of Torch, but the central problem remained.

After Churchill's departure, Roosevelt cabled Stalin to express his regret that he could not join the other two leaders and to assure Stalin of the West's commitment to defeat Germany. He promised that he was doing all that he could to arrange for the shipping of supplies to the Soviet Union, that a thousand tanks would be sent that month, and that other critical supplies, including airplanes, were being expedited. He acknowledged the sacrifices of the Russian forces and that they were "bearing the brunt of the fighting." He asked Stalin to "believe me when I tell you that we are coming as quickly and as powerfully as possibly we can."[47]

On September 7, Roosevelt spoke to the nation with a cautious optimism about the fighting on the interrelated four fronts of the war. He began with

Russia's enormous effort to hold off the German Army and deny it victory. In the process, FDR said, the Soviets were destroying more tanks and planes, and killing more soldiers, than any other nation. He assured his audience that "Russia will hold out" and, with its allies, "ultimately drive every Nazi from her soil." The president noted that, in the Pacific, the United States had stopped a major Japanese offensive and inflicted heavy losses on their fleet. Yet, Tokyo still had great strength and would strike again, but this did not undercut "the significance of our victory at Midway." The news was not as positive in the other two theaters, the Mediterranean–Middle East and Europe. In North Africa the Allies were "fighting a desperate battle with the Germans and Italians"; they were trying to protect the Suez Canal and to thwart Germany's efforts to dominate the area and link up with Japan in the Indian Ocean. The president characterized the situation as dangerous, but said that he was hopeful of success soon. Regarding Europe, he was deliberately vague, speaking of the future aim of an offensive against Germany and the promise that "the power of Germany" would be "broken on the battlefields of Europe." Roosevelt ended by assuring the American people that "vital military decisions have been made"; he promised them that they would learn about these in due time and that they were all "directed toward taking the offensive."[48]

The American people would learn what some of these decisions were on November 8. The invasion of North Africa that day finally brought American ground forces into battle with the Germans and started the process of pushing back the German armies from their greatest point of expansion. The fall and winter of 1942–1943 marked the turning point in the war, even if two and a half years of hard and costly fighting remained ahead; as the period of defeat and defense ended, the Grand Alliance started to take the offensive in the fighting for the first time. The first of these offensive operations had already begun in August with the battle at Guadalcanal. It would last until February 1943 when the combined naval, air, and land forces of the United States ended the final Japanese advance in the Pacific and started to push Japanese forces back. Also in August the Germans drove toward Stalingrad, marking the start of the epic battle that would turn the fortunes of the war on the Eastern Front.

The fighting in North Africa went very well. American troops quickly moved forward, pushing toward the British armies that were driving to the west out of Egypt, and, in a classic pincer action, defeated the famed German forces of General Erwin Rommel. While not a second front, this action hit Germany on its rear flank, split most French forces from Germany, threatened Italy, and ensured Spanish neutrality. It also allowed Roosevelt to tell the nation on Armistice Day that the momentum of the war was changing. The Axis powers, he declared, had sought to "drive history into reverse" by using modern weapons to conquer the world and rule by sheer force. At first, they seemed to be winning, overrunning nations as they enslaved and killed. "But, today, we know and they know that they have conquered nothing. Today, they face inevitable, final defeat. Yes, the forces of liberation are advancing."[49]

The quick victory in Vichy-controlled North Africa raised questions about who would rule the French territories that the Allies took over. Expediency and military considerations overruled concerns about working with French officials who had collaborated with the Germans through the Vichy government. The Americans recognized Admiral Jean Darlan's authority in order to obtain a cease-fire with Vichy forces and turn them against Germany; this provided stability and a secure rear for the advancing American troops. Washington supported Eisenhower's decision to strike a deal with Darlan, knowing full well that he had been a collaborator with the Nazis and that the decision would be criticized by many. Eisenhower, and ultimately Stimson and Roosevelt, believed that only Darlan could ensure that French forces would not fight against the United States. Accommodation, therefore, was necessary, as Stimson put it, due to the "hazardous nature of our operation in North Africa and the perilous condition in which our troops would have been in case there had been any delay caused by the obstruction of the French." The consequent criticism was seen as well worth it in return for a short-term measure that cut the risks and increased the chances of military success against the Germans as American forces stretched their communication and supply lines in the push toward Tunisia. In defending the decision, FDR told Stimson that "a Balkan quotation" aptly fit the situation: "If the devil offered to help you over a bridge, it was just as well to let him do so but not to continue to walk with him on the other side." Stimson responded with his own analogy from the Bible "of Joshua sending the spies to Jericho and their making a pact with Rahab the harlot which was ratified by Joshua." Stimson recorded that Roosevelt "roared with delight" when he heard it.[50]

November marked the first time that news on all of the active fighting fronts was positive. The American and British forces were advancing in North

Africa, the Russian Army was taking the offensive in the Battle of Stalingrad, and on November 12 the U.S. Navy defeated the Japanese effort to drive it out of the Solomon Islands. Five days later, FDR told the nation that in the past two weeks "we have had a great deal of good news and it would seem that a turning point of this war has at last been reached." The president avoided describing the turning point as definitive and followed by declaring: "But this is no time for exultation. There is no time now for anything but fighting and working to win."[51] Yet, unmistakably, one phase of the war, the expansion of the Axis powers, was ending, and now the Grand Alliance would dictate the place and terms of the fighting.

In his State of the Union message on January 7, 1943, Roosevelt was cautiously optimistic about the course of the war and spoke at length about the postwar world. This confidence came from what he called "by far the largest and most important developments in the whole world-wide strategic picture of 1942," the "implacable defense of Stalingrad; and, second, the offensives by the Russian armies at various points that started in the latter part of November and which still roll on with great force and effectiveness." These achievements, in addition to those in the Pacific and Africa, showed that the momentum of the war had changed. "The Axis powers knew that they must win the war in 1942—or eventually lose everything. I do not need to tell you that our enemies did not win the war in 1942." The main task ahead remained "to lessen the concentrated pressure on the Russian front by compelling Germany to divert part of her manpower and equipment to another theater of the war," just as had been done in North Africa, by opening up "to attack what Mr. Churchill well described as 'the under-belly of the Axis.'" While he could not tell the people future military plans, he assured them that "we are going to strike—and strike hard."[52]

Winning battles was, of course, important, but Roosevelt reminded his listeners that "we should never forget the things we are fighting for," the four freedoms and a lasting peace. The president continued: "It is of little account for any of us to talk of essential human needs, of attaining security, if we run the risk of another World War in ten or twenty or fifty years. That is just plain common sense. Wars grow in size, in death and destruction, and in the inevitability of engulfing all Nations, in inverse ratio to the shrinking size of the world as a result of the conquest of the air. I shudder to think of what will happen to humanity, including ourselves, if this war ends in an inconclusive peace, and another war breaks out when the babies of today have grown to fighting age." The United States had to take up the role of world leader after the fighting ended, to seize the second chance that was now in front of it. "After the first World War we tried to achieve a formula for permanent peace, based on a magnificent idealism. We failed. But, by our failure, we have learned that we cannot maintain peace at this stage of human development by good intentions alone."[53]

In his effort to create greater cohesion in the Grand Alliance, Roosevelt tried to arrange a meeting of the Big Three in the first part of 1943. Stalin, citing a new offensive against the Germans, would not leave Russia. Still, the developing military situation at the end of 1942 called for a conference by the United States and the United Kingdom to reexamine strategy and plan for the upcoming year. It was decided that Roosevelt and Churchill would meet in Casablanca with their top military aides to discuss strategy, primarily the question of a second front. In a telegram to Churchill, Stalin expressed the fear that his Anglo–American partners were changing their minds "with regard to the promise given in Moscow to establish a second front in Western Europe in the spring of 1943."[54] That concern demanded an answer.

Roosevelt was well aware of the Soviet position and desire for a second front in 1943. The Red Army had alone been fighting the Germans since June 1941, and Stalin still sought an attack into France to force Hitler to move forces to the west. General Marshall, Secretary Stimson, Hopkins, and FDR's other senior military officials still supported a cross-channel invasion. In preparation for the Casablanca Conference, Stimson and Marshall met in January to discuss strategy. Roosevelt's senior military advisors continued to agree that it was time to directly engage the German Army with a cross-channel attack against France in 1943. The war had reached a critical stage, and they believed it was best to follow up on the achievements of late 1942 with a direct offensive to help weaken the German capacity to fight. It was also crucial that the West provide relief to the Russian Army and demonstrate to Moscow that it understood the enormity of the sacrifices the Soviets were making.

Consistent with past positions, the British disagreed. They argued that the United States and the United Kingdom could not create a large enough force or land it on the continent in 1943, and they continued to prefer fighting on the periphery of German power in the Mediterranean. Given that Stalin could not attend the Casablanca Conference, Roosevelt asked Marshall, in a meeting with the Joint Chiefs of Staff before he left for Africa, if he would go to Moscow after the conference. When the general asked to what end, FDR responded "that the visit would be particularly for the purpose of giving impetus to the Russian morale." He also revealed for the first time that he intended to talk with Churchill about "the advisability of informing Mr. Stalin that the United Nations were to continue until they reach Berlin, and that their only terms would be unconditional surrender." In addition, he wanted to discuss postwar disarmament with Churchill and to have a meeting with Stalin later that year on these matters. Marshall would be the emissary to inform Stalin of the outcome of the Casablanca meeting.[55]

Marshall agreed to go, but he worried that the president's request meant there would be no second front in 1943. He informed the president that the British were determined to continue fighting in the Mediterranean; they argued that it was essential to keep pushing the Germans rather than take time to reorganize for a cross-channel attack. Moreover, London stressed that a collapse of Italy would have the advantage of forcing the Germans to move divisions in order to hold the country and replace Italian forces. If the United States went along with Churchill's approach, continued operations in the Mediterranean would lead to a significant loss of shipping tonnage, which would preclude another large operation that year, thereby cancelling Bolero. The consensus was that the United States would give priority to the attack on France in the meetings with England, but as Marshall and Stimson feared, the North African campaign, and the necessary movement of so many troops and supplies to the Mediterranean for its success, already placed the momentum in favor of the British policy and threatened to derail any action against France that year. It appeared the second front might be doomed before they even got to West Africa.

As expected, in Casablanca the British proposed expanded bombing operations against Germany and an attack on Sicily followed by one against the Italian peninsula. The British wedge was the issue of logistics and the time it would take to redeploy forces and supplies to launch an attack on France. General Marshall noted that "he was perfectly willing to take some tactical hazards or risks" but said that they had "no right to take logistical hazards." If there were not enough supplies and ships in England for an attack, it should not be done.[56]

Ultimately, FDR agreed to the Mediterranean operations. The president wanted to keep American forces fighting and advancing and to keep the public focused on the war in Europe. He also continued to believe that, at this juncture, unity with Great Britain remained critical to victory and peace. In the end, therefore, Roosevelt again sided with the British. In the Pacific, the strategy would remain the same, with the United States seeking to move forward and capture islands to provide bases for bombing the Japanese home islands. As Marshall informed Stimson, the second front would again be delayed due to "the absolute refusal of the British to go on with Bolero."[57]

Yet, Stalin was given a more optimistic version that implied that a second front, as previously promised, would open in the fall. In a February 9 message that Roosevelt approved, Churchill informed the Soviet dictator that once the North African campaign was finished the Anglo–American forces would seize Sicily and clear the Mediterranean, seeking a collapse of Italy. While this operation would involve all of the landing crafts available, along with shipping and troops, the West was "also pushing preparations to the limit of our resources for a cross channel operation in August" or, if shipping was not yet ready, in September. Stalin worried about how long these operations were taking and specifically registered his concern that the attack on France was scheduled for the late summer as "the present situation demands that this date should be brought nearer as much as possible, and that the second front in Europe should be opened considerably earlier." He noted that Hitler was shifting forces from Western Europe to the Russian front, and that by only pursuing campaigns in the Mediterranean the Western allies would allow this to continue.[58]

In his press conference in Casablanca on January 24, 1943, Roosevelt claimed that the strategic studies undertaken over the past ten days were "unprecedented in history" because they discussed global strategy. "It isn't just one front, just one ocean, of one continent—it is literally the whole world." The guiding principle was "the determination that peace can come to the world only by the total elimination of German and Japanese war power." To that end, Roosevelt announced that Washington and London would accept only an "unconditional surrender" from the Axis nations. This would provide "a reasonable assurance of future world peace. It does not mean the destruction of the population of Germany, Italy, or Japan, but it does mean the destruction of the philosophies in those countries which are based on conquest and the subjugation of other people."[59]

Roosevelt had several motivations in announcing the policy of unconditional surrender at this time, none more important than seeking to demonstrate the resolve of the United States and its commitment to its Russian ally. Knowing that the second front would now be put off until 1944, the president saw the policy of unconditional surrender as a means to ease Soviet disappointment about the lack of a campaign in Western Europe by assuring the Russians that he was committed to the defeat of Nazi Germany. As the official communique of the conference noted, "the President and Prime Minister realized to the full the enormous weight of the war which Russia is successfully bearing along her whole land front, and their prime object has been to draw as much of the weight as possible off the Russian armies by engaging the enemy as heavily as possible at the best selected points." The Soviet premier, it noted, had been informed of the military proposals.[60]

Also, as Roosevelt pointed out in the press conference, the policy of unconditional surrender aligned closely with his vision of how to maintain peace; the four policemen would have a crucial role and the Grand Alliance would be kept intact. The president was concerned about the risk of nations making separate peace deals with Germany or Japan. While all nations had signed off on the Atlantic Charter, each had also noted exceptions. For example, in the fall of 1942, Churchill had stated in a speech that Great Britain would look out for its interests. "I have not become the King's First Minister in order to preside over the liquidation of the British Empire."[61] There was, therefore, worry that the war goals of Great Britain, with its concern for its empire, and the Soviet Union, with its desire for its 1941 borders, were not necessarily aligned with those of the United States. Unconditional surrender bound the Grand Alliance to a common policy of continuing to fight until Germany, Japan, and Italy were beaten and occupied. Finally, seeking the complete defeat of the Axis through unconditional surrender would avoid the problems encountered after World War I with the armistice, Versailles, and the claims made by the Nazis that Germany was never defeated.

Having failed at Casablanca, Stimson and Marshall were determined that British opposition to a second front be overcome and a plan for a cross-channel attack on France in 1944 be agreed to once and for all by Washington and London. While they understood the president's position, and did not wish to launch an attack without the proper preparation, the secretary of war and chief of staff remained convinced that the British approach was a less effective use of Anglo–American power than an attack on France and, thus, that it served to prolong the war. They did not see any other strategy toward winning the war that would be as effective as a second front in France.

Stimson also knew that with the Russian victory at Stalingrad, and the American successes in North Africa and Guadalcanal, it was now possible and proper to begin to think specifically about peace and the postwar world. The latter points shaped much of his arguments with the president to set a firm plan for a second front when Churchill came to Washington in May 1943 for the Trident Conference.

When negotiations resumed between U.S. and U.K. officials, both sides rehearsed the same arguments they had made back in January; the Americans pushed for a definite commitment to a second front in 1944 and their British counterparts argued for further campaigns in the Mediterranean. As Stimson noted, a "very decided deadlock" remained as the British were "holding back dead from going on with Bolero." Roosevelt, however, refused to compromise this time. As he told his secretary of war, "he was coming to the conclusion that he would have to read the Riot Act to the other side and would have to be stiff." Knowing Roosevelt's fondness for historical analogies, and worried about the Russian view of any more delays, Stimson told FDR that the British position reminded him of a story Lincoln told of a general who, "although he couldn't skin the deer, could at least hold a leg." He went on, "The British are trying to arrange the matter so that Britain and America hold the leg for Stalin to skin the deer." Any further postponement, Stimson continued, "will be a dangerous business for us at the end of the war. Stalin won't have much of an opinion of people who have done that and we will not be able to share much of the post-war world with him."[62]

Roosevelt held his ground at the conference, insisting that the planning for Bolero, now renamed Overlord, had to be the top priority for the next year, and that all other planning would be based off of that. The president, now fully asserting his leadership of the Anglo–American partnership, would determine for the rest of the war how American forces and resources would be deployed. The British Prime Minister ultimately agreed but not without a condition. He asked that General Marshall join him for an inspection tour of the preparations for the attacks on Sicily and Italy in North Africa. Apparently, Churchill thought he could get Marshall to see the correctness of the British position and then convince FDR. If that was the intention, it failed. Marshall, Stimson later wrote, "returned safe, and unconverted, to the Pentagon."[63]

Roosevelt sent the joint message to Stalin this time. It began by noting that in the "overall strategy," agreed to by the United States and Great Britain, the first priority was to continue the recent success in protecting the shipping lanes of the Atlantic in order to allow supplies to reach the Soviet Union and to "employ every practical means to support Russia." The West also sought to continue its pressure on Japan, to provide all practical support to China to maintain it as an effective ally against Japan, and to take direct action "to eliminate Italy from the war as quickly as possible." Regarding the second front, planning continued with the anticipation that "the concentration of forces and landing equipment in the British Isles" would allow for a full-scale invasion of the continent "at the peak of the great air offensive in the Spring of 1944." The "absorption of large landing-craft in the Mediterranean" and the Pacific "has been our most serious limiting factor regarding operations out of England." Trying to present the best possible interpretation of the news that the second front was now officially delayed again to 1944, Roosevelt noted that the various Anglo–American operations would "heavily engage the enemy in the air and will force a dispersion of his troops on the ground to meet both actual attacks and heavy threats of attack which can readily be converted into successful operations whenever signs of Axis weakness become apparent."[64]

Stalin did not hide his anger at the news and his complete disagreement with the policy. He noted that the latest decision was "in contradiction" with what he had been told after Casablanca, "regarding the terms of the opening of the second front in Western Europe." Then, it had been promised that action preparations were "energetically being carried out" that would "divert considerable German land and air forces from the Russian front" and begin the final defeat of Germany. "Now, in May 1943 you and Mr. Churchill made the decision, postponing the British-American invasion of Western Europe until spring of 1944." This meant that the start of a second front, "which was postponed already from 1942 to 1943, is being postponed again, this time until spring 1944." The Anglo–American decision created "enormous difficulties for the Soviet Union, which has already been fighting for two years . . . against the main forces of Germany," and left the Soviet Army "almost in single combat with yet very strong and dangerous enemy." Stalin concluded by noting the negative impression that leaving the Red Army without support would make in the Soviet Union.[65] Roosevelt saw that these tensions could only be overcome by the actual opening of the second front and through a meeting of the Big Three and personal diplomacy with Stalin. The question that remained for FDR was whether there was enough time to overcome the discord now that he had taken control of the Western Allies' strategy.

The first year and a half of fighting had witnessed a dramatic turn in the war. In early 1942, Japan had gained control of large parts of China and most of Southeast Asia and the Western Pacific Ocean, while Germany dominated Europe from the Atlantic Coast to the outskirts of Moscow and also large parts of North Africa. By the spring of 1943, the United States had gained the momentum in the Pacific, halting Tokyo's expansion, inflicting significant damage on the Japanese Navy at Midway and the Coral Sea, and beginning the arduous process of pushing Japan's forces back toward the home islands in the hard-fought battles at Guadalcanal. Anglo–American forces had liberated North Africa from German control and were poised for further operations in the Mediterranean. Most significantly, the Soviet Union had won a decisive victory against the Germans at Stalingrad and had begun to take the offensive against Germany.

For Roosevelt, the Soviet achievement shifted the nature of the war and the context for decision making; now it was time to pay more attention to the question of peace and the postwar world. The challenge FDR now faced in keeping the Grand Alliance together was to focus less on London and more on Moscow, to demonstrate to the Soviet Union that he understood its concerns and needs. The policy of unconditional surrender was a significant step in that direction; it established that there would be no armistice or negotiations, that fascism would be eliminated, and that Germany would not be allowed to again threaten its neighbors. Over the next year Roosevelt would fully develop his plans for how to maintain peace. His long-sought meeting with Stalin, at Tehran in November 1943, was crucial for a successful conclusion to the fighting and for cooperation among the great powers in the postwar period.

7

Architect of Victory

The year 1943 was the turning point in the military fortunes of the Grand Alliance and the crucial time for postwar planning. In the period between the military victories in the spring of 1943 and the first Big Three meeting in Tehran, the full power of the United States was finally brought to bear in World War II, and the Axis powers began to be overwhelmed by the combined forces of the United Nations. Throughout 1943, Allied forces moved forward on all fronts: taking control of the Mediterranean and toppling Mussolini from power in Italy, pushing the Germans back across the broad front in the Soviet Union, and gaining enough ground in the Pacific to put American planes in position to consistently strike at the Japanese home islands by late in the year. The launching of the second front in Europe and the success of the D-Day landings on the coast of France on June 6, 1944, marked the beginning of the final phase of the fighting that would lead to the defeat of Nazi Germany in May 1945 and Imperial Japan in August 1945; but it was Roosevelt's decisions and actions in 1943 that made this defeat possible and that made him the architect of victory. Even though over a year and a half of fighting remained, the end of the war began to come into sight. Thus, 1943 also marked the height of the Grand Alliance in terms of cooperation among the Big Three. Roosevelt, Stalin, and Churchill were finally able to meet together in November and December 1943 in Tehran to plan for the final victory and discuss peace and the postwar world. Tehran was the most important meeting of the allied leaders during the war, and the vital decisions reached there carried the Allies through 1944 and to victory in 1945.

As American industrial production continued to set new records, and American forces found victories on the battlefields of Africa, Europe, and the Pacific, Roosevelt gained confidence to begin to speak systematically to the nation's allies and to the American public about the postwar period and his vision for peace. Aiding that confidence was the knowledge of the progress being made on the atomic bomb. A self-sustaining nuclear chain reaction had been achieved by scientists working in Chicago in late 1942, a significant milepost in the creation of an actual weapon and, the president hoped, one that was ahead of German efforts. Important issues that had been delayed due to the intense focus on mobilization and production, halting the Axis expansion, keeping the Soviet Union in the war, and getting American forces into battle, could now be taken up, and FDR began to make crucial decisions about the future in terms of national security and international economic policy.

Roosevelt avoided any grand proclamation of fixed goals; he conducted most of his diplomacy privately and sought to keep his options open for as long as possible so as to be best able to tack when necessary. In the process, Roosevelt's planning moved on two separate and parallel courses. On the one hand, he pursued his internationalist policies through the continuation of the Grand Alliance, which he sought to make permanent with the creation of the United Nations. Roosevelt knew postwar peace and stability required cooperation between Washington and Moscow. Soviet power in Eastern Europe was a reality that had to be recognized and its contribution to victory acknowledged. On the other hand, FDR continued to pursue more unilateral policies, most notably through the building of the atomic bomb, which was done in cooperation with Great Britain alone. He also pursued defense in depth through the plan to station American troops in Europe and acquire military bases outside the Western Hemisphere; he sought to build up China as a great power closely aligned to the United States (despite the misgivings of both England and Russia); and he established liberal-capitalist international economic institutions. To these ends, Roosevelt consistently noted that he did not seek a final peace conference. He understood that the situation would be fluid and that the agreements reached during the war would be a starting point for peace rather than the final word on postwar arrangements. The process and efforts of maintaining the Grand Alliance, he believed, would have to continue after victory was achieved. Roosevelt did not care about the exact route taken as long as he sailed the ship of state to a secure port that would protect American interests and values, prevent future wars, and secure the necessary balance to produce postwar peace and prosperity.

In the first months of 1943, Roosevelt began to address the issues of peace and the postwar international system; he did this privately to convince his allies to accept his concepts, and publicly to educate the America people on what he saw as the proper course of action. In a series of meetings with British Foreign Secretary Anthony Eden in March 1943, Roosevelt set out his thinking on a wide range of issues that would confront the Grand Alliance once Germany and Japan were defeated. Making it clear that he wanted to avoid the numerous problems of Versailles, FDR was emphatic that "he wanted no negotiated armistice after the collapse." Roosevelt would "insist on total surrender with no commitments to the enemy as to what we would or would not do after this action." Indeed, FDR even "doubted if a peace treaty should be signed for some time after the collapse of Germany and Japan."[1]

The two men agreed that Russia would be the most difficult issue facing their respective nations. The reasons were varied: the differences between the political systems of the Western allies and the Soviets, Moscow's historical distrust of the West, which was furthered by the delay of the second front, the divergent postwar goals and needs of the allies, and the differences in economic and military power. Yet, the basis for continued cooperation existed. From his talks in Moscow, Eden believed that, similar to the Anglo–American powers, the Russians' primary hope was a continuation of the Grand Alliance. The Soviets, however, were worried the United States might withdraw again from Europe after the war; therefore, they believed they had to plan for that contingency and how to achieve postwar security on their own. The British foreign secretary thought that the starting point was to understand that Stalin did not trust the Germans, and would insist on disarmament and the dismemberment of Germany. At the same time, the Soviet Union did not want to have full responsibility for Germany after the war as it would have enormous difficulties with its own postwar recovery without taking on extra burdens. Rather, "it was a fixed matter of Russian foreign policy to have both British and United States troops heavily in Europe when the collapse comes." Roosevelt indicated that he understood that unconditional surrender meant the occupation and disarmament of Germany by the

Big Three. The questions of borders and reparations, and whether or not Germany should be broken up into smaller states, would need further discussion that was best taken up at the end of the fighting.[2]

Whatever the configuration of power, Russia would insist on its 1941 borders "for reasons of security," specifically the inclusion of the Baltic States in the USSR and the new boundary with Poland. Roosevelt hoped the absorption of Estonia, Latvia, and Lithuania could be done through a plebiscite and that the absorption of these states was not seen by the Soviets as a fait accompli. Still he understood the security issue and the reality that "none of us can force them to get out" of these lands. Regarding Poland, it was clear that Stalin would not accept the type of anti-Soviet regime that had existed prior to the war. The president and Eden agreed that Poland would get territory from Germany to offset what it lost to Russia, but in the end, Roosevelt stated that "the big powers would have to decide what Poland should have" and that he did not intend to "bargain with Poland or the other small states" at a peace conference. "As far as Poland is concerned," FDR said, "the important thing is to set it up in a way that will help maintain the peace of the world."[3]

Beyond Europe, Roosevelt discussed his hope that China would emerge as a stabilizing power in East Asia. He, therefore, "wanted to strengthen China in every possible way" to allow it to become a pro-Western model of an independent Third Way between continued colonialism and revolution that he envisioned for nations in Asia. The president directly linked China's ability to play this role to a new international organization in which "the real decisions should be made by the United States, Great Britain, Russia and China, who would be the powers for many years to come that would have to police the world." Moreover, the president was confident that China, "in any serious conflict of policy with Russia, would undoubtedly line up on our side." Directly related to his concept of the Third Way were FDR's ideas for a trusteeship system for some former colonies and nations that had been occupied by Axis forces. Roosevelt thought this would provide these countries with a nation committed to assisting them in making the transition from colony to full independence. In Harry Hopkins's words, Roosevelt "made it clear that he did not want a commitment made in advance that all those colonies in the Far East should go back to the countries which owned or controlled them prior to the war," noting specifically French Indo-China and the Dutch possession of Timor. Eden, while agreeing that the United Nations needed to be global in scope, expressed considerable skepticism about China playing the role of a great power. He also indicated concerns about trusteeships, leading Hopkins to note that "the British are going to be pretty sticky about their former possessions in the Far East."[4]

At the same time that he was meeting with Eden, FDR was holding discussions with a reporter he trusted, Forrest Davis, about his plans. The president shared with Davis his views on international relations and the postwar world as a means of starting a public discussion of his ideas and shaping opinion without having to go directly on record about any specific positions. Davis's summary of their talks was published in the *Saturday Evening Post* in April with the misleading title "Roosevelt's World Blueprint." The president did not have a set of "blueprint" plans that he would closely follow; rather he set out his key assumptions, concerns, and broad goals.[5]

What was quickly evident in Davis's piece was Roosevelt's command of strategy and knowledge about the world, his interrelated global views of the issues that would confront the United States after the war, and his perspective that just as Russia was the keystone of the war, so it would be in terms of establishing postwar stability and peace. Davis noted that FDR was a global power theorist who saw the connections of different problems and understood the needs of various nations and regions. The author reported that, as befit such a skilled sailor and geographer, Roosevelt "reads maps with the skill of a professional." The pilots who had flown him to his recent meeting with Churchill at Casablanca "were astonished by his knowledge of the South American and African coasts" and his ability to identify headlands and landmarks. They believed that with good visibility the "President could have made his way to Casablanca by air" by himself.[6]

Three main concerns guided Roosevelt's thinking: establishing a permanent peace, economic reconstruction, and anticolonialism. To achieve his goals, FDR knew he had to avoid the mistakes of Versailles and the peacemaking of 1919. Thus, his first concern was national security. Placed in terms of the four freedoms, this meant that freedom from fear was the most important and that the others could only be achieved after a durable peace was established. Peace would allow for economic recovery and prosperity, or freedom from want. As for freedom of speech and worship, it was not up to the United States to impose these on others, but Roosevelt believed, Davis reported, "that in a world free of fear of aggression those values can be propagated by example and moral suasion." All of this meant the Grand Alliance had to continue in order to provide collective security in the postwar period so as to avoid another war. The great powers would be responsible for "policing a peace."[7]

The Good Neighbor Policy, Davis informed his readers, served as an overarching guide to the president's thinking. Roosevelt saw it as a model for an international organization that would be flexible, consultative, and representative of all nations; there would be no issues about surrendering sovereignty, which had led the U.S. to reject the League of Nations. At the same time, a United Nations organization would not preclude the fact that peace would ultimately depend on the "genuine association of interest on the part of the great powers," anticipating, in Davis's words, "a security commission" composed of the United States, Russia, and Great Britain. Peace was a process, not a fixed point, and it depended on relationships, trust, cooperation, and finding common interests.[8]

For FDR, a stable and secure world order would also provide a means to peacefully move away from empire and the danger of aggression against weaker nations. The president was opposed to the automatic reestablishment of all colonies by the imperial powers. Rather, he foresaw the need for mandates for administrating the transition from colonial possession to independence under trusteeships set up by the international community. He also favored the use of plebiscites for helping to determine what nations would gain possession of disputed territories, noting it would take "a conclusive majority, say two thirds," before sovereignty was granted. Ultimately, collective security guaranteed by the great powers would protect the smaller nations from attack and allow for disarmament by all countries.[9]

Risks would need to be taken, most notably in relations with the Soviet Union. Roosevelt fully understood the tensions that existed between Moscow and London–Washington. Some were historical and ideological, while others stemmed from the questions of wartime strategy and postwar aims. Russia's successes on the battlefield meant it would emerge from the war as a great power; its sacrifices would have to be taken into account and its needs respected. Roosevelt was confident, however, that agreements could be reached, cooperation could be fostered, and Western and Russian goals could be reconciled. There were, Roosevelt believed, certain common interests to build on: the desire for peace, the need for reconstruction, and the need for protection in the future from aggression through collective security. Through assistance in all of these areas, the United States could find a "common denominator" with the Soviet

Union. Once Germany was defeated, all of the powers would see the advantages in putting behind them previous grievances and rivalries and would collaborate in rebuilding Europe and establishing a firm foundation for an enduring peace. The alternative would be a collapse of the Grand Alliance, a return to a balance of power system, and an inevitable conflict between the West and Russia in Central Europe. Roosevelt was confident and determined that if he could demonstrate the good faith of the United States to the Soviet Union and show how the framework for peace that he envisioned would protect Russian security and preserve peace, the distrust could be overcome and a cooperative international order established.[10]

In public statements in May and June, Roosevelt noted the hierarchy he now placed on the four freedoms, as first set out in the Davis article. In May, in Hot Springs, Virginia, a letter from Roosevelt was read to delegates to the first international conference held under the auspices of the United Nations, which was attended by forty-four nations. Roosevelt praised the work they were about to begin to assist people after the war; he regretted he could not attend but told them his attention had to be fully on victory over the Axis before anything else. "We know that in the world for which we are fighting and working the four freedoms must be won for all men," he stated, adding that these freedoms were all interrelated. "Freedom from fear, for example, is dependent on freedom from want." Only in securing these can all people "be free to live out their lives in peace, prosperity, and security." When the delegates visited the White House in June, FDR reiterated the points from his letter about the freedom from fear and told them that a return to peacetime economies "will depend on world political security." The work of the United Nations would be to put into practice "the principles of the Atlantic Charter" to meet the needs of all people. "The United Nations," the president declared, "are united in the war against fear and want, as solidly and effectively as they are united on the battle front in the world war against aggression."[11] This is what Roosevelt was alluding to when he stated later in the year that Dr. New Deal had become Dr. Win the War. National security—the freedom from fear—was essential if the nation, and the world, wanted prosperity—the freedom from want—and social progress after the war.[12]

One of the most controversial aspects of Roosevelt's wartime leadership was his response to the Holocaust. The historical debate over the administration's policy has been described by Richard Breitman and Allan J. Lichtman as "unforgiving, passionate, and politically charged."[13] Roosevelt's position and policies were based on his view that the best way to end the Nazi effort to annihilate all Jews was to win the war as quickly as possible. While efforts were made to rescue people, he believed that the crisis had to be approached within the context of the war and what was possible, and that ultimately only victory would end the barbarity of the gas chambers.

Critics, most notably David S. Wyman, contend that Roosevelt failed to do all he could to save Jews from the Nazis, claiming that there were ways that would not have detracted from the fighting of the war. Wyman argued that Roosevelt was aware of Nazi atrocities early enough, by late 1942, and that the United States had the ability to intervene and mount a more significant rescue operation to save Europe's Jews. He attributed the failure to several factors: a slow response by the president, especially the delay in creating the War Refugee Board, which did save over 200,000 Jews, until late 1943; anti-Semitism in America; and the failure on the part of American Jewry and the media to create public pressure. All of this led to a policy characterized by too little action taken too late. In particular, Wyman asserted that the United States could have bombed the concentration camps, and specifically Auschwitz, by late 1944, thereby halting its deadly use. Wyman claimed that, had Roosevelt made "a substantial commitment" to rescue the Jews, such as creating the War Refugee Board just months earlier, "almost certainly [such an action] could have saved several hundred thousand of them [Jews], and done so without compromising the war effort."[14]

Rejecting Wyman's analysis, William D. Rubinstein argued that Hitler alone bore the responsibility for the genocide and that there was little more Roosevelt could have done. Rubinstein directly challenged Wyman's thesis, arguing that "no Jew who perished during the Nazi Holocaust could have been saved by any action which the Allies could have taken at the time" based on what was known then, what was actually proposed, and what was possible to accomplish. A critical point for Rubinstein was that the Jews in Nazi Europe were not refugees but prisoners after the war began in September 1939. This crucial distinction explained the fundamental problem facing U.S. efforts at rescue. As he concluded: "Only refugees can flee to havens of safety; prisoners cannot, and corpses cannot." In addition, Rubinstein dismissed the idea that the Allies could have bombed Auschwitz and ended the killing in the concentration camps any earlier.[15]

Breitman and Lichtman rejected "both extremes in this dispute" and have provided the most convincing interpretation of the president's policy.[16] They acknowledge that because of his focus on victory, "for most of his presidency Roosevelt did little to aid the imperiled Jews of Germany and Europe." Yet, "at times Roosevelt acted decisively to rescue Jews, often withstanding contrary pressures from the American public, Congress, and his own State Department," and he did more than any other leader to help Europe's Jewish population.[17] Thus, they found that "FDR was neither a hero of the Jews nor a bystander to the Nazi's persecution and then annihilation of the Jews."[18] It was "only during his first term [that Roosevelt] was a bystander to Nazi persecution, well before the beginning of the Holocaust," because of his focus on the New Deal and the problems of the Great Depression.[19]

By his second term, Roosevelt had shifted his focus to the Jewish peril in Europe, opening immigration restrictions and supporting the Zionist movement. The president had supported the British Balfour Declaration, and its promise of the "establishment in Palestine of a nation home for the Jewish people," since its proclamation in 1917. Germany's actions reinforced FDR's conviction of the need for a Jewish state, a position he reiterated as late as March 1945. The coming of the war to the United States necessitated a shift to military policy and a focus on victory, with all other issues now secondary to security and the defeat of the Axis. Still, Roosevelt remained concerned about the fate of the Jews, leading him to establish the War Refugee Board and to make other efforts on behalf of Jews in Europe. It is difficult to argue with Breitman and Lichtman's conclusions that the "story of FDR and the Jews is ultimately a tragic one," but that even if the president had been willing to take more risks politically "he could not have stopped the Nazis' mass murder of some six million Jews."[20] Roosevelt understood that the Holocaust was a central part of Hitler's war, and that only Germany's military defeat could end it and save the most lives.

The Anglo–American assault on Sicily on July 9–10 quickly smashed the Italian defenses and plunged Rome into chaos. On July 16, the United States and Great Britain released a joint statement to the Italian people declaring that their armed forces were "carrying the war deep into the territory of your country." Making a distinction between the fascist government and the citizens of Italy, it noted that the attack on Italy was the "direct consequence of the shameful leadership to which you have been subjected by Mussolini and his Fascist regime" that had required Italians to fight for the interests of Nazi Germany. It called upon them to overthrow the "false and corrupt leaders" who had betrayed their nation and to unconditionally surrender "to the overwhelming power of the military forces of the United Nations" or face destruction. It was up to the Italian people to decide if they would continue to die for Mussolini and Hitler "or live for Italy, and for civilization."[21]

As American planes bombed Italy, and final preparations were being made for the allied attack on the Italian peninsula, word arrived in Washington on July 25 that Mussolini had been forced out of power. The king of Italy, Victor Emmanuel III, had survived the Fascist Council's ouster of Mussolini and appointed Marshal Pietro Badoglio as prime minister. This immediately raised questions of surrender and how Washington and London would approach the new government should it send out peace feelers, a situation made more difficult by earlier criticism of the Darlan Deal and the fact that Badoglio had led the Italian forces in Ethiopia.

Speaking to the nation in a fireside chat on July 28, Roosevelt announced that these stunning developments did not change American policy. He began by recalling his words from the January 6, 1942, State of the Union message when he declared to Congress that "the militarists of Berlin and Tokyo started this war. But the massed, angered forces of common humanity will finish it." That prophecy was now "in the process of being fulfilled." Allied forces were on the march, moving forward on the Russian front, in the Mediterranean, and across the Pacific Ocean, "converging upon their ultimate objectives: Berlin and Tokyo." In the process, "the first crack in the Axis has come. The criminal, corrupt Fascist regime in Italy is going to pieces." But Mussolini could not evade justice by resigning. All leaders responsible for the war "will be brought to book." Given this, "our terms to Italy are still the same as our terms to Germany and Japan—'Unconditional Surrender.' We will have no truck with Fascism in any way, shape or manner. We will permit no vestige of Fascism to remain." At the same time, the forces of the United Nations would help the Italian people rid themselves of the vestiges of fascism and reestablish a free society. "It is our determination," FDR stated, to restore all "conquered peoples to the dignity of human beings, masters of their own fate, entitled to freedom of speech, freedom of religion, freedom from want, and freedom from fear."[22]

While the news from Italy was welcomed, Roosevelt declared that "ahead of us are much bigger fights" in Europe and Asia. "The heaviest and most decisive fighting today is going on in Russia." The ability of the Red Army to retreat in 1941 and 1942 without breaking, and to counterattack in 1943, was "helping to save all the world from the Nazi menace." The president praised the Russians for their "devotion, determination, and self-sacrifice," and noted that with such a nation "this country of ours should always be glad to be a good neighbor and a sincere friend in the world of the future." Where Russia now had the initiative on the Eastern Front, the United States was gaining the initiative in the Pacific from the Aleutians to New Guinea. The United States was destroying more planes and ships than the Japanese could replace and was moving toward the home islands. "We are still far from our main objectives in the war against Japan," Roosevelt cautioned. Yet he reminded his listeners that a year ago they had been far from their objectives in Europe and now the Allies were pushing the Germans back. Similarly in Asia, American forces "are pushing forward to occupation of positions which in time will enable us to attack the Japanese Islands themselves." While the first part of the plan for victory, knocking out Mussolini and Italy, was succeeding, the toughest battles remained. "We still have to defeat Hitler and Tojo on their own home grounds." In doing so, "we shall not settle for less than total victory."[23]

Prior to their meeting in Quebec in mid-August, the president set out for Churchill his priorities concerning the fighting in Italy. Despite the positive developments and Mussolini's fall, "our thoughts at this moment above all others must be directed at the supreme goal namely the destruction of Hitlerism and Hitler." Should Italy surrender, the terms must be determined with this objective in mind. That meant control of all Italian territory and military assets, most importantly its navy, and "to whatever extent we find needful and useful, of Italian ground and air forces." The Allies, Roosevelt wrote, "cannot afford in our struggle with the German Army and with Hitler to deny ourselves any means that will kill Germans."[24]

The fighting in Italy proved to be more difficult than it had appeared when Roosevelt addressed the nation on July 28. Unlike the situation in North Africa, Italy was one of the three main enemy nations. As a military issue, there was enormous gain in having any Italian government surrender and turn over bases and the Italian fleet to the Allies without any battles. Anglo–American forces had not yet landed on the Italian peninsula, and Germany was moving reinforcements to Italy. On the political side, whatever action was taken would have an impact on relations with Russia, the war against Germany and Japan, and the structure of the postwar world. Roosevelt indicated this in a press conference two days after his fireside chat. Responding to a question on whether or not the United States should strike a deal with Badoglio or the king of Italy, FDR stated that there were two circumstances that they were looking for, an end to armed opposition and the avoidance of anarchy. "I don't care with whom we deal in Italy, so long as it isn't a definite member of the Fascist Government, as long as they get them to lay down their arms, and so long as we don't have anarchy. Now he may be a King, or a present Prime Minister, or a Mayor of a town or a village." From there, the long-range goal, as set out in the Atlantic Charter, was self-determination, but "you can't get self-determination in the first week that they lay down their arms. In other words, common sense."[25]

To discuss the situation in Italy and other questions on the war, Roosevelt and Churchill met in Quebec City along with Canada's Prime Minister Mackenzie King. The Quadrant Conference commenced right after the first official efforts by Rome to strike a surrender deal. Stalin was informed about the contact from Italy and was kept up to date on the discussions with the Italians, including the fact that General Eisenhower had been instructed by the Western leaders to send representatives to Lisbon to meet with Italy's General Giuseppe Castellano. It was clear that military conditions would determine the surrender and that it again would be left to General Eisenhower to set the terms. An agreement on Italy's surrender to the United Nations forces was reached on September 3 and announced on September 8. The Badoglio government agreed to turn over Italy's fleet to the Allies and allow Anglo–American forces to land on the Italian peninsula without having to face the Italian Army. Germany quickly responded, attacking Italian forces, taking control of much of the nation from Rome to the north, and reinstalling Mussolini in power in the so-called Republic of Salò. Badoglio and King Victor Emmanuel III fled from Rome to the south, and no Italian resistance to the Germans materialized. The fighting in Italy against the Germans would continue for another twenty months, until April 1945.

The issue of the second front, now named Overlord, again dominated the discussions of the Anglo–American leaders. Stimson and Marshall remained determined that Churchill would not derail the cross-channel invasion with other plans for fighting in the Eastern Mediterranean. The American chiefs of staff rejected all the British efforts to place conditions on the promised invasion of France, and the final decisions represented a triumph for Stimson and Marshall. The target date for Overlord was set as May 1, 1944, with an American commander in charge. In conjunction with this decision, Roosevelt and Churchill agreed to a Four Power Declaration, to include the Soviet Union and China, calling for the establishment of a postwar international organization. This was the beginning of direct collaboration between the Western Allies and the Soviet Union, which was designed to provide better coordination in the war, address any tensions in the Grand Alliance, and prepare for peace. Word arrived from Moscow that Stalin agreed to the Foreign Ministers meeting to be held in the Soviet capitol in October as a precursor to a Big Three meeting in Tehran at the end of November.

The president and prime minister informed Stalin on August 25 of their key military decisions in the wake of Italy's collapse. The air campaign against Germany would be increased with the use of bases in Italy as well as Great Britain, with the objective "to destroy the German air combat strength, to dislocate the German military, industrial, and economic system, and to prepare the way for a cross channel invasion." To that end, "a large-scale buildup of American forces in the United Kingdom is now under way." While the war in the Mediterranean would be "pressed vigorously," the second front "will be the primary British and American ground and air effort against the Axis." There would be no offensive in the Balkans; operations would be limited to supplying anti-German forces and bombing strategic targets. As for the Pacific, the Soviet premier was informed that the island campaigns against Japan would be accelerated "to exhaust Japanese air, naval, and shipping resources, to cut the Japanese communications and to secure bases from which to bomb Japan proper."[26]

Inevitably, as military progress was made, postwar considerations played a larger role in influencing decisions. Roosevelt had no doubt that cooperation with Great Britain would continue; for him, the more difficult and significant question was relations with the Soviet Union. As the War Department noted in preparation for the Quadrant meeting, "Russia's post-war position in Europe will be a dominant one. With Germany crushed, there is no power in Europe to oppose her tremendous military forces." The implications, it noted, were obvious. "Since Russia is the decisive factor in the war, she must be given every assistance and every effort must be made to obtain her friendship." Because Russian power would be dominant after the defeat of the Axis, then after the war it would be "even more essential to develop and maintain the most friendly relations with Russia." The report concluded by stating that "*the most important factor the United States has to consider in relation to Russia is the prosecution of the war in the Pacific.*" Written at a time when estimates for the fighting against Japan extended into 1947, it noted that "with Russia as an ally in the war against Japan, the war can be terminated in less time and at less expense in life and resources than if the reverse were the case. Should the war in the Pacific have to be carried on with an unfriendly or a negative attitude on the part of Russia, the difficulties will be immeasurably increased and operations might become abortive."[27]

Before returning to the United States, Roosevelt addressed the Canadian Parliament about his meeting with King and Churchill. "It is no secret," FDR noted, "that at Quebec there was much talk of the postwar world." People were anxious to return to peacetime, but this was "not a longing to go back to what they call 'the good old days.' I have distinct reservations as to how good 'the good old days' were. I would rather believe that we can achieve new and better days." Victory would provide a great opportunity to the world for progress. "Surely we can make strides toward a greater freedom from want than the world has yet enjoyed," Roosevelt declared. "Surely by unanimous action in driving out the outlaws and keeping them under heel forever, we can attain a freedom from fear of violence." The president was angered by "those who assert vociferously that the four freedoms and the Atlantic Charter are nonsense because they are unattainable. If those people had lived a century and a half ago they would have sneered and said that the Declaration of Independence was utter piffle. If they had lived nearly a thousand years ago they would have laughed uproariously at the ideals of Magna Charta. And if they had lived several thousand years ago they would have derided Moses when he came from the Mountain with the Ten Commandments. We concede that these great teachings are not perfectly lived up to today, but I would rather be a builder than a wrecker, hoping always that the structure of life is growing—not dying."[28]

On September 17, Roosevelt delivered a message to Congress on the progress of the war, with the thesis that as the fortunes in the war turned the United States "could not and cannot be content to drift with this favorable tide." As any sailor like FDR knew, conditions could change quickly, bringing danger and damage. Similarly, the nation could not afford to drift concerning the postwar world. Washington had to follow up its victory with well-planned actions to ensure peace and its national security through the continuation of the Grand Alliance. The starting point for peace was the elimination of the forces that had brought about the war. Roosevelt emphatically stated that he wanted to make one point "perfectly clear." When Germany was defeated, and "when Hitler and the Nazis go out, the Prussian military clique must go with them. The war-breeding gangs of militarists must be rooted out in Germany—and out of Japan—if we are to have any real assurance of future peace." Thus, the Allies could not claim "that we have gained total victory in this war if any vestige of Fascism in any of its malignant forms is permitted to survive anywhere in the world."[29]

While the Allies were "still a long, long way from ultimate victory in any major theater of the war," the planning was in place for victory, the resources for fighting were being produced, and the courage and determination in the soldiers that was necessary for victory was on display around the world. As FDR had always insisted, "we cannot think of this as several wars. It is all one war." The various fronts were connected, and all the actions were having a cumulative impact and weakening the enemy. The same was true in terms of thinking about postwar peace; it was necessary to look at the world as one rather than as separate spheres or regions. National security would come not just from winning the war but through "a national cooperation with other Nations toward the end that world aggression be ended and that fair international relationships be established on a permanent basis." How to do this was already known. "The policy of the Good Neighbor," Roosevelt concluded, "has shown such success in the hemisphere of the Americas that its extension to the whole world seems to be the logical next step." By maintaining the Grand Alliance and implementing his internationalist policies through the Good Neighbor Policy, Roosevelt believed that the nation would achieve its ultimate goals of "freedom and justice and security at home and abroad."[30]

For Roosevelt, a crucial piece in maintaining the Grand Alliance was a new international organization led by the Big Four. Fully cognizant of the failure of Woodrow Wilson and the rejection of the League of Nations by the Senate, FDR made sure he had support for what became the United Nations before he brought the idea to Stalin at Tehran. The president's efforts to gain support for his approach paid off on November 5 when the Senate, by an eighty-five to five vote, approved the Connally Resolution. The resolution endorsed the Four Power Declaration by supporting U.S. collaboration with other nations to maintain peace after the war, and it paved the way for the creation of an international organization designed to secure peace. Roosevelt could now negotiate with the backing of the legislature, and other nations would not have to wonder about Washington keeping its commitments.

Stimson met with Roosevelt and Hopkins prior to their departure to give them a full account of the planning and status of the preparations for the assault on France, assuring them that everything was on schedule, provided there were no new diversions. Stimson followed up with a letter to Hopkins, setting out his thoughts for him to use at Tehran. He noted that "the task of our Commander-in-Chief is to hold the situation firmly to the straight road which has been agreed to and which it is now on." The United States could not tolerate any departures as "the success of Overlord is so much the most important thing in the world horizon." Stimson also believed that Marshall should be given the command of the operation and of all military activity in the European theater; the other joint chiefs disagreed because they wished Marshall to remain in Washington and continue to oversee the whole war effort. Hopkins agreed with Stimson, noting that he, too, was anxious "owing to the very doubtful attitude of the British Prime Minister" but was convinced that going forward with the cross-channel incursion "was the most important problem now before the world."[31]

Prior to their summit with Stalin at Tehran, Roosevelt and Churchill met with Chiang Kai-shek in Cairo to discuss the state of the war with Japan and coordinate planning, particularly regarding how to provide support for China. In public, Roosevelt talked about China as one of the four policemen and at times included China as a member of the Big Four allies. Americans sympathized with China as a victim of brutal Japanese aggression, and the Roosevelt administration adhered to the Stimson Doctrine and opposed all of Tokyo's efforts at territorial conquest. This was a central reason why the United States was fighting Japan. Moreover, the president hoped that China would emerge from the war as a stabilizing force in East Asia and a model for the Third Way, for a pro-Western nationalism between colonialism and revolutionary nationalism.

Still, Roosevelt was unimpressed by Chiang. He and his advisors were aware that Chiang's government was rent with corruption and was ineffective on the battlefield; they realized that the Chinese were in no position, no matter how much aid Washington sent, to defeat the Japanese forces in their country. Victory would come from the steady advance of American naval, ground, and air forces driving toward Japan's home islands. From the view of the United States and Great Britain, China's most important role was to keep a large portion of the Japanese army tied down on the Asian mainland.

The final Cairo Communiqué set out the determination of the Allies to defeat Japan unconditionally. The three powers sought no territorial gain, but made it clear that Japan would be "stripped of all the islands in the Pacific which she has seized or occupied since the beginning of the first World War in 1914, and that all the territories Japan has stolen from the Chinese, such as Manchuria, Formosa, and the Pescadores, shall be restored to the Republic of China." Furthermore, it stated that Japan would be expelled from all other territory it had conquered in East Asia and that "in due course Korea shall become free and independent."[32]

From Cairo, the president and his advisors flew on November 27 to Tehran for the most important meeting of the war, leaving shortly after 7:00 a.m. and arriving in Iran at 3:00 p.m. Roosevelt had his first meeting with Stalin on Sunday afternoon, November 28. Reflecting his efforts to hold such a meeting, Roosevelt greeted Stalin by stating: "I am glad to see you. I have tried for a long time to bring this about." The two men immediately began discussing the state of the war on the Russian front. Stalin provided a mixed picture, in particular noting setbacks due to the fact that the Germans were "exercising strong pressures on the Soviet front" as a result of fresh reinforcements. When the president asked if the Soviet forces still had the initiative, Stalin stated they did "but that the situation was so bad that only in the Ukraine was it possible to take offensive operations." Roosevelt responded that "he wished that it were within his power to bring about the removal of 30 or 40 German divisions from the Eastern front and that that question, of course, was one of the things he desired to discuss." Stalin stated the obvious, that it would be "of great value if such a transfer of German divisions could be brought about."[33]

Determined to establish good relations, FDR noted that after the war the merchant fleets of the United States and Great Britain would be larger than either nation could utilize, and indicated that he was willing to make some of these ships available to the Soviet Union to assist it with postwar recovery. Stalin indicated this would be of "great value" to his nation and to the development of good relations between Moscow and Washington. If the ships were provided, "a plentiful supply of the raw materials" from Russia "could be made available to the United States."[34]

The lengthiest discussion during this meeting concerned France, with both leaders agreeing that it was a collaborationist nation. Roosevelt concurred with Stalin's statement that Vichy represented "the real physical France" that provided aid to Germany. The Soviet leader went so far as to dismiss the leader of the exiled French resistance, General Charles de Gaulle, as a man who commanded little power, and he called for France to be punished for its support of the German war effort. The whole French ruling class had collaborated, Stalin asserted, and their nation should not share in any of the benefits of victory. Roosevelt noted that Churchill thought France would quickly recover as a strong nation, but that he disagreed. Stalin responded that he agreed with FDR. Moreover, he was adamant that the Allies should not fight to restore France's empire in Indochina, and he repeated again his position that Paris must pay for its "criminal collaboration with Germany."[35]

Roosevelt used this opportunity to bring up his views on colonies and trusteeships. He stated that he was "100% in agreement with Marshal Stalin," and noted that "after 100 years of French rule in Indochina, the inhabitants were worse off than they had been before." Chiang Kai-shek had assured FDR that China had no interest in Indochina but that he agreed with the president that its people were not ready for independence. Roosevelt stated that the Philippines had not been ready for independence when the United States gained possession of the archipelago in 1898, but that due to U.S. guidance it would be granted its freedom after the war with Japan. He proposed that the Philippines served as a model for Indochina; a trusteeship set up after the war would have "the task of preparing the people for independence within a definite period of time, perhaps 20 to 30 years." Stalin completely agreed with the president's position. Roosevelt cautioned Stalin not to have this discussion with Churchill, particularly regarding India, since the British had no solution to the problem. It was better, FDR opined, to have that discussion at a later date.[36]

After forty-five minutes together, the two leaders were joined by Churchill for the first meeting of the Big Three. Roosevelt served as the chair of this first meeting and began by welcoming Stalin and the Russians "to the family circle," an allusion to the previous Anglo–American conferences, as these were meetings among friends. The president declared he "was confident that this meeting would be successful and that our three nations would not only work in close cooperation for the prosecution of the war but would also remain in close touch for generations to come."[37]

Before turning to what he called "the most important theater of the war—Europe," Roosevelt provided a summary of the war in the Pacific, where "United States forces were bearing the chief burden" and the largest part of its navy was operating. He did so to note that the United States was the only nation engaged on all fronts of the world war and to establish that it, too, was making enormous sacrifices in the battle against the Axis. The president pointed out the immense logistical difficulties presented by the size of the Pacific Ocean and the long distances of supply lines. Still, the United States was sinking more Japanese tonnage than Tokyo could replace, and this was aiding in the island hopping campaign to Japan's south and east. The other main objective of America was to keep China in the war to tie down a large amount of the enemy's army and resources. As a result, the United States would soon be in position to be able to continually bomb Japan's home islands as it continued to move forward to destroy Tokyo's forces.[38]

Regarding Europe, Roosevelt emphasized that the United States shared with its Allies "the desire to hasten in every way possible the day of victory." All of Washington's military efforts, and each of FDR's meetings with the British, "revolved around the question of relieving the German pressure on the Soviet front." It was "largely because of the difficulties of sea transport that it had not been possible until Quebec to set a date for the cross-channel operations." In an unexpected nod toward British preferences, FDR stated that one of the questions that needed to be considered was how the Allied forces in the Mediterranean could be deployed "in such a way as to bring the maximum aid to the Soviet armies on the Eastern front." Roosevelt noted that further operations in that theater could "involve a delay of one, two or three months in the large cross-channel operation" and that he and Churchill sought Stalin's input on this before making any final decision. The president did, however, emphasize that he did not wish to see a delay in the large cross-channel operation due to secondary operations.[39]

Stalin first responded regarding the Pacific war, noting that the Soviet government "welcomed the successes of the Anglo–American forces against the Japanese" and regretted that due to the fighting within Russia his nation was unable to join in the joint battle against the Japanese. He did state that "once Germany was finally defeated, it would then be possible to send the necessary reinforcements to Siberia" and at that point "we shall be able by our common front to beat Japan." This assurance that the Soviet Union would join the fighting against Japan once the Nazis were beaten was welcomed by Roosevelt and seen as an important step toward a quicker final victory in the Pacific. Turning to the question of the second front, Stalin indicated that he understood the value of the Mediterranean campaigns in freeing the waterway for Allied shipping, but that Italy, and by extension the Balkans, was not a proper place for an attack on Germany. "The best method," in the Soviet view, "was getting at the heart of Germany with an attack through northern or northwestern France and even through southern France." Stalin acknowledged "that this would be a very difficult operation since the Germans would fight like devils to prevent it."[40]

Churchill sought to defend the Allied operations and options in the Mediterranean by arguing that Overlord was still a long way off and that he did not want to leave Anglo-American forces idle for up to six months. Stalin refused to budge. He questioned the wisdom of dispersing Allied forces in different areas, declaring that he believed "it would be better to take overlord as the basis for all 1944 operations." Roosevelt sided with Stalin, noting that the question of timing was very important and that "nothing should be done to delay the carrying out of Overlord which might be necessary if any operations in the eastern Mediterranean were undertaken." While it was agreed that they would return to this discussion at subsequent meetings, there were no fundamental changes in any of the leaders' positions.[41] At the dinner Roosevelt hosted that evening, when the conversation turned to Germany, Roosevelt stated that the concept of a Reich had to be eliminated and "that the very word should be stricken from the language." All agreed that Germany would be disarmed, but Stalin insisted that it was not enough to eliminate the word, but that the "very Reich itself must be rendered impotent ever again to plunge the world into war." That was why he believed it was crucial that the Allies "retained in their hands the strategic positions necessary to prevent any recrudescence of German militarism." If they failed to do so, Germany would recover in fifteen to twenty years to again be a threat. The president concurred with Stalin's views, particularly regarding the approaches to the Baltic Sea, and each was open to an adjustment of Germany's and Poland's borders and the possible dismemberment of the German state. Churchill noted that he was not attached to any specific boundary between Poland and the USSR and that considerations "of Soviet security on their western frontiers was a governing factor."[42] In the only discordant note, Stalin questioned the appropriateness of the policy of unconditional surrender without the exact terms that would be imposed on Germany. He feared that leaving it imprecise would serve to unite Germans, whereas specific conditions would speed up the collapse of German resistance. There is no record of whether or not Roosevelt responded, but the policy was never changed.[43]

The meetings on the first day set out the key issues and decisions that guided the rest of the Tehran Conference. The Big Three discussed the vital importance of the second front in the west, the need for continued cooperation into the postwar period, the future of Europe, particularly postwar Germany, coordination against Japan and Soviet participation in the Pacific War, and the end of colonialism along with the establishment of trusteeships for former Japanese and French colonies. Roosevelt, Stalin, and Churchill would return to all of these issues over the next three days. The only other major topic of discussion was the president's vision for the United Nations and its role in maintaining the postwar peace, which he presented in a bilateral meeting the next day to the Soviet dictator.

In a move designed to facilitate better communication and coordination among the Big Three military operations, and to gain Soviet trust, Roosevelt began his second one-on-one meeting with Stalin by handing him four papers: one on Yugoslavia, one a request for U.S. planes from Great Britain to use air bases in the Soviet Union for the shuttle-bombing of Germany, and two reports on air operations and naval operations in the war against Japan. At that point, FDR raised the question of "a post war organization to preserve peace" based on the wartime United Nations. The president proceeded to outline his general plan. He stated that "there would be a large organization composed of some 35 members of the United Nations which would meet periodically at different places, discuss and make recommendations to a smaller body." It would report to "an executive committee composed of the Soviet Union, the United States, United Kingdom and China, together with two additional European states, one South American, one Near East, one Far Eastern country, and one British Dominion." Regarding the Executive Committee, Roosevelt noted that it "would deal with all non-military questions such as agriculture, food, health, and economic questions, as well as the setting up of an International Committee." Roosevelt noted that Churchill did not like this proposal because the British Empire only had two votes.[44]

Stalin inquired whether the organization was to be worldwide or European, and whether it would have the right to make decisions binding on the nations of the world. The president stated it would be worldwide and not regional. On the second question, FDR replied yes and no. "It could make recommendations for settling disputes with the hope that the nations concerned would be guided thereby, but that, for example, he did not believe the Congress of the United States would accept as binding a decision of such a body." Thus, there was to be a third organization, which he termed the "Four Policemen," the Soviet Union, the United States, Great Britain, and China, that would have the power to respond to any threat to the peace. He used the Ethiopian crisis as an example. Roosevelt noted that when Italy attacked in 1935, the only mechanism available to stop Rome was the League of Nations, an organization that required the whole body of nations to discuss the matter. The result was inaction. The president argued that had the structure of the four policemen existed, it would have been possible to prevent Italy from sending its troops to Africa as the great powers would have acted.[45]

The Soviet leader raised other questions about the structure; he thought the smaller nations of Europe would resent the power of the four policemen and questioned China having a say in European affairs. He suggested, as had Churchill, regional organizations with at least two of the Big Three powers as a member. Reflecting on the long battles with Congress prior to the war, the president doubted that it would agree to U.S. participation in exclusively regional arrangements that would require the use of American troops, noting that "it would take a terrible crisis such as at present before Congress would ever agree to that step." He supposed that any U.S. contribution outside of the Western Hemisphere, to assist England and the Soviet Union in stopping any future threat to the peace of Europe, would be limited to supplies and air. He went on to add that there were other methods to deal with challenges besides force. For example, if a threat arose "from a revolution or developments in a small country, it might be possible to apply the quarantine method, closing the frontiers of the countries in question and imposing embargoes." For more serious threats, collective security would act as the deterrent: "the four powers, acting as policemen," would send "an ultimatum to the nation in question and if refused, [it] would result in the immediate bombardment and possible invasion of that country."[46]

Stalin's final questions focused on Germany and China. He repeated the concerns he had expressed the previous day about safeguarding against the revival of Germany's power, pointing out how quickly it had recovered from the First World War, and his belief that unless specific action was taken Germany would recover again within fifteen to twenty years. He was, therefore, worried that what Roosevelt had outlined was not enough to prevent this. Specifically Stalin thought that parts of Germany needed to be occupied to ensure "that Germany would not embark on another course of aggression." He noted that he had similar concerns about Japan, and that he remained "dubious about the question of Chinese participation" given its weakness and ineffectiveness in fighting against the Japanese. Roosevelt stated "that he agreed 100% with Marshal Stalin" on the need to control Germany. This was why he believed the United Nations, through the four policemen, had to control strategic positions in the world "to prevent a revival of German and Japanese aggression." Regarding China, FDR said he was insistent on its participation as one of the four powers "not because he did not realize the weakness of China at present, but he was thinking farther into the future and that after all China was a nation of 400 million people, and it was better to have them as friends rather than as a potential source of trouble."[47]

The issue of the second front was settled over the next two days. Stalin consistently took the position "that overlord was the most important [military action] and nothing should be done to distract attention from that operation" and that the Soviet Union was willing to attack German forces at the same time to prevent any quick movement of divisions to the Western Front. Roosevelt continued to occupy a position in the middle, noting that "we are all agreed as to the importance of overlord and the only question was one of when." He favored the adherence to the date set in Quebec of the beginning of May, but the question remained whether or not to delay it a few months "for the sake of other operations in the Mediterranean." Churchill did not want "to neglect the great possibilities in the Mediterranean merely for the sake of avoiding a delay of a month or two." From the Soviet perspective, Churchill's position sounded eerily similar to promises made previously regarding a cross-channel invasion that were broken for other options. Stalin held to his position "that the operations in the Mediterranean have a value but they are really only diversions."[48]

It was finally agreed that Overlord was the primary military action for the next year, that it would be launched by June 1, and that the Red Army would "undertake offensive operations, and would demonstrate by its actions the value it places on this decision."[49] It was evident to all participants that a "historic understanding had been reached" and behind it was "the feeling that basic friendships had been established which there was every reason to believe would endure" among the Big Three. Moreover, there was a "strong feeling of optimism" based on the "realization that if the three nations went forward together, there was real hope for a better world future, and that their own most vital interests dictated such a policy."[50] After Tehran, there was no turning back from Overlord. The British had no more hope for other avenues through the Mediterranean; after two years of struggle with London, Washington was finally in complete control of Anglo–American military strategy. As FDR told Stimson upon his return from Tehran, "I have thus brought overlord back to you safe and sound."[51]

Roosevelt was also able to get Stalin's approval of the Cairo Communiqué; this would take away from Japan all territory it had conquered by violence, including Korea, and return the relevant areas to China or grant eventual independence for many of the former colonies of Japan, France, and other nations through the concept of trusteeships. In the process of these adjustments, it was also noted that Russia deserved access to warm water ports, and that these would be part of the final peace settlement.[52] Moreover, concerning the United Nations, Stalin informed Roosevelt on the last day that "he had come to agree with the President that it should be world-wide and not regional."[53]

Regarding the most nettlesome issues, Poland and Germany, all agreed that Poland's border would be moved to the west, and that the Soviet Union's border with Europe would be close to the line of 1941 to provide it greater security, but that final decisions on the governments in Warsaw and Berlin would be delayed until the end of the war. Roosevelt held a side meeting with Stalin to discuss the issue of Poland's postwar government. He told Stalin there would be "an election in 1944 and that while personally he did not wish to run again, if the war was still in progress, he might have to. He added that there were in the United States from six to seven million Americans of Polish extraction, and as a practical man, he did not wish to lose their vote." While he agreed with Stalin's views on borders and the need for a friendly Polish state, FDR hoped that Stalin "would understand that for political reasons outlined above, he could not participate in any decision here in Tehran or even next winter on this subject and that he could not publicly take part in any such arrangement at the present time."[54]

The spirit of the meetings was captured in some of the toasts given at the dinner on November 30. Stalin expressed his appreciation for the lend-lease aid provided to the Soviet Union, what he called the importance of "the machine" in the present war, and "his great admiration for the productive capacity of the United States." The Soviet leader noted that the United States would soon be producing 10,000 planes every month as compared with the 2,500 to 3,000 that the Soviet Union was able to produce and a similar number of planes produced monthly by Great Britain. "Without these planes from America the war would have been lost," Stalin emphasized. He also expressed "his gratitude and that of the Russian people for the great leadership of President Roosevelt which had developed the great production of war machines and made possible their delivery to Russia."[55]

Roosevelt responded that "these meetings at Teheran had raised all our hopes that the future would find a better world, an ordered world in which the ordinary citizen would be assured the possibility of peaceful toil and the just enjoyment of the fruits of his labors." He noted that "there has been discussion here tonight of our varying colors of political complexion." The president stated that he liked "to think of this in terms of the rainbow. In our country the rainbow is a symbol of good fortune and of hope. It has many varying colors, each individualistic, but blending into one glorious whole." The same was true for the United States, Great Britain, and the Soviet Union. "We have differing customs and philosophies and ways of life. . . . But we have proved here at Teheran that the varying ideals of our nations can come together in a harmonious whole, moving unitedly for the common good of ourselves and of the world. So as we leave this historic gathering, we can see in the sky, for the first time, that traditional symbol of hope, the rainbow."[56]

The final communiqué from the Tehran meeting stressed the unity of the Big Three in their determination to cooperate for victory and "in the peace that will follow." The planning and agreements reached were "guarantees that victory will be ours." Roosevelt, Churchill, and Stalin acknowledged the "supreme responsibility" the Big Three nations had to forge a peace "which will command the good will of the overwhelming mass of the peoples of the world and banish the scourge and terror of war for many generations," and they expressed their confidence in being able to do so through continued cooperation after the war. "We came here with hope and determination," the document concluded. "We leave here, friends in fact, in spirit, and in purpose."[57]

At the end of the meeting, Roosevelt confided to Hopkins that these final words were not mere platitudes to him, but represented how he truly felt. The president was certain now, as he put it, that Stalin was "getable" even if the Soviet dictator's methods were often coarse and his views on matters cynical. Every time Stalin saw that Soviet interests were being considered, and his nation's legitimate needs met by the Western nations, he proved cooperative. As the war ended and Stalin was fully convinced that the United States would respect Russia's needs, he would become a dependable ally.[58]

Upon his return to the United States on December 16, Roosevelt spoke to the crew of the battleship USS *Iowa* about Tehran's accomplishments. "One of the reasons I went abroad," the president stated, "was to try . . . to see that this war we are all engaged in shall not happen again. We have an idea—all of us, I think—that hereafter we have got to eliminate from the human race Nations like Germany and Japan" and their ability to wage war again. "We are making real progress," he continued, toward the goal: "when we win the war, to make the possibility of a future upsetting of our civilization an impossible thing. I don't say forever. None of us can look that far ahead. But I do say as long as any Americans and others who are alive today are still alive. That objective is worth fighting for."[59]

Roosevelt spoke to the nation on Christmas Eve, combining his annual Christmas greeting to the American people with a report on his meetings in Cairo and Tehran. His confidence about the course of the war and optimism about relations with the Soviet Union in the wake of their first meeting permeated his fireside chat. "On Christmas Eve this year," Roosevelt declared, "I can say to you that at last we may look forward into the future with real, substantial confidence that, however great the cost, 'peace on earth, good will toward men' can be and will be realized and insured. This year I can say that. Last year I could not do more than express a hope. Today I express a certainty—though the cost may be high and the time may be long." In 1943, "history has been made, and it is far better history for the whole human race than any that we have known, or even dared to hope for, in these tragic times through which we pass." In the meetings at Cairo and Tehran "we devoted ourselves not only to military matters; we devoted ourselves also to consideration of the future—to plans for the kind of world which alone can justify all the sacrifices of this war." These talks, FDR noted, provided him his first opportunity to meet Generalissimo Chiang Kai-shek and Marshal Stalin. "We came to the Conferences with faith in each other. But we needed the personal contact. And now we have supplemented faith with definite knowledge. It was well worth traveling thousands of miles over land and sea to bring about this personal meeting, and to gain the heartening assurance that we are absolutely agreed with one another on all the major objectives—and on the military means of attaining them."[60]

Regarding relations with the Soviet Union, Roosevelt said: "To use an American and somewhat ungrammatical colloquialism, I may say that I 'got along fine' with Marshal Stalin. He is a man who combines a tremendous, relentless determination with a stalwart good humor. I believe he is truly representative of the heart and soul of Russia; and I believe that we are going to get along very well with him and the Russian people—very well indeed." The Big Four, the United States, the United Kingdom, the Soviet Union, and China, represented over three-quarters of the world's population; and as long as they remained united in the pursuit of peace, there would be no possibility of a new aggressor rising that could start World War III. Peace would be maintained through collective security. As the president noted, "We are agreed that if force is necessary to keep international peace, international force will be applied for as long as it may be necessary."[61]

Thus, the ending of the war provided the second chance for the United States to take up its rightful place as a world leader and, in conjunction with the other members of the Grand Alliance, maintain the peace. Roosevelt reminded his audience that in 1918 they had "hoped that the militaristic philosophy of Germany had been crushed," but there had been no one to make sure that this was the case. "The well-intentioned but ill-fated experiments of former years did not work," the president noted, and "it is my hope that we will not try them again. No—that is putting it too weakly—it is my intention to do all that I humanly can as President and Commander in Chief to see to it that these tragic mistakes shall not be made again." The American people, the same as the vast majority of the people in the world, wanted a permanent peace. That meant the United States had to be willing to join with other nations once the war was over to make sure that peace was "as strongly enforced and as durable as mortal man can make it. If we are willing to fight for peace now, is it not good logic that we should use force if necessary, in the future, to keep the peace?" Washington, London, Moscow, and Beijing had all agreed that they "must be prepared to keep the peace by force." It was the only way to deter future aggression by Germany, Japan, and any other nation. This, for Roosevelt, was the best way to honor the message of peace of Christmas and extend it into the future.[62]

8

Victory, Roosevelt's Synthesis, and the Postwar World, 1944–1945

With the battle plans for 1944 confirmed and the military strategy for victory set, Roosevelt and his senior advisors turned more of their attention toward the postwar world. Throughout the war, Franklin D. Roosevelt had set forth two parallel strategies for postwar peace. The first was the continuation of the Grand Alliance. Best symbolized by the United Nations, this course sought continued cooperation between the Anglo–American powers and the Soviet Union, collective security provided by the great powers, and the incorporation of Russia into a cooperative world order led by the United States. The second strategy was based on American power and unilateral planning by the West. It was represented by the development of the atomic bomb by the United States and Great Britain, which Roosevelt refused to share with the Russians. Though Roosevelt desired that peace be made on the first course of action, he was willing to keep his options open and tack to another course if necessary. With his characteristic optimism, the president believed that time would allow him to unite his two courses and overcome the conflicts through personal diplomacy.

The Yalta Conference in February 1945 brought to the fore the tensions in Roosevelt's two-course approach. The Allies disagreed over the composition of Poland's government, and did not fully settle some of the crucial questions regarding the occupation of Germany and postwar reparations. Roosevelt, however, believed he had found a way forward. Unwilling to allow small nations to disrupt the work of the great powers, he was ready to compromise in the short term to keep intact his vision for postwar peace based on the Grand Alliance. In the common desire of the Big Three to prevent a resurgence of German power, in conjunction with Russia's needs for reconstruction, Roosevelt saw a firm basis for continued cooperation among the United States, the United Kingdom, and the Soviet Union. He, therefore, was convinced that concessions to Soviet security concerns in Eastern Europe were necessary in the short run until the West could demonstrate its good faith, through American economic aid in assisting Russia in its recovery and through guarantees against German remilitarization. The president understood that any truly representative government in Warsaw would be anti-Soviet. Ultimately, to demonstrate Washington's intentions to respect Soviet interests, Roosevelt accepted a vague compromise on Poland that allowed the Soviet-imposed government to maintain control without technically violating the agreement. Once Stalin was persuaded that the West did not intend to allow Germany to once again threaten Europe's peace, and that Soviet postwar needs and goals could be best met through cooperation, Moscow would no longer see the need to dominate its neighbors. The Soviet Union would find its security protected within the collective agreements of the United Nations Security Council.

Throughout 1944, FDR set out his vision for peace and prosperity. In his Annual Budget Message on January 10, 1944, the president explained that the goals of the war extended well beyond the defeat of the Axis nations. "Military victory is not enough," FDR declared. "We shall not have completed the defense of our way of life until we also solve the second task, the reconstruction of an economy in which everyone willing to work can find for himself a place in productive employment. The enemy, though beaten on the battlefields, may still rise in our midst if we fail in the task of reconstruction." The final end of the war "will be not only a cause for joy over an accomplishment but at the same time a challenge to another great undertaking."[1]

The next day, in his 1944 State of the Union message, the president elaborated on these points. Roosevelt noted that the "one supreme objective for the future . . . can be summed up in one word: Security." He explained that he was talking about not just "physical security" but also "economic security, social security, moral security—in a family of Nations." No one was content with "mere survival"; the sacrifices made by Americans and their allies "impose upon us all a sacred obligation to see to it that out of this war we and our children will gain something better."[2]

Roosevelt emphatically stated that he was determined "that this war shall not be followed by another interim which leads to new disaster—that we shall not repeat the tragic errors of ostrich isolationism." One of the big mistakes Wilson and the other leaders had made during the Great War was to put off any planning and meetings until after the fighting ended. There were no discussions or agreements prior to the peace conference in Paris. "The result was a peace which was not a peace. That was a mistake which we are not repeating in this war." From the Atlantic Charter and the Casablanca meeting with the British, to the Foreign Ministers Meeting in Moscow and Roosevelt's travels to Cairo and Tehran the previous November, the president noted, vital questions were being discussed and common goals and understandings of what was necessary for peace and prosperity were being achieved through candid conversations.[3]

Franklin Roosevelt held the firm conviction that peace depended on the continuation of the Grand Alliance into the postwar period, and that good relations with Russia were possible. Roosevelt saw two courses of action that the Soviet Union could follow in the postwar period. The first was a return to hostility toward the West, following the Leninist view of inevitable conflict and revolution. The other was for the Soviets to understand that they had a convergence of interests with the Anglo–American powers and that Soviet security and recovery from the war could best be achieved through cooperation with the United States and Great Britain. The president believed he could influence Moscow in the second direction.

The Combined Chiefs of Staff reflected the "consensus" on relations with Russia in a memorandum to Harry Hopkins. All were agreed that the United States needed the Soviet Red Army to defeat Germany. "No arguments are necessary," it stated, as the case was self-evident. Eventually, the memo noted, the United States "will also need [Russia] . . . to defeat Japan." The final point of consensus was that America needed the Soviet Union "as a real friend and customer in the post-war world." Once the war was won, the Joint Chiefs acknowledged, "Russia will be one of the three most powerful countries in the world." In light of this fact, "for the future peace of the world, we should be real friends so that we can help shape world events in such a way as to provide security and prosperity." Regarding the latter point, it was noted that "Russia's post-war needs for the products of America will be simply overwhelming." The Soviet Union would have to "rehabilitate her war losses in homes, industries, raw materials and farms." Thus, it was "evident that Soviet relationships are the most important to us of all countries, excepting only the United Kingdom." This made it essential to provide as much support as possible to the Soviet Union so that it could fight until Germany and Japan were beaten, and so that Moscow would "willingly join with us in establishing a sound peace and mutually beneficial relations in the post-war world." The United States, therefore, had to treat the Soviet Union as a world power, provide significant economic assistance for postwar reconstruction, and "agree to assist, in every proper and friendly way, to formulate a peace that will meet Russia's legitimate aspirations."[4]

In March 1944, Roosevelt again met with the journalist Forrest Davis, this time to discuss the Tehran Conference. A two-part series of articles appeared in the *Saturday Evening Post* in May, right before the D-Day landings in Normandy, entitled "What Really Happened at Teheran." For Roosevelt, this served as a means to continue his effort to gain support for what he termed his "great design" for the postwar world. Davis reported that after his first night in Iran, Roosevelt accepted Stalin's invitation to stay at the Russian embassy because the Russians feared the possibility of Nazi assassins sent to the area. It was certainly more convenient, as the U.S. legation was more than a mile away from the Soviet and British embassies, which were next to each other. This also made security arrangements much easier. Just as important to Roosevelt, the move was a means to demonstrate America's trust in its ally and for him to build a relationship with Stalin, which the president viewed as essential to achieving his goals. Davis informed his readers that Roosevelt and Stalin got along well during the meeting and shared their concerns and interests in good faith, and that each understood the other's positions. The president left confident that Stalin would cooperate toward peace after the war, and that the Soviet Union would join with its Atlantic Allies to maintain the Grand Alliance. The center of the "great design," he wrote, was Roosevelt's "tough-minded determination to enroll the Soviet Union as a sincere and willing collaborator in postwar settlements"; to create "a reciprocal spirit of confidence," Roosevelt wanted to show that he understood the Soviet view of issues relating to Germany and Eastern Europe and to demonstrate "his own complete good faith."[5]

Good relations with Moscow were clearly the focal point for FDR at Tehran. The president revealed to Davis that he had conducted "a seminar" for Stalin on the Good Neighbor Policy. Roosevelt explained how the abandonment of the Roosevelt Corollary and the embrace of collective security had led to improved relations of all nations in the Western Hemisphere, to everyone's benefit. Once small nations did not fear the power of the United States, cooperation followed, as evidenced by the simultaneous declarations of war on the Axis in December 1941 by so many Latin American nations. Roosevelt stated that he saw this as the proper policy for stronger nations that were dominant in their regions, as were the United States in the Western Hemisphere and the Soviet Union in Eastern Europe. In response, FDR noted, Stalin had stated directly that he had "no desire to own Europe." He faced enormous issues related to the reconstruction of the Soviet Union without taking on the burden of governing others. According to Davis, FDR felt that the discussion about the future of smaller nations "afforded him an opportunity to avow his trust in Stalin's word."[6]

Roosevelt held a couple of key assumptions as he pursued his postwar peace plans. First, he acknowledged that the Soviet Union was now a great power, one that had made enormous sacrifices and a critical contribution to the ultimate defeat of Nazi Germany. Second, the president believed Russia's interests could be reconciled with those of the United States and Great Britain. Peace and stability, along with reconstruction and recovery, were just as much in the best interests of the Soviets as they were the American and British, and Roosevelt believed that Stalin was willing to compromise and collaborate with him to obtain them. Because of that belief, the president was willing to accommodate what he saw as legitimate Soviet needs. The alternative, a postwar conflict with Russia and a Soviet Union at odds with its former allies—aggrieved, excluded, and with its historical mistrust of the West confirmed—was the recipe for another war.[7]

The structure for peace would be the United Nations. The president set out for Stalin the importance he saw in the continuation of the Grand Alliance through an international organization designed to ensure peace. For Roosevelt, the collaboration of the great powers was the only route to permanent peace. The United Nations would provide flexibility, while it would guarantee collective security, frequent communication, and a means for the four policemen to act to preserve order and protect small nations. The full details on the organization of the United Nations would be left for future meetings. What was crucial at Tehran was getting Stalin to agree to the fundamental idea. As Davis concluded, "The president, staking much on his good-neighbor diplomacy with Moscow has been undertaking to convince the Russians of two things: (a) the good faith of this country and (b) the need of the Soviet Union for a framework of peace which will remove distrust and the causes of war wherever possible." Roosevelt left Tehran convinced that he had established the necessary basis for continued cooperation toward his goals.[8]

On June 4, Rome finally fell to Allied forces. The timing appeared fortuitous as the D-Day invasion was planned for June 5; this allowed the White House to schedule a fireside chat for the next day without revealing what it hoped would be the main topic. Weather delayed the cross-channel invasion a day, leaving the Italian campaign as the only topic for the president's brief speech. "The first of the Axis capitals," Roosevelt informed the nation, "is now in our hands." The president noted that the achievement was part of a broader drive toward victory over Germany, with Allied troops prepared to strike elsewhere in Western Europe and the Red Army continuing to push the Germans back. Still, Roosevelt cautioned that "it would be unwise to inflate in our own minds the military importance of the capture of Rome. The German army had retreated over a thousand miles in the past year, from North Africa and through Italy, and from the outskirts of Moscow and Stalingrad, but they had not collapsed and remained a formidable foe." With the assault on the French coast, which was just beginning at the time he spoke on the other side of the Atlantic, on his mind, FDR warned that "we shall have to push through a long period of greater effort and fiercer fighting before we get into Germany itself." Given this, "victory still lies some distance ahead. That distance will be covered in due time—have no fear of that." But to achieve the unconditional surrender necessary to make sure Germany "will be unable to recommence world conquest a generation hence" would be costly and hard earned[9]

On June 6, the long-awaited second front in Europe was opened, as Allied forces stormed the northwest coast of France. Operation Overlord was the largest amphibious operation yet, at that point in the war. On the first day, 156,000 American, British, and Canadian troops landed on five beaches in Normandy. By June 11, 326,000 troops, 50,000 vehicles, and 100,000 tons of supplies had crossed the English Channel and all five beaches were secured. Roosevelt again spoke to the nation on the evening of June 6. Prior to his prepared remarks, FDR told the American public that while he was speaking the night before he had known that the D-Day assault was beginning "in another and greater operation," and that now as he spoke "it has come to pass with success thus far."[10]

The president's formal talk was delivered as a prayer. "Almighty God," Roosevelt began. "Our sons, pride of our nation, this day have set upon a mighty endeavor, a struggle to preserve our Republic, our religion, and our civilization, and to set free a suffering humanity. Lead them straight and true; give strength to their arms, stoutness to their hearts, steadfastness to their faith." The task would be hard because the enemy was strong and might deliver defeats, but with God's blessings "and by Thy grace, and the righteousness of our cause, our sons will triumph." With the enemy seeking the domination and destruction of others, the contrast between adversaries was clear. American forces were "men lately drawn from the ways of peace. They fight not for the lust of conquest. They fight to end conquest. They fight to liberate. They fight to let justice arise, and tolerance and good will among all Thy people. They yearn but for the end of battle, for their return to the haven of home."[11]

Many had counseled the president to ask for a single day of prayer from the whole nation. Roosevelt noted that because the road to Berlin was long, he was asking the American people to "devote themselves in continuance of prayer" so that "our hearts be stout, to wait out the long travail, to bear sorrows that may come, to impart our courage unto our sons wheresoever they may be." The president concluded by stating: "With Thy blessing, we shall prevail over the unholy forces of our enemy. Help us to conquer the apostles of greed and racial arrogancies. Lead us to the saving of our country, and with our sister nations into a world unity that will spell a sure peace—a peace invulnerable to the schemings of unworthy men. And a peace that will let all men live in freedom, reaping the just rewards of their honest toil. Thy will be done, Almighty God. amen."[12]

The next day, the president met with Stanislaw Mikolajczyk, the head of the exiled Polish government in London. All of the different parts of policy and postwar planning were now converging, and concrete decisions would soon have to be made about the future of Europe. Roosevelt had already decided that peace depended on good relations with the Soviet Union and demonstrating to Moscow that the West understood its security and reconstruction needs. For the Soviets, a friendly Poland was essential; thus, the president's focus in the meeting was the need for Poland to cooperate with Russia after the war. In his dinner toast, FDR stated that he and Mikolajczyk had had a "very frank talk" about the future of Poland, noting that in both their lifetimes "we have seen the rebirth. In my boyhood and his, there was no independent Poland." Although the Polish state would be restored after the war, historical borders would not determine its extent; rather, Roosevelt stated, "We have got to do the practical thing." He said that postwar Poland would be free and democratic, and that "steps will be taken by which the people of Poland and the very large Nation that lies to the East will become not merely good neighbors—that is an essential—but also two Nations . . . that will be able to work out a mutual economic system by which there will be complete independence on the part of Poland." Roosevelt noted that Stalin had assured him at Tehran that he wanted Poland to be a "completely independent Nation" after the war.[13]

As he wrote Stalin ten days later, the president was confident he had delivered his message. He assured the Russian leader that "no specific plan or proposal in any way affecting Soviet-Polish relations was drawn up," but Roosevelt did want Stalin to know his views on Mikolajczyk. He impressed FDR "as a very sincere and reasonable man whose sole desire is to do what is best for his country. He is fully cognizant that the whole future of Poland depends on the establishment of good relations with the Soviet Union," and he was committed "to achieve that end." Roosevelt concluded by acknowledging that relations with Poland were "a matter which is of special concern" to the Soviet Union and that he was, therefore, seeking to keep Stalin informed about the talk and its content.[14]

Roosevelt spoke to the American people again on June 12 about the state of the war. While he knew the nation's attention was fixed on the English Channel and the beaches of France, FDR did not want the public to lose sight of the fact that American forces were "engaged on other battlefronts all over the world, and that no one front can be considered alone without its proper relation to all." The United States was "on the offensive all over the world—bringing the attack to our enemies." The original strategy of dealing with Europe first and defeating Germany was working, and while Tokyo still seemed a long way to go, once the European enemies were crushed "we can force the Japanese to unconditional surrender or national suicide much more rapidly than has been thought possible." Germany now had "her back against the wall—in fact three walls at once!" In the south, Rome was captured and the German hold on central Italy broken; in the east, "our gallant Soviet allies" had pushed the Nazis out of their territory and into Eastern Europe; and in the west, "the hammer blow which struck the coast of France" the past week was starting the liberation of Western Europe. Now that Allied forces had "a firm foothold" with fewer casualties than expected, General Eisenhower's forces were ready to meet any German counterattacks "with power and confidence" as the war in Europe entered its final phase, the complete defeat of Nazi tyranny.[15]

Within another month, Allied forces were advancing rapidly on all three fronts. The American and British forces continued to drive up the Italian peninsula, pushing the Germans north of Florence and driving toward the Po Valley. The Russian army had moved well into Poland and Lithuania, coming close to East Prussia. The Red Army was also now in Romania and was approaching Czechoslovakia, routing German forces across Eastern Europe. In France, the American Third Army had swept across the Brittany Peninsula and was advancing rapidly to the west, while the buildup of men and supplies proceeded at a quicker rate than anticipated: over one and a half million troops, along with supplies, weapons, and vehicles, had been moved across the English Channel in the six weeks since D-Day.

With success on the battlefields, Roosevelt turned his attention again to postwar concerns and the establishment of the multilateral institutions necessary to carry out his internationalist vision for peace. On June 15, the president set out the current draft of his thinking about the establishment of the United Nations in a statement released by the White House. The purpose of the United Nations was "to maintain peace and security and to assist the creation, through international cooperation, of conditions of stability and well-being necessary for peaceful and friendly relations among Nations." To do so, it had to have a representative body consisting of all nations and "broad responsibilities for promoting and facilitating international cooperation, through such agencies as may be found necessary, to consider and deal with the problems of world relations." It would include a council, to be "elected annually by the fully representative body of all Nations, which would include the four major Nations and a suitable number of other Nations. The council would concern itself with peaceful settlement of international disputes." This would be done through collective security and would become possible "once our present enemies are defeated and effective arrangements are made to prevent them from making war again." Roosevelt's statement was not as specific as his discussion with Churchill and Stalin at Tehran, and did not identify the Big Four as the permanent members of a Security Council; but it did provide the outline of the three bodies that would come to comprise the United Nations.[16]

A concurrent announcement by the administration noted that the Soviet Union, Great Britain, and China would be invited to a meeting to discuss the president's proposal. It convened at Dumbarton Oaks, in Washington, DC, on August 21 and lasted until October 7. Roosevelt spoke to the American, British, and Soviet delegations—the Chinese were not yet in attendance—on August 23 and made clear the importance he placed on the work to be done. The president hoped that "in planning for the peace that is to come we will arrive at the same good cooperation and unity of action as we have in the carrying on of the war." At the end of the fighting, "we have got to make not merely a peace, but a peace that will last." It had to be a "peace in which the larger Nations will work absolutely in unison in preventing war by force." The Grand Alliance had to be maintained and their nations "have to be friends, conferring all the time—the basis of getting to know each other—'putting their feet on the table.'"[17]

Roosevelt could not have been more pleased with the final outcome of the meeting; the proposed structure of the United Nations adhered closely to what he had already outlined. In accepting the plan produced at Dumbarton Oaks for further study, FDR pointed out that the delegates had made the primary purpose of the new organization "the maintenance of international peace and security and the creation of the conditions that make for peace." The actions of Nazi Germany and Imperial Japan demonstrated "the need for such an organization for peace." Unlike the end of the First World War, this time the nations of the world were determined to take actions so that no countries could again threaten their weaker neighbors and bring about war. The will of the peace-loving nations was that through collective security they would assure the world "that no other would-be aggressor or conqueror shall even get started." It was for this reason, FDR stated, that "from the very beginning of the war, and paralleling our military plans, we have begun to lay the foundations for the general organization for the maintenance of peace and security." Indeed, the "projected organization may be regarded as the keystone of the arch" for building peace.[18]

Prior to the meeting at Dumbarton Oaks, delegates from forty-four nations gathered at Bretton Woods, New Hampshire, from July 1 to July 22, 1944, for the United Nations Monetary and Fiscal Conference, to establish a new international monetary system and international bank for reconstruction and development. The conference was organized by the United States, and delegates were greeted by a welcoming message from Franklin Roosevelt.

The president noted that, while the war to liberate Europe was at its height, it was fitting that "the representatives of free men should gather to take counsel with one another respecting the shape of the future which we are to win." The war "has prodded us into the healthy habit of coming together in conference" to examine and solve crucial world problems. Problems already being successfully addressed included military matters, production and supplies, relief, and the distribution of food. These were, however, "essentially emergency matters," FDR stated. At Bretton Woods, the world would meet "for the first time to talk over proposals for an enduring program of future economic cooperation and peaceful progress." While it was "only one phase of the arrangements which must be made between nations to insure an orderly, harmonious world . . . it is a vital phase." Nothing was more important to the peace and health of the world than international finance and trade.[19]

"Commerce is the life blood of a free society," FDR declared. Referencing the trade blocs of the 1930s, the president stated that "we must see to it that the arteries which carry that blood stream are not clogged again, as they have been in the past, by artificial barriers created through senseless economic rivalries." "Economic diseases," he continued, "are highly communicable." Thus, the economic health of all nations "is a proper matter of concern to all its neighbors, near and distant." As good neighbors, they must reach decisions that would allow for an expanding world economy and rising living standards for all countries. Seeking to institutionalize the approach of the Good Neighbor Policy, President Roosevelt believed that the spirit of the discussions "will set a pattern of future friendly consultations among nations in their common interest" and prove that people of "different nationalities have learned how to adjust possible differences and how to work together as friends." Roosevelt concluded his message by noting that Bretton Woods was the crucial first step to a new postwar economic order and peace. "This conference will test our ability to cooperate in peace as we have in war." Its success was essential to guaranteeing that the sacrifices made in the war for a better world were not in vain.[20]

The final outcome was the establishment of the International Monetary Fund (IMF) and the International Bank for Reconstruction and Development, the World Bank, which was designed to help rebuild the world after World War II and stabilize world trade. Both the IMF and the World Bank were to be run through an international board of directors and a designated executive. Each director voted on behalf of the nation or nations it represented; the vote of the United States would count for twenty-seven percent of the votes for the bank and twenty-eight percent of votes for the fund. The International Bank for Reconstruction and Development was authorized to guarantee foreign loans or to make them directly and was created to give loans to European countries to help them rebuild after the devastation of World War II. Of its initial capitalization of $10 billion in U.S. currency, $3.175 billion was subscribed initially by the United States. The IMF asked for $8.8 billion in gold and U.S. currency, $2.75 billion to be supplied by the United States. The IMF was created to ensure that currencies would not be manipulated for financial gain. When countries ran out of normal supplies of foreign exchange, this fund would allow them to buy foreign currency at the agreed upon exchange rates. Additionally, both the IMF and the World Bank stabilized the dollar at $1 equal to 35 oz. of gold, and linked each foreign currency to gold. For every dollar put into the IMF, twenty-five percent had to be in gold; for the World Bank, ten percent had to be in gold. Thus, the United States would maintain the value of gold, which it had more of than the rest of the world, and also stabilize the U.S. dollar on world markets and make it the currency of international trade. Furthermore, the fund and the bank allowed governments to provide jobs through public expenditure. Therefore, the Bretton Woods agreement rested on the belief that to stabilize the world economy and promote prosperity, it was necessary to promote economic recovery, stabilize currencies, increase demand, and allow for the freest exchange of trade possible. These agreements were designed to prevent the economic storms that had plagued the United States and the world prior to World War II.

Roosevelt focused most of his discussions about foreign policy during the 1944 presidential campaign on the postwar world. In his announcement on July 11 that he would accept the nomination of his party if chosen, Roosevelt stressed that he was only doing so because of the war. "All that is within me cries out to go back to my home on the Hudson River." Unfortunately, "we of this generation chance to live in a day and hour when our Nation has been attacked, and when its future existence and the future existence of our chosen method of government are at stake." The first task at hand was to complete the victory over the Axis powers. "To win this war in such a way that there be no further world wars in the foreseeable future is our second objective."[21]

In his formal address to the Democratic Convention via radio from San Diego on July 20, the president repeated these points. He stated that his first goal was "to win the war—to win the war fast, to win it overpoweringly. Second, to form worldwide international organizations, and to arrange to use the armed forces of the sovereign Nations of the world to make another war impossible within the foreseeable future." Roosevelt was sure the "American people know that all Nations of the world—large and small—will have to play their appropriate part in keeping the peace by force, and in deciding peacefully the disputes which might lead to war." The attacks by Germany and Japan had conclusively demonstrated that all parts of the world were interconnected and that "oceans will no longer figure as greatly in our physical defense as they have in the past." The security of all Americans, whether they lived on the coasts or in states such as Oklahoma, was "being defended in Normandy and on Saipan." The United States, therefore, had to "take a leading part in the maintenance of peace and in the increase of trade among all the Nations of the world."[22]

Even in his Labor Day statement, FDR kept the focus on the future and the need for a continuation of the Grand Alliance to maintain the peace. "Once the forces of tyranny have been overcome," the Commander in Chief stated, "we shall be faced with difficult problems of transition from war to peace. There will be matters of international arrangements as well as questions of internal economic policy. What we do in both spheres will affect our success in attaining a durable world peace—a peace that will contribute to the progress of mankind, and will give to all who work and produce, an opportunity constantly to better their lives."[23] Peace and prosperity were intertwined and could only be secured through an internationalist foreign policy.

Soon after, Roosevelt traveled again to Quebec for a second meeting there with Winston Churchill. Here, too, the focus was on the postwar period and Germany. Secretary of War Stimson represented the prevailing thinking that the "essential basis of enduring peace must be economic."[24] The lessons of the failure at Versailles were evident: its agreements hampered reconstruction and failed to prevent "the rise of tariff barriers between the different states of Europe after the war." Germany would have to be punished and both the Nazi and militaristic elements of its government vanquished. As Stimson noted, "Germany had been so under the military clique, the militarist Prussians, that five times during a little over my lifetime she had been responsible for beginning an aggressive war in Europe." For the secretary of war, this "stamped her apart from the ordinary nation" and demanded punishment. Yet, the form of that punishment would determine the future of Europe and whether or not the United States was successful in creating a peaceful and prosperous postwar world. The harsh punishment needed to be political: war crimes trials for Nazi leaders, denazification, and the creation of a democratic German state. It could not take the form of punitive economic action that would cripple Germany and leave it dependent on other nations.[25]

In September, in contradiction to all the historical lessons from World War I, all the postwar planning conducted up to this point, and the agreements reached at Bretton Woods, Secretary of the Treasury Henry Morgenthau proposed a postwar plan based on the deindustrialization of Germany to punish it and prevent a future war. The Morgenthau Plan would have dismantled Germany's factories and transformed the Ruhr and the Saar into agrarian areas, making Germany dependent on other nations for many basic goods and leaving it incapable of producing weapons of war. When he found out about this plan, an appalled Stimson wrote Roosevelt, setting out the reasons he found it dangerous. Germany, the secretary of war argued, was the central nation upon which the "industrial and economic livelihood of Europe [was] based." Any effort to destroy it as an industrial nation would cause "great dislocation to the trade upon which Europe has lived." Germany's productive capacity was essential to the recovery of both Allied and enemy nations, after the destruction of the war and given the current economic conditions. The Morgenthau Plan would be a replay of 1919; it would "create tensions and resentments far outweighing any immediate advantage of security and would tend to obscure the guilt of the Nazis and the viciousness of their doctrines and acts." Those leaders had to be punished, and Nazism expunged from Germany, but "economic oppression" should not be part of America's postwar program. "Such methods," Stimson reminded the president "do not prevent wars; they tend to breed wars."[26]

Roosevelt's cabinet discussed the differences between Stimson and Morgenthau on September 6 and 9. At first, FDR sided with Stimson, noting that Great Britain would be in "sore straits after the war" and that German production could benefit it. Morgenthau countered this argument at the second meeting; he claimed that Germany was not vital to Europe's recovery and that, on the contrary, its production was replaceable by British industry and, thus, would be in competition with Great Britain and would damage England's economy. This claim that English industry could replace Germany's in the markets of Europe played directly to Roosevelt's known desire to aid England, especially as it would be losing its empire after the war.[27]

The president left for his meeting with Churchill in Quebec without resolving the matter. Morgenthau was called to Canada on September 13 to present his plan. Stimson responded by sending a new memorandum that summarized his objections to what he termed the Carthaginian proposal that ignored the lessons of the interwar period. He added to his argument the point that the secretary of the treasury's plan was impossible to carry out without a permanent Allied occupation of Germany, which would be an additional source of tension destined to bring about yet another war.[28] On September 15, Roosevelt and Churchill initialed a document that approved the fundamental aspects of the Morgenthau Plan. In order to punish Germany and prevent its rearmament, and "in accordance with justice," the nations it harmed "should be entitled to remove the machinery they require in order to repair the losses they have suffered." All of the industry "in the Ruhr and in the Saar would . . . be necessarily put out of action and closed down." As the final sentence stated, the goal of the program was to eliminate the war-making capacity of these regions and to look "forward to converting Germany into a country primarily agricultural and pastoral in its character."[29]

As Roosevelt returned to Hyde Park the next day, Stimson sent him a third memorandum via Harry Hopkins that again set out his strenuous objections to the Morgenthau Plan. The secretary of war knew FDR would not welcome another paper on the subject, but he insisted that it be given to the president. Roosevelt read it when Hopkins gave it to him and let Stimson know that he wanted to discuss the issue further with him. Word of the draconian policy toward Germany had already reached the press and was receiving broad criticism. The president called Stimson at his home in Huntington, New York, and told him he had "made a false step and was trying to work out of it." His motive was not, FDR said, to turn Germany into a pastoral nation, but to find a way to help an impoverished England acquire more business and markets in Europe.[30]

Roosevelt had acted hastily in approving the document based on the Morgenthau Plan. Stimson understood this, and, confident that FDR would find a way forward, he kept his criticisms of the policy and discussions with the president private, even after the information got leaked to the press. Roosevelt quickly began to tack away from the agreement. Churchill had joined Roosevelt at Hyde Park and was made aware of Roosevelt's reconsideration of his position. Neither the president nor his spokesmen ever publicly acknowledged reports that an agreement had been reached with Great Britain, and no mention of it appeared in any record of the Quebec meeting or any statement made about the conference.

As part of his effort to correct his course, Roosevelt and Stimson met the next week when both had returned to Washington from their respective homes in New York. The president again repeated that he did not intend to turn Germany into an agricultural nation. Stimson tersely responded, "Mr. President, I do not like you to dissemble to me," and read him the final line of the document he had approved in Quebec. The president was "frankly staggered"; he stated that he had "no idea how he could have initialed this" and that he had "evidently acted without much thought."[31] Roosevelt wrote Hull on September 29 that he saw no need for the administration to "sound out the British and Russian views on the treatment of German industry." The issue that concerned FDR was how "to keep Britain from going into complete bankruptcy at the end of the war." It was unfortunate, Roosevelt stated, that someone was "talking not only out of turn to the papers or on facts which are not fundamentally true." Contrary to these reports, "no one wants to make Germany a wholly agricultural nation again."[32]

The policy of the United States was, therefore, reset to its former course; it would be a tough policy toward Germany that centered on Allied occupation, putting Nazi leaders on trial for war crimes, demilitarization, denazification, economic recovery, and ultimately democratization. On September 29, the Department of State sent Roosevelt a memorandum outlining the important issues and decisions to be made about Germany. In a specific rebuke of the Morgenthau Plan, FDR responded that he did not like the idea of making "detailed plans for a country which we do not yet occupy." He fully agreed with the State Department on the demilitarization of Germany, a policy that was, "of course, correct," and with the dissolution of the Nazi Party. Moreover, he concurred that no decisions could be made on a possible partition of Germany until it was occupied and the situation could be evaluated and discussed by the Allies. He also affirmed the position that the postwar economic policy should be structured "to render Germany incapable of waging war" and to end its "economic domination of Europe"; but he said that the specifics were "dependent on what we and the Allies find when we get into Germany—and we are not there yet."[33]

After meeting with Acting Secretary of State Edward Stettinius on November 10—Hull having stepped down due to poor health—the State Department produced for the president a revised memorandum on the "Economic Treatment of Germany." The goals remained the same as in the earlier policy statements—demilitarization and the end of Germany's economic dominance in Europe. The current document made clear, however, that "a program of sweeping deindustrialization does not provide an adequate basis for sustained international security cooperation, nor does it provide a satisfactory alternative to such cooperation." A long-term program that imposed restraints on Germany's industrial output involved "the danger of generating serious, new rivalries in Europe and of weakening the basis for international security cooperation." Roosevelt responded that he was "determined to be tough with Germany," and that the current draft met that demand. Stettinius summarized all these points on November 22, noting that "Allied occupation policy should be *severe*" and that "an effective international security organization" was necessary "to keep Germany disarmed," but that it would be a mistake to "make Germany so weak that it will be impossible for her to recover." It would only breed resentment if the "country is left alone 'to stew in its own juice.'" The ultimate objective was "a German economy geared into a liberal world economy on the basis of efficient specialization."[34] President Roosevelt had successfully steered his policy out of the troubled waters caused by his action in Quebec and back on course with his overall approach to peace and prosperity after World War II.

The only other significant outcome from Roosevelt's meeting with Churchill came when the prime minister joined him at his home following the Quebec meeting. There they initialed the Hyde Park memorandum; it rejected a proposal to inform the world about the research on the atomic bomb "with a view to an international agreement regarding its control and use." Rather, the United States and Great Britain would continue to treat the work "as of the utmost secrecy" between the two nations. Not knowing exactly when a bomb would be produced, and sure that the war with Japan would last longer than the one with Germany, the two leaders agreed that "when a 'bomb' is finally available, it might perhaps, after mature consideration, be used against the Japanese, who should be warned that this bombardment will be repeated until they surrender." Moreover, the joint Anglo–American collaboration on atomic power "for military and commercial purposes should continue after the defeat of Japan" unless jointly terminated. Thus, the Anglo–American

Allies would continue to withhold knowledge about the Manhattan Project from the Soviets throughout the rest of the war.[35]

Roosevelt used his campaign speeches to update the American people on the progress of the war and his plans for the postwar world. The president was now confident a complete victory would be achieved over Germany in the next year and that it would prepare the way for peace and prosperity. In FDR's view, his two goals were inseparable: postwar prosperity could only be achieved and maintained if there was peace, and peace was only possible with American leadership in the world. He declared in his September 23 speech to the Teamsters, "I think that the victory of the American people and their allies in this war will be far more than a victory against Fascism and reaction and the dead hand of despotism of the past." It would be "a victory for democracy" and "an affirmation of the strength and power and vitality of government by the people as history has never before witnessed." Thus, the tasks at hand were to achieve complete victory as quickly as possible, establish the "international machinery to assure that the peace, once established, will not again be broken," and reconvert the economy from war production "to the purposes of peace."[36]

On October 5, Roosevelt felt compelled to remind voters that "this war for the preservation of our civilization is not won yet." Although Allied forces "under General Eisenhower have waged during the past four months one of the most brilliant campaigns in military history," which had brought his army to the border of Germany, and although American forces in the Pacific continued to advance and were now operating "more than five thousand miles west of Pearl Harbor," German and Japanese resistance remained determined. Nonetheless, Allied forces would not stop short of the final goal of victory and unconditional surrender. More importantly, the president continued, "nor will our goals have been achieved when the shooting stops." Returning soldiers should find a nation that was "stronger and more prosperous, and more deeply devoted to democracy, than ever before," with even greater opportunity for all. That would be possible with a continuation of the Grand Alliance to ensure peace after the war.[37]

On October 20, Roosevelt announced to the nation that American forces, supported by the most powerful air and naval forces employed in the Pacific War, had landed in the Philippines. "We promised to return; we *have* returned." The president was "glad to be back in the Philippines but we do not intend to stop there." This was another step on the way to Tokyo that would help cut Japan's lifelines to Southeast Asia and China and allow for even more destructive blows against its home islands. Before the war, Roosevelt noted, the United States trusted Japan and treated it as a "civilized neighbor." That trust was betrayed and "the price of the lesson was high. Now we are going to teach Japan her lesson." The United States would continue to liberate the people of Asia, and ultimately "we shall strangle the Black Dragon of Japanese militarism forever."[38] This good news provided the backdrop to the president's talk the next day in New York City to the Foreign Policy Association.

The speech represented Roosevelt's most extensive comments on foreign policy during the campaign. It had two key themes. The first was that Roosevelt had been correct about foreign policy since he took office in 1933 and that the policies he had pursued prior to the war had made possible the success of the United States in fighting in Europe and Asia. The other theme was that it was imperative that the United States seize its second chance for world leadership and that it do so in cooperation with its allies. Roosevelt began by noting that he had always believed "that enduring peace in the world has not a chance unless this Nation—our America—is willing to cooperate in winning it and maintaining it." In the Great War, the United States had only carried out half of that mandate. The war had been won, but "we failed to organize the kind of world in which future generations could live—with freedom. Opportunity knocks again." Indeed, FDR stated that "it was with recognition of that fact away back in 1933" that he set out "as the basis of our foreign relations, the Good Neighbor policy" of respecting equally the rights of other nations. It worked in the Western Hemisphere, Roosevelt declared, and "it is my conviction that this policy can be, and should be, made universal throughout the world."[39]

For these reasons, the United States was taking the lead in establishing a new world organization that would embody the ideals of the Good Neighbor Policy and collective security, to act to stop international lawlessness. It was "obvious that we cannot attain our great objectives by ourselves." Cooperation was imperative. "If we do not catch the international felon when we have our hands on him," Roosevelt implored his audience, "if we let him get away with his loot because the Town Council has not passed an ordinance authorizing his arrest, then we are *not* doing our share to prevent another world war." Establishing and maintaining peace would not be easy. "Indeed," FDR stated, "it will be as difficult and complex as any task as has ever faced any American administration." Nonetheless, Roosevelt had "unlimited faith that the task can be done." The president was as effusive in his praise as he was serious about the mission ahead. "I speak to the present generation of Americans with a reverent participation in its sorrows and in its hopes. No generation has undergone a greater test, or has met the test with a greater heroism and I think greater wisdom, and no generation has had a more exalted mission." It was now up to this generation of Americans to act for itself, "as a trustee for all those who fell in the last war—a part of their mission unfulfilled," and, ultimately, "it must act for the generations to come—that must be granted a heritage of peace." In taking up this challenge and "in embarking on the building of a world fellowship, we have set ourselves a long and arduous task, which will challenge our patience, our intelligence, our imagination, as well as our faith."[40]

On October 27, in his last extended remarks about the war during the campaign, Roosevelt spoke at Philadelphia's Shibe Park about the decisions he had made during the war and the victories achieved. The president reminded his audience that it was Navy Day, and that it was celebrated on this date because it was Theodore Roosevelt's birthday. The twenty-sixth president, his distant cousin stated, would be impressed by the American fleet, which was larger than all other naval forces combined. This included the former Japanese navy, which three days earlier had been routed by America's Third Fleet in the Battle of Leyte Gulf. Overall, in the last year, American forces "have participated in no fewer than twenty-seven different D-Days—twenty-seven different landings in force on enemy held soil." In the face of this record, the president noted that an unnamed "prominent Republican" had criticized his administration, claiming that there were not five civilians in it who had the respect of the public, and had described the administration as "'the most spectacular collection of incompetent people who ever held office.'" FDR noted that this was a serious but obviously ridiculous charge, and that he was proud of his appointments of Stimson, Knox, Admiral Leahy, General Marshall, Admiral King, and General Arnold as the leaders of America's forces. Moreover, the president stated that the only conclusion one could draw from the Republican description of his administration was that the United States must be losing the war. "If so, that will be news to most of us—and it will certainly be news to the Nazis and the Japs." Roosevelt countered that he preferred to base his claims on his administration's record of preparedness, noting that, for example, every battleship in Admiral Halsey's victorious Third Fleet had been authorized prior to the war and their construction had begun by 1940, and on the victories won over the nation's enemies.[41]

The day after his election to a fourth term in office, Roosevelt issued a statement designed to highlight the significance of the event. "For the first time in eighty years we have held a national election in the midst of a war," FDR noted. "What is really important is that after all the changes and vicissitudes of fourscore years, we have demonstrated to the world that democracy is a living, vital force, that our faith in American institutions is unshaken; that conscience and not force is the source of power in the government of man." "In that faith," he appealed to the American people, "let us unite to win the war and to achieve a lasting peace."[42]

At the outset of 1945, victory in Europe was in sight. The last German counteroffensive, the Battle of the Bulge, had been stunted, and Allied forces were again closing in on Germany. On January 6, 1945, Roosevelt delivered what turned out to be his last State of the Union message. Speaking on the radio to the nation, he was upbeat and confident that victory over the Nazis was assured. For that reason, most of his discussion on foreign policy was about the postwar period and the need for the United States "to stand together with the United Nations not for the war alone but for the victory for which the war is fought. It is not only a common danger which unites us, but a common hope." The Grand Alliance was more than an alliance of governments; it was an association of the world's people for peace. "Here, as in England; in England, as in Russia; in Russia, as in China; in France, and through the continent of Europe, and throughout the world; wherever men love freedom, the hope and purpose of the people are for peace—a peace that is durable and secure."[43]

There was still much fighting to be done, and the transition from fighting to peacetime would not be easy. "We delude ourselves," Roosevelt stated, "if we attempt to believe wishfully that all these problems can be solved overnight." Still, a firm foundation of multilateral international institutions and relationships based on the wartime alliance was being built. And, with the essential principles of the four freedoms and the Atlantic Charter serving as guideposts, peace could be made and maintained through the united determination of people and their governments, as they worked together, respected each other, and cooperated to resolve differences and problems. "In the future world the misuse of power, as implied in the term 'power politics,' must not be a controlling factor in international relations. That is the heart of the principles to which we have subscribed. In a democratic world, as in a democratic Nation, power must be linked with responsibility, and obliged to defend and justify itself within the framework of the general good." This was the key lesson learned from the failures of the First World War, and those failures could not be repeated. Now it was up to the United States to seize its second chance at world leadership, which would require taking up both political and economic responsibilities following the war. "In our disillusionment after the last war we gave up the hope of achieving a better peace because we had not the courage to fulfill our responsibilities in an admittedly imperfect world. We must not," FDR declared, "let that happen again, or we shall follow the same tragic road again—the road to a third world war. We can fulfill our responsibilities for maintaining the security of our own country only by exercising our power and our influence to achieve the principles in which we believe, and for which we have fought."[44]

Ultimately, Roosevelt concluded, "an enduring peace cannot be achieved without a strong America—strong in the social and economic sense as well as in the military sense." The United States must make a commitment that, after the battles were won, it would take up the necessary effort for peace; otherwise, the sacrifices of the American soldiers and "their magnificent fight will have been in vain if this war should end in the breaking of the unity of the United Nations. We need the continuing friendship of our Allies in this war. Indeed, that need is a matter of life and death. And we shall need that friendship in the peace."[45]

Due to the war, Roosevelt eschewed the normal ceremonies of a presidential inauguration. His goals were to spend only $2,000 of the $25,000 appropriated for the event and to save the time and effort of members of the armed forces. There was no elaborate ceremony in front of the Capitol Building, and no parade or parties. Instead, FDR delivered his Fourth Inaugural Address from the front of the White House. His brief comments were all on the war, the test it provided to democracy, and his hope for the future. As he had many times before, Roosevelt returned to the lessons he had learned from his headmaster at Groton, Endicott Peabody, to explain his view of history and optimism about the future. "I remember that my old schoolmaster, Dr. Peabody, said—in days that seemed to us then to be secure and untroubled, 'Things in life will not always run smoothly. Sometimes we will be rising toward the heights—then all will seem to reverse itself and start downward. The great fact to remember is that the trend of civilization itself is forever upward; that a line drawn through the middle of the peaks and the valleys of the centuries always has an upward trend.'"[46]

The key takeaway for President Roosevelt was that it was crucial to learn the correct lessons from the war, lessons that in 1945 came at great cost. "We have learned that we cannot live alone, at peace" Roosevelt declared; "that our own well-being is dependent on the well-being of other Nations, far away. . . . We have learned to be citizens of the world, members of the human community." Finally, he noted, "We have learned the simple truth, as Emerson said, that, 'The only way to have a friend is to be one.'" Thus, the United States had to take on the role of world leader. "We can gain no lasting peace if we approach it with suspicion and mistrust—or with fear," Roosevelt warned. "We can gain it only if we proceed with the understanding and the confidence and the courage which flow from conviction." He concluded by stating what he found obvious, that peace would come from living up to the principles and values that had guided the nation throughout the war. "The Almighty God has blessed our land in many ways. He has given our people stout hearts and strong arms with which to strike mighty blows for freedom and truth. He has given to our country a faith which has become the hope of all peoples in an anguished world."[47]

Planning for the second Big Three meeting at Yalta on February 4–11, 1945, began in September 1944. As victory in Europe came into view, Roosevelt's priorities were to reach a final agreement on policy toward Germany, secure Soviet entry into the war against Japan, and ensure Soviet cooperation in the United Nations as the centerpiece of his efforts to maintain the Grand Alliance and achieve postwar peace. In all three areas, the general parameters of the policies had been set out at Tehran and in other meetings. Now, they needed to be finalized so that the Allies were not working at cross-purposes.

In the run-up to the Yalta Conference, Poland was the most difficult issue. At the end of the year, the Soviet Union unilaterally recognized the Lublin Committee as the provisional government of Poland despite Roosevelt's direct appeals to Stalin to wait until Yalta to settle the issues of the government in Warsaw and Poland's postwar borders. Writing to Stalin on December 16, the president reiterated the American position that it "stands unequivocally for a strong, free, independent and democratic Poland." He also noted that while the United States would prefer to wait until the Big Three meeting to settle all territorial questions, Washington would not object if a border agreement was reached prior to Yalta among all the groups directly concerned. Roosevelt added to these well-known positions that he believed it was "of the highest importance that until the three of us can get together and thoroughly discuss this troublesome question" that no action be taken on establishing the Lublin Committee as the provisional government of Poland. Although the president noted that he did "fully appreciate" the Soviet Union's desire to clarify who had authority in Poland as the Red Army moved into that nation, he asked Stalin to understand the "great political implications" that recognizing the Lublin Poles would have on opinion in the West.[48]

In Marshal Stalin's reply on December 27, he represented his support for recognizing what he referred to as the Polish National Committee as being "especially important for the Allies and for the solution of our common task—the speeding of the defeat of Hitlerite Germany." Stalin depicted the London Poles as obstructionist and obstacles to victory, and not in any way representative of Poland. "For the Soviet Union, which is bearing the whole burden for the liberation of Poland . . . the question of relations with Poland under present conditions is the task of daily close and friendly relations with a power which has been stablished by the Polish people on its own soil." If the Polish Committee was to "transform itself into a Provisional Polish Government then, in view of the above-said, the Soviet Government will not have any serious ground for postponement of the question of its recognition." Finally, Stalin pointed out that not only was the Soviet Union doing all of the fighting in Poland but also its interests were greater than those of its Western Allies "because Poland is a border state with the Soviet Union and the problem of Poland is inseparable from the problem of security of the Soviet Union."[49]

Roosevelt repeated his objections in a December 30 message to Stalin, noting that he was "disturbed and deeply distressed" that the Soviet Union could not "hold in abeyance the question of Poland" until the meeting in Yalta. The president could see no inconvenience or problem that could be caused by a delay in recognition as "there was not suggestion in my request that you curtail your practical relations with the Lublin Committee nor any thought that you should deal with or accept the London Government in its present composition." "I had urged this delay," FDR explained, because he believed the Soviets "would realize how extremely unfortunate and even serious it would be at this period in the war in its effect on world opinion" should Russia recognize one government in Poland when the United States and Great Britain, along with the majority of the other United Nations, continued to formally recognize the Polish government in London. Furthermore, given that Germany still held most of Poland west of the Curzon Line, the proposed postwar eastern boundary of Poland, it was "an unquestioned truth that the people of Poland have had no opportunity to express themselves in regard to the Lublin Committee." Roosevelt agreed with Stalin that Mikolajczyk's departure from the London Poles had made the situation worse and had heightened the tensions between that group and Moscow. Mikolajczyk was, FDR believed, committed to "settling all points at issue between the Soviet Union and Poland" and was "the only Polish leader in sight who seems to offer the possibility of a genuine solution of the difficult and dangerous Polish question." This was all the more reason that the Soviet Union should delay. "I am more than ever convinced that when the three of us get together we can reach a solution of the Polish problem," Roosevelt assured Stalin, adding again that he could not see any negative impact on the Soviet Union in delaying for a month a decision.[50]

Roosevelt, while greatly disappointed by Stalin's rejection of his request and recognition of the Lublin Poles, nonetheless understood the Soviet Union's security concerns and views on Poland. It was evident Moscow was not going to allow the establishment of a democratic Poland that was independent from the Soviet Union. The president had pushed as hard as he could on the issue. His priority was the Grand Alliance, and FDR was not going to allow the disagreement over Poland to derail the Big Three meeting at Yalta. The war still had to be won, and there were the crucial issues of Germany, the war with Japan, and the United Nations to settle. Roosevelt would, therefore, tack in a new direction regarding Poland at Yalta to avoid a conflict with Russia.

President Roosevelt left the United States on January 22, 1945, aboard the USS *Quincy*, arriving in Malta on February 2. He and Churchill then flew the next day to Yalta for the first sessions on February 4. It is old news that the decisions reached at Yalta have been deliberately misrepresented and distorted over time by critics of the president to paint a picture in which Roosevelt was duped by Stalin, appeased Russia, and gave away Eastern Europe. None of these claims stand up against the evidence of what happened in the meetings and the compromises made by all participants. The record demonstrates that FDR had specific goals, was in full command of the issues, and was able to gain numerous concessions and agreements from Stalin related to Germany, the United Nations, and the war with Japan that greatly served American interests. Just as important to Roosevelt, the unity of the Big Three was maintained throughout the meeting.[51]

Concerning the final defeat of Germany, the Allies agreed to coordinate their military operations to bring an end to German resistance, and to establish zones of occupation and a German control commission to coordinate activities. It was also decided that France would have an occupation zone. Still, throughout most of the meeting, the Soviets strongly opposed allowing France to be part of the control commission; they ultimately yielded to the argument that it would be impossible to have any consistent policies throughout the zones if France was not included. Two other issues related to Germany were deferred: whether the country would be dismembered and whether the Allies would receive reparations from Germany after the war. Dismemberment had been part of the discussions among the Big Three going back to Tehran, but the issue quickly disappeared after Yalta. Occupation zones superseded the perceived need. Germany was going to lose territory, particularly in the East, but would not be disassembled into multiple states. Reparations was a different matter.

Throughout the Yalta Conference, the Russians raised the issue of reparations from Germany in the amount of $20 billion, with half going to the Soviet Union. The United States and Great Britain consistently expressed opposition to the idea, citing the negative consequences and postwar problems caused by the reparations required by the Treaty of Versailles. By the last day of the meeting the issue remained unresolved, and it was decided to refer it to an Inter-allied Commission to meet in Moscow for further discussion. Yet, that group would need guidance, and there was no area of overlap for a compromise proposal. At this juncture, Harry Hopkins gave Roosevelt a note that encouraged him to break the logjam. "The Russians have given in so much at this conference," Hopkins wrote, "that I don't think we should let them down. Let the British disagree if they want—and continue their disagreement at Moscow. Simply say it is all referred to the Reparations Commission with the minutes to show the British disagree about any mention of 10 billion." The president agreed and did so, and the decision on reparations was deferred without causing a serious rift between the Western Allies and the Soviets.[52]

Roosevelt considered the final agreements concerning the United Nations just as crucial as the decisions on Germany. In the discussion of the "World Organization" during the Third Plenary session on February 6, Roosevelt reminded his colleagues that the Tehran Declaration stated: "We recognize fully the supreme responsibility resting upon us and all the nations to make a peace which will command good will from the overwhelming masses of the peoples of the world." Thus, it was incumbent on them to compromise on this key issue to maintain the Grand Alliance. Roosevelt believed "that the unity of the Great Powers was one of our first aims" in deciding matters. "Should there unfortunately be any differences between the Great Powers, and there might well be, this fact would become fully known to the world."[53]

The biggest compromise was made by the Soviet Union, which yielded on its request that the powers on the Security Council be allowed to veto the discussion of items, not just actions. The Big Three also agreed that a final meeting to establish the United Nations would be held on April 25 in San Francisco, rather than waiting until the war was over to issue the call for nations to gather, as Great Britain desired. Finally, the United States switched its position and agreed to allow the Soviet Union three votes in the General Assembly, by including the Ukraine and Belarus as voting members, but only on the condition that the issue was put to the vote of the full assembly and with the Soviet Union's agreement that it would back giving the United States three votes should Washington make that request.[54]

Poland was the subject of the lengthiest discussions over the course of the conference and was the only issue that created real tensions. The Soviet Union held to its position that the Lublin Committee it had recognized was the legitimate government of Poland. The United States continued to oppose this, but the president's position reflected a fundamental contradiction in goals. On the one hand, Washington refused to recognize the Lublin Poles and sought to create a genuinely democratic state in Poland (as well as in all the other liberated nations of Europe). Roosevelt stated that he wanted "to see the creation of a representative government which could have the support of all the great powers" while representing the principal parties of that nation. On the other hand, FDR understood that the Soviets had security concerns regarding Poland and that there would have to be a government in Warsaw friendly toward Moscow. As part of his effort to continue to build trust, Roosevelt would assure Stalin over and over that he understood the Soviet Union's needs and that they would be best obtained through the continuation of the

Grand Alliance. Thus, while Roosevelt sought to create a democratic government in Poland, he noted that it was necessary to keep in mind one certain point: "that Poland should maintain the most friendly and co-operative relations with the Soviet Union."[55]

On February 6, Roosevelt wrote to Stalin after that day's discussion about Poland to express his frustration with the deadlock, in the hope of finding a compromise. He noted he was "greatly disturbed that the three great powers do not have a meeting of minds about the political setup of Poland." It undercut all they were doing to have the U.S. and the United Kingdom recognize one group and the USSR another. Still, FDR indicated his commitment to make sure that the issue of Poland did not create a fissure in the Grand Alliance. "I am determined that there shall be no breach between ourselves and the Soviet Union. Surely there is a way to reconcile our differences." The United States, he emphasized, would "never lend its support in any way to a provisional government in Poland that would be inimical to your interests," but it could not recognize the Lublin Government as currently constituted.[56] Stalin remained unmoved, remarking at a subsequent meeting that he did not understand the push for elections right away in Poland. The Soviet dictator noted that "he saw little difference between the position of de Gaulle [in France] and that of the Polish Provisional Government. Neither had been elected, and he could not say which one enjoyed the greatest degree of popularity—yet we all had dealt with de Gaulle and the Soviet Government concluded a treaty with him."[57]

The deadlock was broken by the American delegation through the "United States Proposal on Poland, February 8, 1945," and the "Declaration on Liberated Europe" that was submitted the next day. The American compromise called for the details on the future government in Warsaw to be worked out by the U.S., British, and Soviet Foreign Ministers meeting in Moscow with representatives of the main Polish parties to form a new provisional government based on broader representation. This new interim government "will pledge itself to the holding of free elections in Poland as soon as conditions permit" to create a constituent assembly to draft a new Polish constitution that would be the basis for the election of a permanent government in Warsaw. This was linked to the Declaration on Liberated Europe, in which the United States, the Soviet Union, and the United Kingdom agreed to assist all "peoples liberated from the domination of Nazi Germany and the peoples of the former Axis satellite states of Europe to solve by democratic means their pressing political and economic problems" in line with the principle from the Atlantic Charter to the right of self-determination and self-government. The two proposals were presented on February 9 and were endorsed by Roosevelt, Stalin, and Churchill. "We were now very near agreement," FDR stated, "and it was only a matter of drafting" the final language for the communiqué.[58]

In bilateral meetings with Stalin, Roosevelt addressed issues related to the war with Japan and postwar security in East Asia. This was not part of the official Yalta Conference, because Churchill was not included; however, although they were not announced with the other agreements due to the need for secrecy, Roosevelt's and Stalin's decisions on the war in the Pacific were equally as important as other arrangements made by the Big Three. The United States was eager to obtain a firm commitment from Russia that it would enter the war with Japan after the defeat of Germany. In February 1945, the Pacific War seemed far from over. By this time, Japanese naval losses were significant, and its air power was reduced to mainly kamikaze missions. Nonetheless, Japan still had a significant army in China, upwards of two million troops, in addition to the forces on its home islands. The United States had yet to take Iwo Jima or Okinawa, and the planned American attack on Japan itself was still nine months away—scheduled for November 1945—if all went well. The atomic bomb was still being developed, and no one knew for sure when it would be tested, much less ready for use. In that context, the participation of the Red Army was seen as vital in taking on Japan's forces in China and helping to shorten the war.

Stalin agreed to enter the war two or three months after the fall of Berlin. In turn, Roosevelt consented to the "restoration" of territory and rights that Russia had lost to Japan in the 1904–1905 Russo–Japanese War: a return of the southern half of Sakhalin Island, the use of Port Arthur as a naval base, the internationalization of Darien as a commercial port, and joint control, with China, of the Manchurian railway and the Chinese Eastern Railway. In addition, the Soviet Union would gain control of the Kuril Islands. Roosevelt also gained Stalin's approval of the idea to establish trusteeships over former colonies in Indochina—overriding Churchill's desire to see the area returned to France—and Korea. The two leaders concurred that Chiang Kai-shek should be leading China and that he had their support, while acknowledging that he needed new people around him to be successful.

On February 11, Churchill, Roosevelt, and Stalin released their "Joint Statement on the Crimea Conference." It began by noting that coordinated plans for the final defeat of Germany were in place to achieve the goals of total victory and unconditional surrender. "Nazi Germany is doomed," the statement declared; and, with it, German militarism would be destroyed to ensure "that Germany will never again be able to disturb the peace of the world." The mechanisms to ensure this would be the occupation of Germany—which would produce disarmament, denazification, and the trial of war criminals—and the establishment of the United Nations and its Security Council to oversee collective security. The most extensive and significant parts of the communiqué were the publication of the "Declaration on Liberated Europe" and the section on Poland. The three leaders pledged that in the rebuilding of Europe, the people liberated from Nazi occupation would be able "to creat[e] democratic institutions of their own choice." The Declaration on Liberated Europe stated that it was "the right of all peoples to choose the form of government under which they will live—the restoration of sovereign rights and self-government to those peoples who have been forcibly deprived of them by the aggressor nations." For Poland, the application of the Declaration on Liberated Europe meant the current provisional government would be "reorganized on a broader democratic basis with the inclusion of democratic leaders from Poland itself and from Poles abroad."[59]

The Joint Statement concluded with this section: "Unity for Peace as for War." The meeting, the Big Three stated, "reaffirmed our common determination to maintain and strengthen in the peace to come the unity of purpose and of action which has made victory possible." Incorporating Roosevelt's statement from the February 6 Plenary Meeting about the importance of the meeting, the leaders declared that "we believe that this is a sacred obligation which our Governments owe to our peoples and to all the peoples of the world." Only through a continuation of the Grand Alliance could the "highest aspiration of humanity be realized—a secure and lasting peace which will, in the words of the Atlantic Charter, 'afford assurance that all men in all the lands may live out their lives in freedom from fear and want.'" Victory and the establishment of the United Nations "will provide the greatest opportunity in all history to create in the years to come the essential conditions of such a peace."[60]

All of those close to Roosevelt who were at the meetings or who spoke to him right afterward agreed on how the president understood the meaning of Yalta. Commenting on his and President Roosevelt's sentiments at the end of the conference, Harry Hopkins said that the ideas in the final section of the

Joint Statement fully reflected their views and were what he and FDR had been talking about for so many years. "We were absolutely certain that we had won the first great victory for peace—and by 'we,' I mean *all* of us, the whole civilized human race. The Russians had proved that they could be reasonable and farseeing and there wasn't any doubt in the minds of the President or any of us that we could live with them and get along with them peacefully for as far into the future as any of us could imagine." Hopkins did add one qualifier: "I think we all had in our minds the reservation that we could not foretell what the results would be if anything should happen to Stalin. We felt sure that we could count on him to be reasonable and sensible and understanding—but we never could be sure who or what might be in back of him there in the Kremlin."[61]

In his memoir on Yalta, Secretary of State Stettinius captured Roosevelt's thinking at the time. "From my close association with Franklin D. Roosevelt, I know that he was primarily motivated by the great ideal of friendly co-operation among nations." "At the same time," Stettinius noted, "[Roosevelt] had no illusions about the dangers and difficulties of dealing with the Soviet Union. He emphasized many time that we must keep trying with patience and determination to get the Russians to realize that it was in their own selfish interest to win the confidence of the other countries of the world. We must help them see, he said, that co-operation with other nations was the only way they or we could have a peaceful world. If the Russians would acquire confidence in a world organization, the President was convinced that much could be accomplished." Roosevelt, of course, understood that this was not going to be easy, but the alternative was the danger of another war. "Although he knew that the winning of Russian confidence in a world organization would be difficult, and would take time and patience, peace was too vital a necessity not to make a supreme effort toward achieving this goal." As Stettinius accurately observed, Roosevelt had "a strong sense of history" and was sure that "no society was static." Given this, "he believed that the United States could do much, through firmness, patience, and understanding, over a period of time in dealing with the Soviet Union to influence its evolution away from dictatorship and tyranny," which the president was well aware was the nature of the Soviet regime, "in the direction of a free, tolerant, and peaceful society."[62]

This explained the president's comment to his chief of staff Admiral William Leahy regarding the Declaration on Liberated Europe and the agreement on Poland. Leahy told the president that he thought the arrangement was "so elastic that the Russians can stretch it all the way from Yalta to Washington without ever technically breaking it." Roosevelt reportedly replied, "I know, Bill, I know it. But it's the best I can do for Poland at this time."[63] Realizing he could not force a change in the Soviet Union's position, Roosevelt was just being realistic about what he could accomplish and what he should risk to do more. For FDR, it was worthwhile to establish a principle as an aspiration, one that could be worked toward regarding Poland, even if it did not change anything immediately. It would take time to establish the United Nations, occupy Germany, and begin the postwar reconstruction of Europe. As the Soviet Union's needs for security and recovery were met, Roosevelt was sure that its policies would start to change.

The day after the release of the Joint Statement from the Crimea, President Roosevelt sent a message to Congress to urge the adoption of the Bretton Woods agreements, which linked the just concluded Yalta meeting with the need to establish the International Monetary Fund and the International Bank for Reconstruction and Development. "As we dedicate our total efforts to the task of winning this war," the president wrote, "we must never lose sight of the fact that victory is not only an end in itself but, in a larger sense, victory offers us the means of achieving the goal of lasting peace and a better way of life." If the nations of the world were to succeed in peace as they had done in the war, "we must see that the institutions of peace rest firmly on the solid foundations of international political and economic cooperation." The keystone for political cooperation was the proposed United Nations and, for economic cooperation, the Bretton Woods institutions.[64]

The Allies would provide relief to all nations that needed it, but that was not the main job. As FDR noted, the key to economic recovery was reconstruction; in this, the United States could play its most important role in the world while also benefiting itself. Nations would need capital and markets. "Unless a means of financing is found . . . countries will be unable to restore their economies and, in desperation, will be forced to carry forward and intensify existing systems of discriminatory trade practices, restrictive exchange controls, competitive depreciation of currencies, and other forms of economic warfare." The stakes could not be higher, Roosevelt warned. "That would destroy all of our good hopes. We must move promptly to prevent its happening, and we must move on several fronts, including finance and trade." The nations of the world were economically interconnected, and no countries could produce all the goods they needed. It was, FDR declared, "time for the United States to take the lead in establishing the principle of economic cooperation as the foundation for expanded world trade."[65]

Roosevelt concluded by claiming that the decisions now being made would determine the future direction of the world and whether there would be peace or a return to chaos and conflict. "The point in history at which we stand is full of promise and of danger. The world will either move toward unity and widely shared prosperity or it will move apart into necessarily competitive economic blocs." The United States needed to lead the world "in favor of a more united and cooperating world. Whether we do so will determine, as far as it is in our power, the kind of lives our grandchildren can live."[66]

The combination of the Joint Declaration from the Yalta Conference and Roosevelt's submission to Congress of the legislation to enact the decisions from the Bretton Woods Conference completed the president's synthesis of his foreign policy. Roosevelt's grand strategy placed good relations with the Soviet Union at its center. Permanent peace was impossible without the maintenance of the Grand Alliance, and the president knew that the only way to accomplish that was to provide the Soviets with a stake in a stable world order that protected its primary postwar interests—security and reconstruction. And it was clear that there would be tensions. These stemmed from various sources: the brutal nature of the Soviet regime and its actions in Eastern Europe, Moscow's distrust of the West, and the divergent economic systems among the Allies. Still, FDR was convinced that the overriding shared interests in prevention of another war and recovery from the devastation caused by the Nazis could overcome these issues.

Postwar prosperity was just as vital in preventing conflict. Peace depended on rebuilding former enemies as well as reconstruction for the victims of aggression. The United States could not be prosperous over the long term without European and Japanese economic revival. This was the key to avoiding another victor's peace like that which marked the end of World War I. Roosevelt stated while on his way to Tehran that he felt like Aeneas, from Virgil's *Aeneid*, wandering the Mediterranean. While in Tunis with General Dwight Eisenhower, Roosevelt discussed Rome's destruction of Carthage and examined the site of that ancient city. The warnings of Aeneas's father, Anchises, to his son about power were clearly applicable to the decisions he faced; it was the duty of the enlightened victor, Anchises said, "To teach the ways of peace to those you conquer/to spare defeated peoples, tame the proud."[67] To avoid a Carthaginian peace, economic reconstruction and the Bretton Woods agreement were central to establishing a liberal, international economic system that could provide loans, credits, and assistance while integrating the economies of the world.

On his way home from Yalta, in a February 23 press conference held aboard the USS *Quincy*, the president wove in a final thread of his synthesis regarding the future of empires. Asked about French Indochina, Roosevelt stated that "for two whole years I have been terribly worried about Indo-China. I talked to Chiang Kai-shek in Cairo, Stalin in Teheran." They all agreed it "should not go back to the French, that they have been there over a hundred years and have done nothing about educating them, that for every dollar they have put in, they have taken out ten." The president said he asked Chiang: "'Do you want Indo-China?' He said, 'It's no help to us. We don't want it. They are not Chinese. They would not assimilate into the Chinese people.'" Given this, FDR suggested a trusteeship, modeled on the U.S. policy in the Philippines, to help the people of Indochina make the transition from colonialism to independence and, in Roosevelt's paternalistic words, to "educate them for self-government." Both leaders, he said, liked that idea. The British, however, balked. Churchill feared that "it might bust up their empire, because if the Indo-Chinese were to work together and eventually get their independence, the Burmese might do the same thing to England." China and Russia would cooperate with the United States. "As for the British, it would only make the British mad. Better to keep quiet just now." On matters regarding colonies, Roosevelt stated that Churchill "is mid-Victorian on all things like that." When a reporter noted that Churchill's views were "inconsistent with the policy of self-determination," and undercut the Atlantic Charter, FDR responded, "Yes, that is true." He further opined: "The Atlantic Charter is a beautiful idea. When it was drawn up, the situation was that England was about to lose the war. They needed hope, and it gave it to them." A reporter recalled the speech the prime minister made "about the fact that he was not made the Prime Minister of Great Britain to see the empire fall apart." "Dear old Winston," Roosevelt sighed, "will never learn on that point. He has made his specialty on that point. This is, of course, off the record."[68]

President Roosevelt went to Congress immediately upon his return from his fourteen-thousand-mile trip to Yalta and declared that "we have made a good start on the road to a world of peace." Here he set out the full scope of his Grand Strategy and how the course he had sailed throughout the war would lead to peace. The meeting had two main purposes: to complete the defeat of Germany as quickly as possible, and to establish plans for peace. At Tehran, he noted, the Big Three had set the framework for peace and the shape of the postwar world. The Crimea Conference had confirmed as well as added details that would "continue to build the foundation for an international accord that would bring order and security after the chaos of the war, that would give some assurance of lasting peace among the Nations of the world." Roosevelt noted that "I have never for an instant wavered in my belief that an agreement to insure world peace and security can be reached." Yalta had confirmed that position. All sides, FDR stated, had worked hard and in cooperation to reach decisions, and "at the end, on every point, unanimous agreement was reached."[69]

The first big decision was on the meaning of unconditional surrender for Germany: a temporary occupation by Great Britain, Russia, France, and the United States, with each controlling an administrative zone; an end to Nazism and "all its barbaric laws and institutions"; the trial of Nazi leaders as war criminals; the demilitarization of Germany and expunging of militarism from its society; and reparations for the damages done to other nations. "Our objective in handling Germany is simple—it is to secure the peace of the rest of the world now and in the future. Too much experience has shown that that objective is impossible if Germany is allowed to retain an ability to wage aggressive warfare." It was all enough to convince him "that there is not room enough on earth for German militarism and Christian decency." These actions would not harm the German people. Rather, they would spare them from another war similar to those waged by the Kaiser and Hitler.[70]

The second great achievement, "of equal importance with the military arrangements" according to Roosevelt, was that decisions had been made regarding the United Nations and other international organizations. He informed Congress and the American people that agreements regarding the Security Council would soon be announced, and that a conference of all nations would meet in San Francisco on April 25 to establish a "charter of organization under which the peace of the world will be preserved and the force of aggression permanently outlawed." The president noted that the Senate would have to approve the agreement, that members of that body had been continuously kept informed about the establishment of the United

Nations and the Security Council, and that the American delegation to the San Francisco Conference would be bipartisan, with an equal number of Democrats and Republicans and the Senate and the House of Representatives both represented at the meeting.[71]

"World peace is not a party question," FDR declared, "any more than is military victory." A structure for world peace was also not something that could be achieved by one nation alone. The Big Three agreed that during the transition phase to peace and the establishment of postwar governments, the "political and economic problems of any area liberated" from the Axis were their joint responsibility. Still, peace would only be accomplished through the cooperation of all the nations in the world and through the protection of each nation's rights. Moreover, although the postwar institutions would not, at first, be able to perfectly handle all of the problems facing the world, peace, "and it will be peace" Roosevelt declared, would be built on the "sound and just principles of the Atlantic Charter—on the concept of the dignity of the human being—and on the guarantees of tolerance and freedom of religious worship."[72]

This was the second chance for the United States to avoid the mistakes made at the end of World War I and to take up the duties and obligations of world leadership. "Responsibility for political conditions thousands of miles away," the president argued, "can no longer be avoided by this great Nation. Certainly, I do not want to live to see another war." Preventing this required active American involvement in creating a peaceful international order given that "the United States now exerts a tremendous influence in the cause of peace throughout the world." Yet, that influence would only be effective "if we are willing to continue to share in the responsibility for keeping the peace." Otherwise, FDR warned, "it will be our own tragic loss . . . if we were to shirk that responsibility." Ultimately, the "final decisions in these areas are going to be made jointly; and therefore they will often be a result of give-and-take compromise." None of the Big Three would get its way all of the time, but the president was "sure that under the agreements reached at Yalta, there will be a more stable political Europe than ever before."[73]

In addition to international political cooperation, postwar peace demanded economic cooperation, as set out in the agreements reached at the Bretton Woods Conference. It was imperative, Roosevelt insisted, that the United Nations assist the "liberated areas adequately to reconstruct their economy so that they are ready to resume their places in the world." The Nazis had stripped them of raw materials, tools, machines, and transportation and had "left the industry of these places stagnant and much of the agricultural areas . . . unproductive." This demanded action. The necessary assistance was not merely the provision of relief aid, but the economic recovery of nations. "It is in the national interest that all of us see to it that these liberated areas are again made self-supporting and productive so that they do not need continuous relief from us." For FDR, this was "an argument based on plain common sense."[74]

The most difficult decisions reached at the Crimea Conference related to Poland. From determining its postwar boundaries to choosing the government in Warsaw, the decisions were reached by compromise. The president stated that his goal was "to help create a strong, independent, and prosperous Nation" with a government "ultimately to be selected by the Polish people themselves." Roosevelt understood that the Polish question was the most vexing and the greatest "potential source of trouble in postwar Europe." He considered the solution an excellent example of the "joint action of the three major Allied powers in the liberated areas" as the leaders were determined to find common ground. "Steps were taken at Yalta to reorganize the existing Provisional Government" in Lublin "on a broader democratic basis, so as to include democratic leaders now in Poland and those abroad" that were part of the London Polish government. This arrangement was temporary but necessary as "Poland needs a temporary government in the worst way." Noting the strong Soviet influence and interest in this matter, FDR pointed out that "throughout history, Poland has been the corridor through which attacks on Russia have been made. Twice in this generation, Germany has struck at Russia through this corridor." Therefore, "to insure European security and world peace, a strong and independent Poland is necessary to prevent that from happening again." Given the circumstances, Roosevelt conceded, this was "the most hopeful agreement possible."[75]

Franklin Roosevelt wanted the nation to know that, while the Yalta Conference was only concerned with the war and problems in Europe, the war with Japan was not being overlooked. For the obvious reason of wartime security, the president did not discuss the agreements reached with Russia regarding the war in the Pacific. Nonetheless, FDR noted that plans had been made with the British to step up the attacks against Japan, and that American forces were moving ever closer toward Japan's home islands. Tokyo knew this better than anyone, he said, as the "Japanese war lords . . . have felt the force of our B-29's and our carrier planes; they have felt the naval might of the United States" and "know what it means to hear that 'The United States Marines have landed.'" Still, the road to Tokyo was going to be longer than the one to Berlin, and the fall of Hitler would not mean an end to the war against Japan. Roosevelt declared that "the unconditional surrender of Japan is as essential as the defeat of Germany. I say that advisedly, with the thought in mind that that is especially true if our plans for world peace are to succeed. For Japanese militarism must be wiped out as thoroughly as German militarism."[76]

The United States was now committed to providing stability and security in East Asia. Since the beginning of the war, American policy toward postwar Japan had been similar to its policy toward Germany. America would demilitarize Japan, remove its ruling class from power, and prevent it from threatening its neighbors again. Central to this, Washington would seek to reform Japan, not punish it. The goal was to make Japan a democratic nation and to reposition its economy to integrate Japan into the liberal international economic order being established by the United States. That would ensure that Japan would be peaceful and would be able to recover from the war.[77] As Roosevelt stated after Yalta, "It seems obvious that we will be more or less responsible for security in all the Pacific waters." The only potential danger to the region "is from Japanese forces; and they must be prevented, in the same way Germany is prevented, from setting up a military force which would start off again on a chapter of aggression." Moreover, the U.S. commitment to the Philippines demanded that it "accept a mandate to keep security in that part of the world."[78]

In the conclusion to his speech to Congress, FDR praised the American men fighting abroad, stating that all Americans should be proud of them. "Against the most efficient professional soldiers and sailors and airmen of all history, our men stood and fought—and won." Now the nation had another chance "to see to it that the sons and grandsons of these gallant fighting men do not have to do it all over again in a few years." It was only twenty-five years earlier that "American fighting men looked to the statesmen of the world to finish the work of peace for which they fought and suffered. We failed them then. We cannot fail them again, and expect the world again to survive." For this reason, Roosevelt called Yalta "a turning point" in American history and the history of the world. "The Crimea Conference was a successful effort by the three leading Nations to find a common ground for peace." The Senate would soon have the opportunity to consider joining the

United Nations, "a great decision that will determine the fate of the United States—and of the world—for generations to come." Roosevelt was emphatic. "There can be no middle ground here. We shall have to take the responsibility for world collaboration, or we shall have to bear the responsibility for another world conflict."[79]

For reasons that are not clear, Roosevelt omitted any mention of the agreement that, if approved by the delegates in San Francisco, would potentially allow for three votes each by the Soviet Union and the United States in the United Nation's General Assembly. Inevitably, it was leaked to the press after FDR's return, with the focus on why he had assented to give Russia three votes. At an April 5 press conference, the president sought to set the record straight on what was agreed to and why. He began by noting the complete devastation of large areas of the Soviet Union, particularly in the Ukraine and Belarus, where, Stalin had informed him, all buildings and farm houses were leveled and millions left destitute. It was "very important from the point of view of humanity—and we thought, as a gesture, they ought to be given something as a result of this coming victory." That gesture was a vote in the U.N. Assembly. Furthermore, Roosevelt informed the press, it was not yet settled, but would be put to a vote; and, if it passed, the United States could also request three votes. In any event, FDR concluded, "it is not really of any great importance." The General Assembly, he said, "is an investigative body only. I told Stettinius to forget it. I am not awfully keen for three votes in the Assembly. It is the little fellow who needs the vote in the Assembly. This business about the number of votes in the Assembly does not make a great deal of difference" as that group did not decide on important matters.[80]

The final days of the war in Europe came with new tensions over Poland. By late March 1945, it was clear that the Soviet Union had no intention of allowing a complete reorganization of the Polish government and that it was content to just add a few people to the existing provisional regime in Warsaw. Roosevelt could not understand the Russians' obstinacy on this point as he had made it very clear that, while he could not recognize the old Lublin Polish government under a name, any reorganized government would have to be friendly toward Moscow and acceptable to the Soviet Union. His concern, as always, was that this issue might lead to larger problems. He wrote to Stalin on March 31 that "I cannot conceal from you the concern with which I view the development of events of mutual interest since our fruitful meeting at Yalta." The Big Three, he noted, had solved many problems and reached decisions that were widely hailed by the people of the world, "who saw in our ability to find a common basis of understanding the best pledge for a secure and peaceful world after the war." It was incumbent upon the great powers not to disappoint them. For this reason, FDR said, he was discouraged by the "lack of progress made in the carrying out, which the world expects, of the political decisions which we reached at the Conference particularly those relating to the Polish question." He could not reconcile the delay in making changes in Warsaw with the agreement that had been reached; and FDR insisted that "any solution which would result in the continuance of the present Warsaw regime would be unacceptable" and would lead people to "regard the Yalta agreement as *having failed*." The issue needed to be settled quickly or "all the difficulties and dangers to Allied unity which we had so much in mind in reaching our decision at the Crimea will face us in an even more acute form."[81]

Also in late March, as German forces were collapsing on all fronts, another incident threatened to drive a wedge into the Grand Alliance. The Soviets claimed that Allied officers were meeting with the Germans in Bern, Switzerland, to arrange the surrender of German troops in Italy, and that Soviet representatives were barred from the meeting. In a series of messages, Roosevelt assured Stalin that there had been no negotiations in Bern. The meeting that took place was solely to ascertain whether the German troops in Italy might surrender, FDR said; he added that if there were any negotiations regarding surrender, then Soviet officers would be welcomed, and that "in any surrender of the enemy army in Italy there could be no violation of our agreed principle of unconditional surrender."[82] Stalin wrote the president that his concern was not that a meeting was held to hasten the surrender of German troops, but that the Germans might be using the occasion to manipulate the Allies to allow them to move forces to the Soviet front. Without a Soviet officer present, the circumstances were "irritating" and created the "ground for distrust."[83]

Astonished that his first two messages had not resolved the problem, Roosevelt wrote Stalin on April 4; he repeated his assurance that no negotiations had taken place and sought to return their focus to the bigger issues at stake as the war ended. The president understood the damage such an issue could cause to the Grand Alliance as the war was getting close to an end.

Roosevelt wrote that he assumed that Stalin had "the same high confidence in my truthfulness and reliability that I have always had in yours," and that he fully appreciated the efforts of "your gallant army" and the "effect that your forces will have hereafter on the eventual collapse of the German resistance to our combined attacks." Given this, "it would be one of the great tragedies of history if at the very moment of the victory, now within our grasp, such distrust, such lack of faith should prejudice the entire undertaking after the colossal losses of life, material and treasure involved." Roosevelt concluded that he felt a "bitter resentment toward your informers . . . for such vile misrepresentation of my actions or those of my trusted subordinates."[84]

Stalin quickly responded to say that he had never questioned the "honesty and dependability" of Roosevelt or Churchill. It came down to a difference of opinion about the preliminary meeting held in Bern and who should have attended.[85] Roosevelt chose to accept the latest message from Stalin as an apology and to bring an end to the issue. His final message to the Russian leader thanked him for his "frank explanation of the Soviet point of view of the Bern incident which now appears to have faded into the past without having accomplished any useful purpose." With that resolved, the president returned to his greater concerns, the war and the overall state of relations between Washington and Moscow. "There must not, in any event," FDR wrote, "be mutual distrust and minor misunderstandings of this character should not arise in the future. I feel sure that when our armies make contact in Germany and join in a fully coordinated offensive the Nazi Armies will disintegrate."[86]

That same day, Roosevelt sent his final message to Churchill, in which he tied together the continuing tensions over Poland and the Bern incident. In a message he drafted personally, the president sought to keep Churchill from reacting too strongly to events in Poland. "I would minimize the general Soviet problem as much as possible because these problems, in one form or another, seem to arise every day and most of them straighten out as in the case of the Bern meeting." This was not the time to tack and change directions; the course had been properly set. Roosevelt advised the British prime minister, to whom he often referred as the Former Naval Person: "We must be firm, however, and our course thus far is correct."[87]

Franklin Roosevelt would not live to witness the victory in World War II that he had done so much to achieve. The president traveled to Warm Springs, Georgia, on March 29 to rest and prepare for his trip to San Francisco to speak to the delegates from around the world at the United Nations Conference. On the morning of April 12, 1945, FDR complained of a terrible headache. He died that afternoon at the age of sixty-three of a massive cerebral hemorrhage, with the fall of Berlin less than a month away. The next day, Harry Hopkins captured the thoughts of millions when he telegraphed his son Robert in France that "the news is a terrible shock." Noting that he had lost his "greatest friend," Hopkins stated that "it is of far greater importance that the poor and impoverished of the world have lost their greatest champion and the hope of a just peace has been grievously wounded."[88]

When Pearl Harbor was attacked, Roosevelt's optimistic assurances notwithstanding, there was no guarantee that the Grand Alliance would hold together and that Germany and Japan would be defeated. With the United States at its center, the Allies met the challenge. Following his telegraph to his son, Hopkins also telegraphed each of the other leaders of the Big Four. Churchill had written that they had lost "one of the most valiant champions of the causes for which we fight" and a great friend, a sentiment Hopkins agreed with, adding that the world had lost "its most outstanding champion of human freedom and justice." Stalin, as well, sent his sympathies to the American people, for which Hopkins thanked him, noting that "I feel that Russia has lost her greatest friend in America. The President was ever deeply impressed by your determination and confidence that the Nazi tyrants of the world will be driven from power forever."[89] To Chiang Kai-shek, Hopkins wrote that Roosevelt was "unswerving in his devotion and confidence in you and the Chinese people" and that those who remained in Washington would "do everything in our power to promote the cause of a free China."[90] The unspoken question behind Hopkins's messages was, could the Grand Alliance stay together? Roosevelt had set out his grand strategy and blueprint for his vision of postwar peace, but it would be up to the new president, Harry S. Truman, to oversee the final phases of the war and the efforts to establish a peace that would last.

Conclusion

Before he died, Franklin Roosevelt completed a Jefferson Day talk, to be broadcast over the radio on April 13, 1945, which set out his views for a peaceful postwar world order. The president's undelivered speech contained all of the main elements of his internationalist approach to foreign policy, optimism, and grand strategy for peace. Approaching the end of what he called "this greatest of all tests of men and the leaders of men, of nations and the community of nations" he was confident that the American people were united with him "in the resolve to make this work endure" into a permanent peace. "More than an end of this war," FDR wrote, he sought "an end to the beginnings of all wars. Yes, an end, forever, to this impractical, unrealistic settlement of the differences between governments by the mass killing of peoples."[1]

The president was well aware that there were plenty of skeptics who would say it could not be done. They would agree that, although "war is hell," it could never be eliminated, that war was the fate of the world, and, therefore, one should not even try to find a course forward to peace. Roosevelt rejected this view, what he called the "awe and adoration" of war, an activity that did not, in his opinion, deserve such emotions. He refused "to concede that we were put here on earth for no better purpose." War, he stated, was "stupidity—not plain stupidity, but enormous, brutal stupidity, a crime that makes no more sense to its perpetrator than it does to its victim." It would be impossible to eliminate all the tyrants who sought to conquer others and rule the earth, "but we can and we will stop these murderous hallucinations from reaching us." America now had a second chance to create a postwar peace in which "we can stop them from wrecking the lives of sane, sound, peace-loving, practical humanity. This we can do. This we will do." Moreover, it had to be done in cooperation with allies, and the "other peoples of the world will be with us every step of the way." Together, the Grand Alliance and the United Nations would maintain the peace.[2]

"I remember saying," FDR recalled, "once upon a time in the long, long ago when I was a freshman, that the only thing our people had to fear was fear itself. We were in fear then of economic collapse. We struck back boldly against that fear, and we overcame it." Now, as the nation moved against the "terrible scourge of war," it went "forward towards the greatest contribution that any generation of human beings can make in this world—the contribution of lasting peace." It could be done if Americans kept the faith in their values, institutions, and commitment to freedom and if they embraced the responsibilities and the necessity of world leadership. The only limit to realizing a lasting peace would be doubt. In the last words he wrote to the American people just before his death, Franklin D. Roosevelt made a final request of his fellow citizens: "Let us move forward with strong and active faith."[3]

The international crisis of the 1930s compelled changes in American foreign policy, and events demonstrated that Roosevelt made the correct decisions on the major issues confronting America and that his policies were the right ones to meet the challenges. By proceeding cautiously at first, and then more fervently in 1940 and 1941, Roosevelt was able to confront and undercut the logic of neutrality and the anti-interventionists without ever losing his popularity. The period between June 1940, when Roosevelt formed his war cabinet, and the passage of the Lend-Lease Act in March 1941 was the fulcrum for change, the critical time when the nation embraced Roosevelt's understanding of the crisis. The president secured the foundation for the buildup of the American military through the draft and the mobilization of the American economy for its massive effort to produce the weapons of war as the arsenal of democracy. Just as important, FDR set out the four freedoms, which expressed what the nation was defending and why it would fight if necessary.

Roosevelt was a skilled hand at the tiller as he guided the nation through the stormy seas and the challenges that faced the nation. When war came, the American people were ready to make the sacrifices necessary for victory over Germany and Japan, and were willing to take up the responsibility of being a great power. Displaying the same optimism, confidence, and navigational skills, FDR forged the Grand Alliance through lend-lease, unconditional surrender, and military victories and also by his willingness to cooperate and compromise with Stalin and Churchill.

In his final toast to President Roosevelt at Yalta, Stalin noted that the Soviet Union and the United Kingdom "had relatively simple decisions" in facing Germany as they were fighting to survive. The United States was not as immediately threatened, but was led by a man who was "the chief forger of the instruments which had lead [*sic*] to the mobilization of the world against Hitler." This was because the American president "had perhaps a broader conception of national interest" than other leaders. Roosevelt characteristically responded to Stalin's words by noting that his vision meant making sure that victory brought about changes that benefited all people. Fifty years ago, FDR stated, "there were vast areas of the world where people had little opportunity and no hope." Now, it was possible "to give every man, woman and child on this earth the possibility of security and wellbeing."[4]

Franklin Roosevelt saw World War II as the second chance for the United States to create a lasting peace, one based on the Grand Alliance, collective security, the Atlantic Charter, and the United Nations. The war was about more than just the defeat of German and Japanese aggression; it was a battle to build a world order that would produce peace and prosperity through a cooperative, multilateral international system. The postwar period, of course, did not turn out entirely as President Roosevelt desired. Certainly, he had sought to create international organizations designed to carry forward his policies. However, if there was one flaw in FDR's handling of foreign policy, it was his overreliance on personal diplomacy and his relationships with Stalin and Churchill to hold the Grand Alliance together as the war was coming to an end. Yet, in many ways, this was necessary. As Hopkins had learned in July 1941, the only way to get decisions from the Soviets was to deal directly with Stalin. Even though Roosevelt was unable to get Stalin to change his mind on Poland, FDR did persuade him to accept the Declaration on Liberated Europe, which helped entrench the concepts of the Atlantic Charter and established a principle that was important throughout the Cold War.

Moreover, as Secretary of State Stettinius wrote four years after the Yalta Conference, if the United States had not reached an agreement with the Soviet Union over Poland "the Russians still would have been in full possession of the territory." On the other hand a failure to reach an accord at the time "would have been a serious blow to the morale of the Allied world, already suffering from five years of war; it would have meant the prolongation of the German and Japanese wars; it would have prevented the establishment of the United Nations; and it would probably have led to other consequences incalculable in their tragedy for the world." The decision was part of a series of agreements reached by Roosevelt, Stalin, and Churchill that "speeded up the end of the war and greatly reduced American casualties." It was, Stettinius concluded, "a wise and courageous attempt by President Roosevelt . . . to set the world on the road to lasting peace."[5]

This was Roosevelt's great legacy, to envision a different world than the one that proceeded the war and to begin to establish the values, concepts, and institutions it would be built on. In doing so, he transformed American foreign policy and redefined how to provide for the security of the United States through cooperation with allies, collective security, and the involvement of the nation in international organizations. Roosevelt's approach was founded on his great vision; his confidence in democracy, the values of the United States, and the expansion of freedom; and his belief that all nations should respect the rights of others. Greater balance in the international system and the involvement of all countries would bring peace and prosperity. His grand strategy was sound; the four freedoms, the Atlantic Charter, the United Nations, the International Monetary Fund and the World Bank, the Nuremburg trials, and the concept of universal human rights, all became the cornerstones of the Western alliance system. The postwar world was, in numerous ways, Roosevelt's world.

Secretary of War Henry L. Stimson, a lifelong Republican born two years after the Civil War, whose father fought for the Union under President Abraham Lincoln, believed that Roosevelt was "without exception the best war President the United States has ever had."[6] This is correct, but too limited an assessment. Franklin Delano Roosevelt was the most important and most successful foreign policymaker in the nation's history.

Acknowledgments

It is an honor and a privilege to have my work in the series Studies in Conflict, Diplomacy, and Peace. I thank George Herring, Andrew Johns, and Kathryn Statler, the series editors, and Natalie O'Neal, for including my book. Natalie's editorial skill brought greater clarity and precision to the book, and it has been a pleasure to work with all of them.

The archivists at the Franklin D. Roosevelt Presidential Library have been unfailingly professional and helpful during all of my trips there over the years. In particular, Virginia Lewick and Patrick Fahy went out of their way in providing assistance for the research on this book. Dana Bronson and Lee Keene of Whitman College's Penrose Library provided assistance in finding documents and sources, and Dana helped me with the images and some last minute material. I greatly appreciate their knowledge and professionalism. Claire Singer of Reads Between the Lines provided expert copy editing.

This work would not be possible without the generous support from Whitman College that allowed me to travel to the various archives to conduct research and to employ, through the Lewis B. Perry Summer Research Scholarship Program, Cade Beck, Destiny Calahan, and David Young as research assistants. All three traveled with me at different times on research trips to the Roosevelt Library, where Cade worked on World War II and, in particular, the response to the Holocaust; Destiny examined American nationalism and support for Roosevelt's policies during World War II; and David assisted with materials on East Asia in the 1930s. My former student Gabrielle Westcott joined Cade and me at the Roosevelt Library and helped with identifying images for this book. Other students also provided assistance: Jessi Anderson did work with the Gallup Polls and read drafts of the first three chapters; Steven Aslin looked at the founding of the United Nations; Maura Flaherty helped me with research on public opinion; Emily Krank conducted research on Japanese American internment and read drafts of the first three chapters; Erin Lopez examined the 1944 presidential election campaign; Lucy Palmersheim provided assistance with the research on Lend-Lease, particularly in the *Congressional Record*; Jack Percival read a completed draft of the book and provided many useful suggestions for improvements; Sara Youmans did research on the Yalta Conference; and Joseph Zimmer provided assistance on the Bretton Woods Conference. I thank them all.

I first began studying the international crisis of the 1930s in a seminar with Carolyn "Rusti" Eisenberg; she has remained a good friend and colleague who continues to teach me. Lloyd Gardner directed my first research on Franklin Roosevelt, and his continued mentoring, friendship, and scholarship continue to inspire me and improve my work. Warren Kimball encouraged me to write this book, and I have greatly benefited from his support and vast knowledge of Franklin D. Roosevelt's foreign policy throughout the project.

I dedicate this book to my wife, Polly. Our regular visits together to the Roosevelt Presidential Library to take walks and discuss FDR's work are just another way that she enhances it all.

Notes

Preface

1. Forrest Davis, "What Really Happened at Teheran," *Saturday Evening Post,* May 13, 1944, 13.

2. Arthur Schlesinger Jr., "The Man of the Century," *American Heritage* (May/June 1994): 93. A slightly revised version of his original quote appeared in *Time 100,* April 13, 1998. It is the latter one that is on the wall at the Arthur M. Schlesinger Jr. Reading Room at the Franklin D. Roosevelt Presidential Library, Hyde Park, New York.

3. Robert Dallek, *Franklin D. Roosevelt and American Foreign Policy, 1932–1945* (New York: Oxford University Press, 1979).

4. See also Robert Divine, *Roosevelt & World War II* (Baltimore: Johns Hopkins University Press, 1969), and *The Reluctant Belligerent: American Entry into World War II,* 2nd ed. (New York: John Wiley & Sons, 1979).

Introduction

Epigraph: Euripides, *Euripides IV: Helen, The Phoenician Women, Orestes,* translation by Richard Lattimore and Elizabeth Wyckoff (Chicago: University of Chicago Press, 2013), 211:703–6.

1. Robert F. Cross, *Sailor in the White House* (Annapolis: Naval Institute Press, 2003), 43.

2. Gaddis Smith was the first historian to note that "FDR was a sailor, literally and metaphorically." Gaddis Smith, "Forty Months: Franklin D. Roosevelt as War Leader, 1941–1945," *Prologue* (Fall 1994): 132.

3. Frank Kingdon, *As FDR Said: A Treasury of His Speeches, Conversations, and Writings* (New York: Duell, Sloan and Pearce, 1950), 68.

4. Frank Freidel, *Franklin D. Roosevelt: A Rendezvous with Destiny* (Boston: Little, Brown and Company, 1990), 15.

5. Roger Daniels, *Franklin D. Roosevelt: Road to the New Deal, 1882–1939* (Urbana: University of Illinois Press, 2015), 23.

6. See Daniel M. Smith, *The Great Departure: The United States and World War I, 1914–1920* (New York: Wiley, 1965).

7. Brooke L. Blower, "From Isolationism to Neutrality: A New Framework for Understanding American Political Culture, 1919–1941," *Diplomatic History* 38, no. 2 (2014): 345–76.

8. David M. Kennedy, *Freedom from Fear: The American People in Depression and War, 1929–1945* (New York: Oxford University Press, 1999).

9. Samuel Rosenman, ed., *The Public Papers and Addresses of Franklin D. Roosevelt*, vol. 7 (New York: Random House, 1941), 239–42 (hereafter *PPA* followed by volume and page numbers).

10. Grace Tully Collection, Marguerite A. ("Missy") LeHand Papers, Box 10, "Draft Article about FDR and Working in the White House ca. 1937–1938," Franklin D. Roosevelt Presidential Library, Hyde Park, New York (hereafter FDRL).

11. James Tertius de Kay, *Roosevelt's Navy: The Education of a Warrior President, 1882–1920* (New York: Pegasus, 2012), 10.

12. Kenneth S. Davis, *FDR: The Beckoning of Destiny, 1882–1928* (New York: Random House, 1971), 167.

13. De Kay, *Roosevelt's Navy*, 11.

14. Franklin D. Roosevelt, *Whither Bound?* (Boston: Houghton Mifflin, 1926), 6–7.

15. Theodore Roosevelt, *The Naval War of 1812* (New York: G. P. Putnam's, 1882); Alfred Thayer Mahan, *The Influence of Sea Power on History 1660–1773* (Boston: Little, Brown, and Co., 1890); and Alfred Thayer Mahan, *The Interest of America in Sea Power, Present and Future* (Boston: Little, Brown, and Co., 1897).

16. Roosevelt was an avid collector. In addition to the materials he owned on naval history, he had an extensive stamp collection. Most of the stamp collection was sold, but the other documents are in the archives at the Roosevelt Presidential Library in Hyde Park, New York.

17. Warren F. Kimball, *The Juggler: Franklin Roosevelt as Wartime Statesman* (Princeton: Princeton University Press, 1991), 8, 4.

18. Arthur M. Schlesinger Jr., *The Age of Roosevelt: The Crisis of the Old Order, 1919–1933* (Boston: Houghton Mifflin, 1957), 322–23.

19. De Kay, *Roosevelt's Navy*, 15.

20. Frances Perkins, *The Roosevelt I Knew* (New York: Viking, 1946), 3–10.

21. *PPA*, 6:406–11.

22. George McJimsey, ed., *Documentary History of the Franklin D. Roosevelt Presidency*, vol. 2, *The Lend-Lease Act, December 1940-April 1941* (Bethesda, MD: University Publications of America, 2001), 71, 89–90 (hereafter *Documentary History of FDR* followed by volume number and document number); Susan Dunn, *A*

Blueprint for War: FDR and the Hundred Days that Mobilized America (New Haven: Yale University Press, 2018).

23. Cross, *Sailor in the White House*, 62.

24. Rexford Tugwell, *The Democratic Roosevelt: A Biography of Franklin D. Roosevelt* (Garden City, NY: Doubleday, 1957), 332.

1. Exceptionalism and Internationalism

1. Franklin D. Roosevelt, Address before the People's Forum, Troy, New York, March 3, 1912, Master Speech File (hereafter MSF), Series 1, FDRL.

2. Quoted in Davis, *FDR: Beckoning*, 233.

3. Kingdon, *As FDR Said*, 69–71.

4. Quoted in Davis, *FDR: Beckoning*, 305.

5. Franklin D. Roosevelt, "Montcalm's Victory and Its Lessons," September 13, 1913, MSF, Series 1, FDRL.

6. Franklin D. Roosevelt, "The Future of Our Navy," January 30, 1915, MSF, Series 1, FDRL; see also Speech to the First Women's National Defense Conference, November 15, 1915, MSF, Series 1, FDRL (emphasis in the original).

7. De Kay, *Roosevelt's Navy*, 128–30.

8. De Kay, *Roosevelt's Navy*, 151–55.

9. Frank Freidel, *Franklin D. Roosevelt: The Apprenticeship* (Boston: Little, Brown and Company, 1952), 253, 261, and 267.

10. Freidel, *Franklin D. Roosevelt: The Apprenticeship*, 268–69.

11. Daniels, *Franklin D. Roosevelt: Road to the New Deal, 1882–1939*, 35.

12. Franklin D. Roosevelt, "The Future of the Submarine," *North American Review* 202, no. 4 (1915): 508. FDR was also quick to understand the changes and impact of airpower.

13. Franklin D. Roosevelt, "Speech on the Submarine Menace," July 7, 1917, MSF, Series 1, FDRL.

14. Graham Cross, *The Diplomatic Education of Franklin D. Roosevelt, 1882–1933* (New York: Palgrave Macmillan, 2012), 56.

15. Franklin D. Roosevelt, "Address to the Democratic National Committee," May 29, 1919, MSF, Series 1, FDRL.

16. Franklin D. Roosevelt, "Address at Worcester Polytechnic Institute," June 25, 1919, MSF, Series 1, FDRL.

17. Franklin D. Roosevelt, "Speech at Syracuse, New York," July 4, 1919, MSF, Series 1, FDRL; see also "Speech at Utica, New York," September 15, 1919, MSF, Series 1, FDRL.

18. Cross, *The Diplomatic Education of Franklin D. Roosevelt*, 66.

19. Roosevelt, "Speech at Syracuse, New York."

20. Franklin D. Roosevelt, "Speech at Poughkeepsie, New York," July 18, 1919, MSF, Series 1, FDRL.

21. Franklin D. Roosevelt, "Acceptance of Vice Presidential Nomination," August 9, 1920, MSF, Series 1, FDRL.

22. Franklin D. Roosevelt, "Speech at Milwaukee, Wisconsin," August 12, 1920, MSF, Series 1, FDRL (emphasis in the original).

23. Franklin D. Roosevelt, "Speech at Milwaukee, Wisconsin," August 12, 1920, MSF, Series 1, FDRL (emphasis in the original).

24. Franklin D. Roosevelt, "End of Maine Campaign," September 11, 1920, MSF, Series 1, FDRL.

25. Franklin D. Roosevelt, "End of Maine Campaign," September 11, 1920, MSF, Series 1, FDRL.

26. Franklin D. Roosevelt, "End of Maine Campaign," September 11, 1920, MSF, Series 1, FDRL.

27. Franklin D. Roosevelt, "End of Maine Campaign," September 11, 1920, MSF, Series 1, FDRL.

28. Franklin D. Roosevelt, "End of Maine Campaign," September 11, 1920, MSF, Series 1, FDRL.

29. Franklin D. Roosevelt, "End of Maine Campaign," September 11, 1920, MSF, Series 1, FDRL.

30. Franklin D. Roosevelt, "Press Release from Helena, Montana," August 18, 1920, MSF, Series 1, FDRL; Franklin D. Roosevelt, "Campaign Speech, in Cincinnati, Ohio," October 16, 1920, MSF, Series 1, FDRL.

31. Davis, *FDR: Beckoning*, 655, 676–81.

32. Franklin D. Roosevelt, "Shall We Trust Japan?" *Asia* (July 1923): 475–78, 526–28.

33. Franklin D. Roosevelt, "Shall We Trust Japan?" *Asia* (July 1923): 475–78, 526–28.

34. Davis, *FDR: Beckoning*, 690.

35. "Plan to Preserve World Peace," in Eleanor Roosevelt, *This I Remember* (New York: Harper and Brothers, 1949), 353–66.

36. Roosevelt, *Whither Bound?*

37. *PPA*, 1:76.

38. Franklin D. Roosevelt, "Our Foreign Policy: A Democratic View," *Foreign Affairs* 6 (July 1, 1928): 573.

39. Franklin D. Roosevelt, "Our Foreign Policy: A Democratic View," *Foreign Affairs* 6 (July 1, 1928): 573–76.

40. Franklin D. Roosevelt, "Our Foreign Policy: A Democratic View," *Foreign Affairs* 6 (July 1, 1928): 576, 582–83, 585.

41. Franklin D. Roosevelt, "Our Foreign Policy: A Democratic View," *Foreign Affairs* 6 (July 1, 1928): 583–85.

42. Franklin D. Roosevelt, "Our Foreign Policy: A Democratic View," *Foreign Affairs* 6 (July 1, 1928): 586.

43. Franklin D. Roosevelt, "Problems of Adequate Markets for American Industry and Agriculture," February 2, 1932, MSF, Series 1, FDRL.

44. Franklin D. Roosevelt, "Problems of Adequate Markets for American Industry and Agriculture," February 2, 1932, MSF, Series 1, FDRL.

45. Franklin D. Roosevelt, "Problems of Adequate Markets for American Industry and Agriculture," February 2, 1932, MSF, Series 1, FDRL.

46. Franklin D. Roosevelt, Address before the Commonwealth Club of San Francisco, September 23, 1932, MSF, Series 1, FDRL.

47. Franklin D. Roosevelt, Address before the Commonwealth Club of San Francisco, September 23, 1932, MSF, Series 1, FDRL.

48. Franklin D. Roosevelt, Address before the Commonwealth Club of San Francisco, September 23, 1932, MSF, Series 1, FDRL.

49. Daniels, *Franklin D. Roosevelt: Road to the New Deal, 1882–1939*, 102.

2. Constructing an Internationalist Framework, 1933–1936

1. H. W. Brands, *Traitor to His Class* (New York: Doubleday, 2008), 268.

2. *PPA*, 2:1–4.

3. *PPA*, 2:1–4.

4. *PPA*, 2:1–4.

5. Stimson Diary, January 9, 1933; Stimson, "Memorandum of Conversation with Franklin D. Roosevelt," January 8, 1933, Henry L. Stimson Diaries, Sterling Library, Yale University (hereafter HLSD).

6. Henry L. Stimson, "The United States and the Other American Republics," February 6, 1931 (Washington, DC: Government Printing Office, 1931).

7. Welles to Roosevelt, January 20, 1928, Sumner Welles Papers (hereafter SWP), Major Correspondence, Box 148, FDRL (emphasis in the original); Roosevelt to Welles, February 24, 1928, SWP, Major Correspondence, Box 148, FDRL.

8. Welles Memorandum, no date (January 1928), SWP, Major Correspondence, Box 148, FDRL.

9. Roosevelt to Welles, March 7, 1928; Welles Memorandum, no date (January 1928); Welles to Roosevelt, March 15, 1928; Welles to Eleanor Roosevelt, October 15, 1928; and Eleanor Roosevelt to Welles, October 29, 1928, SWP, Major Correspondence, Box 148, FDRL.

10. "Uncle Sam as Good Neighbor," *New Republic* 77 (1933): 240.

11. Welles to Roosevelt, May 5, 1932 (emphasis in the original); Roosevelt to Welles, May 19, 1932, SWP, Major Correspondence, Box 148, FDRL.

12. On the continuation of support for right-wing dictators and the pendulum swings in this policy see David F. Schmitz, *Thank God They're On Our Side* (Chapel Hill: University of North Carolina Press, 1999).

13. *PPA*, 2:129–33.

14. *PPA*, 2:263–64.

15. *PPA*, 2:322–24.

16. *PPA*, 2:499–501.

17. *PPA*, 3:270–71.

18. Edgar B. Nixon, ed., *Franklin D. Roosevelt and Foreign Affairs*, vol. 1 (Cambridge, MA: Belknap Press of Harvard University Press, 1969), 527, 552–53 (hereafter *Franklin D. Roosevelt and Foreign Affairs* followed by volume and page numbers).

19. *Franklin D. Roosevelt and Foreign Affairs*, 1:560.

20. *Franklin D. Roosevelt and Foreign Affairs*, 1:560–62.

21. *PPA*, 5:72–74.

22. *PPA*, 5:597–602.

23. *PPA*, 5:604–10.

24. *PPA*, 5:615–17.

25. *Franklin D. Roosevelt and Foreign Affairs*, 3:560.

26. *PPA*, 5:641.

27. *PPA*, 7:411–13.

28. *PPA*, 2:129–33.

29. *PPA*, 2:167.

30. Cordell Hull, *Memoirs* (New York: Macmillan, 1948), 1:355, 81, 365.

31. *Franklin D. Roosevelt and Foreign Affairs*, 1:269, 265.

32. Engelbrecht, Helmuth Carol and Frank Cleary Hanighen, *Merchants of Death* (New York: Dodd, Mead & Company, 1934); Seldes, George, *Iron, Blood and Profit* (New York: Harper & Brothers, 1934).

33. David F. Schmitz, *The United States and Fascist Italy, 1922–1940* (Chapel Hill: University of North Carolina Press, 1988.

34. *PPA*, 4:345–46; Hull, *Memoirs*, 1:229–30.

35. Quoted in Robert Divine, *The Illusion of Neutrality* (Chicago: University of Chicago Press, 1962), 115.

36. Department of State, *Foreign Relations of the United States: Japan, 1931–1941*, 1:76 (hereafter *FRUS* followed by the year and volume).

37. Grew to Hull, 11 May 1933, and Hull to Roosevelt, 27 May 1933, President's Secretary File (hereafter PSF): Japan, Box 42, FDRL.

38. Grew to Hull, 11 May 1933, and Hull to Roosevelt, 27 May 1933, PSF: Japan, Box 42, FDRL.

39. Cross, *Sailor in the White House*, 133–34.

40. "Problem of Japanese-American Relations," 5 April 1934, PSF: Japan, Box 42, FDRL.

41. "Memorandum of Conversation between Secretary Hull and the Japanese Ambassador, Mr. Hirosi Saito," 16 May 1934, PSF: Japan, Box 42, FDRL.

42. "Memorandum of Conversation between Secretary Hull and the Japanese Ambassador, Mr. Hirosi Saito," 19 May 1934, PSF: Japan, Box 42, FDRL.

43. *FRUS* 1935, 3:831.

44. Grew to Hull, "Urge toward Expansion in Japan," 6 February 1935, and Hull to Roosevelt, 13 March 1935, PSF: Japan, Box 42, FDRL.

45. Grew to Hull, "Urge toward Expansion in Japan," 6 February 1935, and Hull to Roosevelt, 13 March 1935, PSF: Japan, Box 42, FDRL.

46. Grew to Hull, "Urge toward Expansion in Japan," 6 February 1935, and Hull to Roosevelt, 13 March 1935, PSF: Japan, Box 42, FDRL.

47. *PPA*, 4:442–43.

48. Roosevelt to Straus, 13 February 1936, PSF: Diplomatic, Box 42, FDRL.

49. Douglas Little, *Benevolent Neutrality* (Ithaca, NY: Cornell University Press, 1985), 69–70, 11. Alexander Kerensky had led the government in Russia between the fall of the czar and the coming to power of the Bolsheviks. See also Dominic Tierney, *FDR and the Spanish Civil War* (Durham, NC: Duke University Press, 2007).

50. Bullitt quoted in Little, *Malevolent Neutrality*, 201.

51. Phillips Diary, 4 August 1936, William Phillips Papers, Harvard University, Houghton Library (hereafter WPP).

3. International Crises, 1937–1940

1. *Franklin D. Roosevelt and Foreign Affairs*, 3:12–377–84.

2. *Franklin D. Roosevelt and Foreign Affairs*, 3:12–377–84.

3. *Franklin D. Roosevelt and Foreign Affairs*, 3:12–377–84.

4. *Franklin D. Roosevelt and Foreign Affairs*, 3:12–377–84.

5. *Franklin D. Roosevelt and Foreign Affairs*, 3:12–377–84.

6. *PPA*, 5:230–36.

7. Bernard Baruch, "Neutrality," *Current History* (June 1936): 44.

8. *FRUS* 1933, 2:328–30.

9. State Department, "Memorandum for the Honorable Norman H. Davis: A Contribution to the Peace Settlement," February 16, 1937, Box 24, Norman H. Davis Papers, Library of Congress, Washington, DC.

10. Roosevelt to Phillips, May 13, 1937, WPP.

11. *Franklin D. Roosevelt and Foreign Affairs*, 3:590.

12. Sumner Welles, "Trade Recovery through Reciprocal Trade Agreements," October 16, 1936, SWP, Box 194, FDRL.

13. Sumner Welles, "Present Aspects of World Peace," July 7, 1937, SWP, Box 194, FDRL.

14. Sumner Welles, "Our Foreign Policy and Peace," October 19, 1936, SWP, Box 194, FDRL.

15. Welles, "Present Aspects of World Peace," July 7, 1937, SWP, Box 194, FDRL.

16. Welles, "Present Aspects of World Peace," July 7, 1937, SWP, Box 194, FDRL.

17. Donald B. Schewe, ed., *Franklin D. Roosevelt and Foreign Affairs*, vol. 5 (New York: Garland Press, 1979) document 195 (hereafter Schewe, *Franklin D. Roosevelt and Foreign Affairs* followed by volume number and document number).

18. Elliot Roosevelt, ed., *FDR: His Personal Letters, 1928–1945*, 2 vol. (New York: Duell, Sloan and Pearce, 1950) 1: 680–81 (hereafter *FDR: His Personal Letters, 1928–1945* followed by volume and page number).

19. *FDR: His Personal Letters, 1928–1945*, 1:688–89.

20. Schewe, *Franklin D. Roosevelt and Foreign Affairs*, 6: doc. 373.

21. Dallek, *Franklin D. Roosevelt*, 147.

22. Welles, "Seven Decisions," SWP, Box 205, FDRL.

23. *Time*, October 18, 1937, 18.

24. Adolf A. Berle Diary, September 14, 1937, Adolf A. Berle Papers (hereafter ABP), Box 210, FDRL.

25. *PPA*, 6:359–67.

26. Welles, "Seven Decisions," SWP, Box 204, FDRL.

27. Schewe, *Franklin D. Roosevelt and Foreign Affairs*, 7: doc. 524.

28. Schewe, *Franklin D. Roosevelt and Foreign Affairs*, 7: doc. 524.

29. Schewe, *Franklin D. Roosevelt and Foreign Affairs*, 7: doc. 524.

30. Schewe, *Franklin D. Roosevelt and Foreign Affairs*, 7: doc. 524.

31. Schewe, *Franklin D. Roosevelt and Foreign Affairs*, 7: doc. 524.

32. Schewe, *Franklin D. Roosevelt and Foreign Affairs*, 7: doc. 530.

33. *PPA*, 6:429–38.

34. *FDR: His Personal Letters, 1928–1945*, 1:716–19.

35. Stimson to Roosevelt, 15 November 1937, President's Personal File (hereafter PPF), Box 20, FDRL.

36. Roosevelt to Hull, 22 November 1937; Roosevelt to Stimson, 24 November 1937, PPF, Box 20, FDRL.

37. Roosevelt to Hull, 13 December 1937, PSF, Box 42, FDRL.

38. *PPA*, 6:554–55.

39. Schewe, *Franklin D. Roosevelt and Foreign Affairs*, 7: doc. 686.

40. *FRUS* 1937, 1:655–70.

41. Sumner Welles, *Time for Decision* (New York: Harper and Brothers, 1950), 50, 65.

42. *FRUS* 1938, 1:115–20.

43. Schewe, *Franklin D. Roosevelt and Foreign Affairs*, 8: doc. 792.

44. Schewe, *Franklin D. Roosevelt and Foreign Affairs*, 8: doc. 792.

45. *FDR: His Personal Letters, 1928–1945*, 2:757–58.

46. *PPA*, 7:236–48.

47. *PPA*, 7:248–49.

48. Schewe, *Franklin D. Roosevelt and Foreign Affairs*, 7: doc. 1309.

49. *FDR: His Personal Letters, 1928–1945*, 2:810–11.

50. Quoted in John Morton Blum, *From the Morgenthau Diaries* (Boston: Houghton Mifflin, 1959), 524.

51. *PPA*, 7:563–66.

52. *PPA*, 7:596–601.

53. Schewe, *Franklin D. Roosevelt and Foreign Affairs*, 16: doc. 2011.

54. Dallek, *Franklin D. Roosevelt*, 173; Reynolds, *From Munich to Pearl Harbor*, 45–46. See also Max Paul Friedman, *Nazis and Good Neighbors: The United States Campaign against Germany in Latin America in World War II* (New York: Cambridge University Press, 2003), for the extent of Roosevelt's concerns about the Nazi threat in Latin America.

55. Schewe, *Franklin D. Roosevelt and Foreign Affairs*, 12: doc. 1403a.

56. Schewe, *Franklin D. Roosevelt and Foreign Affairs*, 12: doc. 1403a.

57. *Documentary History of FDR*, 7:107.

58. *Documentary History of FDR*, 7:107.

59. *PPA*, 8:1–12.

60. *PPA*, 8:1–12.

61. *PPA*, 8:1–12.

62. Schewe, *Franklin D. Roosevelt and Foreign Affairs*, 13: doc. 1565; Berle Diary, May 16, 1939, Box 210, ABP, FDRL.

63. Schewe, *Franklin D. Roosevelt and Foreign Affairs*, 16: doc. 1925.

64. *PPA*, 8:389–397.

65. *PPA*, 8:455–58, 460–64.

66. *PPA*, 8:512–25.

67. *PPA*, 8:xxiii–xl.

68. *PPA*, 8:xxiii–xl.

69. *PPA*, 8:xxiii–xl.

4. The Fulcrum of Roosevelt's Foreign Policy

1. *FDR: His Personal Letters, 1928–1945*, 2:967–68.

2. *PPA*, 9:1–10.

3. *PPA*, 9:1–10.

4. *PPA*, 9:10–24.

5. J. Simon Rofe, *Franklin Roosevelt's Foreign Policy and the Welles Mission* (New York: Palgrave Macmillan, 2007) is the most comprehensive examination of Sumner Welles's diplomatic mission.

6. Welles's report is in *FRUS*, 1940, 1:20–117; see also Sumner Welles, *The Time for Decision* (New York: Harper & Brothers, 1944).

7. *FRUS*, 1940, 2:691–98.

8. *PPA*, 9:198–212.

9. *PPA*, 9:198–212.

10. *PPA*, 9:198–212.

11. *PPA*, 9:230–40.

12. Stimson Diary, June 25, 1940, HLSD.

13. *PPA*, 9:286–91.

14. *PPA*, 9:391–407.

15. *FRUS* 1940, 4:586.

16. Stimson Diary, October 8, 1940, HLSD.

17. See Andrew Johnstone, *Against Immediate Evil: American Internationalists and the Four Freedoms on the Eve of World War II* (Ithaca, NY: Cornell University Press, 2014) for a complete examination of the main internationalists organizations in the United States prior to World War II.

18. *PPA*, 9:473–75, 499–510, 514–24.

19. *PPA*, 9:604–08.

20. *PPA*, 9:633–44 (emphasis in the original).

21. *PPA*, 9:633–44.

22. *PPA*, 9:633–44.

23. *PPA*, 9:663–72.

24. *PPA*, 9:663–72.

25. *PPA*, 9:663–72.

26. *The Gallup Poll: Public Opinion 1935–1971* (Wilmington, DE: Scholarly Resources, 1972), 262.

27. Warren F. Kimball, *The Most Unsordid Act: Lend Lease, 1939–1941* (Baltimore: Johns Hopkins University Press, 1969) provides the authoritative account of the passage of the bill.

28. *Congressional Record-Senate.* Vol. 87, pt. 1, 1109.

29. *Congressional Record-Senate.* Vol. 87, pt. 2, 1281–82.

30. Welles, "The United States and the World Crisis," January 30, 1941, SWP, Box 195, FDRL.

31. *PPA*, 10:51–52.

32. *PPA*, 10:60–69.

5. Internationalism and War

1. Hadley Cantril, ed., *Public Opinion, 1935–1946* (Princeton: Princeton University Press, 1951), 410; PSF: Public Opinion, Box 157, FDRL; *The Gallup Poll: Public Opinion, 1935–1971*, vol. 1, *1935–1948* (New York: Random House, 1972), 280; Adam J, Berinsky, Eleanor Neff Powell, Eric Schickler, and Ian Brett Yohai, "Public Opinion in the 1930s and the 1940s," *PS: Political Science and Politics* 44, no. 3 (July 2011): 515–20.

2. *PPA*, 8:xxxix–xl.

3. Kent Roberts Greenfield, *American Strategy in World War II: A Reconsideration* (Baltimore: Johns Hopkins University Press, 1963), 2, 49–53.

4. *PPA*, 9:645–50.

5. Stimson Diary, March 3, 1941, HLSD.

6. Daniels, *Franklin D. Roosevelt: The War Years, 1939–1945*, 150.

7. Greenfield, *American Strategy in World War II*, 5, 75.

8. *Complete Presidential Press Conferences of Franklin D. Roosevelt*, September 3, 1940, 182.

9. *PPA*, 9:460–67.

10. Lowell T. Young, "Franklin D. Roosevelt and the Expansion of the Monroe Doctrine," *North Dakota Quarterly* 42, no. 1 (Winter 1974): 29.

11. *PPA*, 10:96–99 (emphasis in the original).

12. Einstein to Roosevelt, August 2, 1939, PSF, Box 5, FDRL.

13. Stimson Diary, December 16, 1940, December 19, 1940, December 29, 1940, January 22, 1941, April 10, 1941, April 15, 1941, April 22, 1941, April 24, 1941, and April 25, 1941, HLSD.

14. *PPA*, 10:132–38.

15. Stimson Diary, May 23, 1941, HLSD.

16. Harold Ickes, *The Lowering Clouds, 1939–1941*, vol. 3, *The Secret Diary of Harold Ickes* (New York: Simon and Schuster, 1955), 523.

17. Berle Diary, May 26, 1941, Box 211, ABP, FDRL.

18. *PPA*, 10:194–95.

19. *PPA*, 10:181–94.

20. *PPA*, 10:181–94.

21. *PPA*, 10:181–94.

22. *PPA*, 10:255–57.

23. "Map of the North Atlantic with Franklin Roosevelt's Notes," July 11, 1941, in Robert Sherwood, *Roosevelt and Hopkins: An Intimate History* (New York: Harper & Brothers, 1948), 310.

24. Stimson to Roosevelt, June 23, 1941, Harry L. Hopkins Papers (hereafter HLHP), Sherwood Collection (hereafter SC), Box 305, FDRL.

25. Stimson to Roosevelt, June 23, 1941, HLHP, SC, Box 305, FDRL.

26. *FDR: His Personal Letters, 1928–1945*, 2:1177.

27. See Edward M. Bennett, *Franklin D. Roosevelt and the Search for Security: American-Soviet Relations, 1933–1939* (Wilmington, DE: Scholarly Resources, 1985); and *Franklin D. Roosevelt and the Search for Victory: American-Soviet Relations, 1939–1945* (Wilmington, DE: Scholarly Resources, 1990).

28. *PPA*, 9:85–94.

29. *FRUS: 1941*, 1:770–72.

30. Sherwood, *Roosevelt and Hopkins*, 318.

31. Sherwood, *Roosevelt and Hopkins*, 321–22.

32. *FRUS: 1941*, 1:815.

33. Ickes, *The Lowering Clouds, 1939–1941*, 592–93.

34. Roosevelt to Coy, August 2, 1941, PSF, Box 49, FDRL.

35. "Conference at the Kremlin on July 30, 1941," HLHP, SC, Box 306, FDRL.

36. "Conference Held on July 31, 1941"; Hopkins Memorandum with Stalin's Request in Russian, with Translation, HLHP, SC, Box 306, FDRL.

37. "Conference Held on July 31, 1941," Part 2, HLHP, SC, Box 306, FDRL.

38. Sherwood, *Roosevelt and Hopkins*, 345.

39. Roosevelt to Stimson, August 30, 1941, PSF, Box 84, FDRL.

40. Sherwood, *Roosevelt and Hopkins*, 410–18.

41. Sherwood, *Roosevelt and Hopkins*, 410–18 (emphasis in the original).

42. Memorandum of Conversation, "British-American Cooperation," August 11, 1941, SWP, Major Correspondence, Box 151, FDRL (emphasis in the original); "Record of Conversation Between the Prime Minister and the President, Augutst 11th, 1941," SWP, Major Correspondence, Box 151, FDRL.

43. "Record of Conversation Between the Prime Minister and the President, Augutst 11th, 1941," SWP, Major Correspondence, Box 151, FDRL.

44. *PPA*, 10:314–15.

45. Memorandum of Conversation, "British-American Cooperation," August 11, 1941, SWP, Major Correspondence, Box 151, FDRL (emphasis in the original).

46. *PPA*, 10:317–18.

47. *PPA*, 10:319–24.

48. Roosevelt to Stalin, October 30, 1941, PSF, Box 5, FDRL; Roosevelt to Stalin, October 31, 1041, PSF, Box 5, FDRL; Stalin to Roosevelt, November 4, 1941, PSF, Box 5, FDRL; Sherwood, *Roosevelt and Hopkins*, 386–96. See also, Stalin to Roosevelt, February 20, 1942 and Roosevelt to Stalin, February 23, 1942 PSF, Box 5, FDRL.

49. *PPA*, 10:325–36.

50. *PPA*, 10:384–92.

51. *PPA*, 10:384–92.

52. *PPA*, 10:406–11.

53. *PPA*, 10:438–44. Evidence suggests that British intelligence altered, if it did not create, the map. See Friedman, *Nazis and Good Neighbors*, 58, 251.

54. Stimson Diary, October 2, 1940, HLSD.

55. Grew to Roosevelt, December 14, 1940, PSF: CF Box 9, FDRL.

56. Roosevelt to Grew, January 21, 1941, PSF: CF Box 9, FDRL.

57. *PPA*, 10:277–83; See also Waldo Heinrichs, "FDR and the Entry into World War II," *Prologue* (Fall 1994): 119–29.

58. *FRUS*, 1941, 4:378–80.

59. *FRUS: Japan 1931–41,* 2:546–79.

60. Sherwood, *Roosevelt and Hopkins*, 410–18 (emphasis in the original).

61. Memorandum of Conference between Secretary Hull and Secretary Stimson, 6 October 1941; Stimson Diary, October 16 and 28, 1941, HLSD.

62. *FRUS*, 1941, 4:648–49.

63. Sherwood, *Roosevelt and Hopkins*, 431.

64. Stimson Diary, December 7, 1941, HLSD.

65. Sherwood, *Roosevelt and Hopkins*, 431.

66. Sherwood, *Roosevelt and Hopkins*, 441.

67. Sherwood, *Roosevelt and Hopkins*, 431.

68. *PPA*, 10:514–15.

69. *PPA*, 10:522–30.

70. *PPA*, 10:522–30.

6. Forging the Grand Alliance

1. Henry R. Luce, "The American Century," *Life*, February 17, 1941, 61–65.
2. Henry R. Luce, "The American Century," *Life*, February 17, 1941, 61–65.
3. *PPA*, 11:32–42.
4. *PPA*, 10:522–30.
5. Stimson, "Statement at Press Conference," April 17, 1942, HLSD.
6. *PPA*, 11:32–42, 61.
7. *FRUS: The Conferences at Cairo and Tehran, 1943* (Washington, DC: Government Printing Office, 1961), 584 (hereafter *FRUS: Tehran*).
8. Stimson to Roosevelt, December 20, 1941, HLSD; "Memorandum of Decisions at White House," December 21, 1941, HLSD.
9. *FRUS: Conferences at Washington, 1941–1942, and Casablanca, 1943* (Washington, DC: Government Printing Office, 1968), 50 (hereafter *FRUS: Casablanca*)
10. Sherwood, *Roosevelt and Hopkins*, 445.
11. A new theater of war, termed ABDA (American, British, Dutch, Australian), was also established in the Indian Ocean and waters around Australia, with the British General Sir Archibald Wavell placed in command and the American Admiral T. C. Hart under him.
12. *PPA*, 11:3–5.
13. *PPA*, 11:32–42.
14. "Facing the Japanese Issue Here," *Los Angeles Times*, January 28, 1942, A4.
15. Commission on Wartime Relocation and Internment of Civilians, 1981, Japanese-American Internment File, James Rowe Papers, FDRL, Box 9.
16. Japanese-American Internment File, Francis Biddle Papers, February 7, 1942, FDRL, Box 9.
17. Stimson Diary, February 3, 1942, February 10, 1942, and February 18, 1942, HLSD.
18. Executive Order 9066, February 19, 1942, Japanese-American Internment File, Official File 161, Box 1, FDRL.
19. *PPA*, 11:116.
20. *PPA*, 11:105–16.
21. *PPA*, 11:105–16.
22. *PPA*, 11:32–42.
23. *PPA*, 11:105–16.
24. Stimson Diary, March 5, 1942, HLSD.
25. Sherwood, *Roosevelt and Hopkins*, 519–20.
26. Stimson Diary, March 6, 1942, HLSD.
27. Stimson to Roosevelt, March 27, 1942, PSF, Box 84, FDRL.
28. Sherwood, *Roosevelt and Hopkins*, 528.
29. *PPA*, 11:227–38.
30. *PPA*, 11:227–38.

31. *The Gallup Poll: Public Opinion, 1935–1971*, vol. 1, *1935–1948* (New York: Random House, 1972), 334.

32. Helmut Norpath, *Unsurpassed: The Popular Appeal of Franklin Roosevelt* (New York: Oxford University Press, 2018).

33. *FRUS: 1942*, 3:575–78.

34. Sherwood, *Roosevelt and Hopkins*, 569–70.

35. *FRUS: 1942*, 3:593–94.

36. Hopkins to Winant, June 12, 1942, HLHP SC, Box 311, FDRL.

37. Stimson Diary, June 21, 1942, HLSD.

38. Stimson Diary, June 21, 1942, HLSD.

39. Sherwood, *Roosevelt and Hopkins*, 602–3.

40. Sherwood, *Roosevelt and Hopkins*, 603–5.

41. Bryce Wood, *The Making of the Good Neighbor Policy* (New York: Columbia University Press, 1961), 131.

42. Memorandum of "The President's Conversation at Luncheon with G.G.T and S.I.R." (Grace Tully and Samuel Rosenman), November 13, 1942, *F.D.R.: His Personal Letters, 1928–1945*, 2:1366–1367.

43. *FRUS: 1942*, 3:572–74.

44. *FRUS: 1942*, 3:572–74.

45. *PPA*, 11:330; see also 410.

46. Hopkins to Winant, October 25, 1943, HLHP, Box 218, FDRL.

47. Sherwood, *Roosevelt and Hopkins*, 622.

48. *PPA*, 11:368–77.

49. *PPA*, 11:468–70.

50. Stimson Diary, November 16, 1942, December 11, 1942, HLSD.

51. *PPA*, 11:485.

52. *PPA*, 12:21–34.

53. *PPA*, 12:21–34.

54. *FRUS: Casablanca*, 494.

55. *FRUS: Casablanca*, 505–14.

56. *FRUS: Casablanca*, 505–14.

57. Stimson Diary, January 30, 1943, HLSD.

58. Susan Butler, ed., *My Dear Mr. Stalin: The Complete Correspondence between Franklin D. Roosevelt and Joseph V. Stalin* (New Haven: Yale University Press, 2005), 116–18.

59. *FRUS: Casablanca*, 726–31.

60. *FRUS: Casablanca*, 847–49.

61. Sherwood, *Roosevelt and Hopkins*, 656.

62. Stimson Diary, May 17, 1943, HLSD.

63. Henry L. Stimson and McGeorge Bundy, *On Active Service in Peace and War* (New York: Harper and Brothers, 1947), 428.

64. Butler, ed., *My Dear Mr. Stalin*, 136–38.

65. Butler, ed., *My Dear Mr. Stalin*, 138–39.

7. Architect of Victory

1. Sherwood, *Roosevelt and Hopkins*, 715.

2. Sherwood, *Roosevelt and Hopkins*, 708–16.

3. Sherwood, *Roosevelt and Hopkins*, 708–16.

4. Sherwood, *Roosevelt and Hopkins*, 716–18.

5. Forrest Davis, "Roosevelt's World Blueprint," *Saturday Evening Post*, April 10, 1943, 20–21, 109–10.

6. Davis, "Roosevelt's World Blueprint," *Saturday Evening Post*, April 10, 1943, 20–21, 109–10.

7. Davis, "Roosevelt's World Blueprint," *Saturday Evening Post*, April 10, 1943, 20–21, 109–10.

8. Davis, "Roosevelt's World Blueprint," *Saturday Evening Post*, April 10, 1943, 20–21, 109–10.

9. Davis, "Roosevelt's World Blueprint," *Saturday Evening Post*, April 10, 1943, 20–21, 109–10.

10. Davis, "Roosevelt's World Blueprint," *Saturday Evening Post*, April 10, 1943, 20–21, 109–10.

11. *PPA*, 12:211–13, 238–41.

12. *PPA*, 12:571.

13. Richard Breitman and Allan J. Lichtman, *FDR and the Jews* (Cambridge, MA: The Belknap Press of Harvard University Press, 2013), 2.

14. David S. Wyman, *The Abandonment of the Jews: America and the Holocaust, 1941–1945* (New York: Pantheon Books, 1984), ix.

15. William D. Rubinstein, *The Myth of Rescue* (London: Routledge, 1997), x. 92.

16. Breitman and Lichtman, *FDR and the Jews*, 2.

17. Breitman and Lichtman, *FDR and the Jews*, 2.

18. Breitman and Lichtman, *FDR and the Jews*, 315.

19. Breitman and Lichtman, *FDR and the Jews*, 3.

20. Breitman and Lichtman, *FDR and the Jews*, 6–7.

21. *PPA*, 12:305–6.

22. *PPA*, 12:326–36.

23. *PPA*, 12:326–36.

24. Roosevelt to Churchill, July 30 1943, Map Room File, Box 16, FDRL.

25. *PPA*, 12:340–45.

26. Roosevelt and Churchill to Stalin, August 25, 1943, Map Room File, Box 16 FDRL.

27. Sherwood, *Roosevelt and Hopkins*, 748–49 (emphasis in the original).

28. *PPA*, 12:368–69.

29. *PPA*, 12:388–406.

30. *PPA*, 12:388–406.

31. Stimson Diary, October 28, 1943, and November 9, 1943; Stimson to Hopkins, November 10, 1943, HLSD.

32. *FRUS: Tehran*, 448–49.
33. *FRUS: Tehran*, 482–86.
34. *FRUS: Tehran*, 482–86.
35. *FRUS: Tehran*, 482–86.
36. *FRUS: Tehran*, 482–86.
37. *FRUS: Tehran*, 487–97.
38. *FRUS: Tehran*, 487–97.
39. *FRUS: Tehran*, 487–97.
40. *FRUS: Tehran*, 487–97.
41. *FRUS: Tehran*, 487–97.
42. *FRUS: Tehran*, 509–12.
43. *FRUS: Tehran*, 513–14.
44. *FRUS: Tehran*, 529–33.
45. *FRUS: Tehran*, 529–33.
46. *FRUS: Tehran*, 529–33.
47. *FRUS: Tehran*, 529–33.
48. *FRUS: Tehran*, 533–40.
49. *FRUS: Tehran*, 564–65.
50. *FRUS: Tehran*, 582.
51. Stimson Diary, December 18, 1943, HLSD.
52. *FRUS: Tehran*, 566.
53. *FRUS: Tehran*, 596.
54. *FRUS: Tehran*, 594.
55. *FRUS: Tehran*, 582–85.
56. *FRUS: Tehran*, 582–85.
57. *FRUS: Tehran*, 640–41.
58. Sherwood, *Roosevelt and Hopkins*, 799.
59. *PPA*, 12:546–48.
60. *PPA*, 12:553–62.
61. *PPA*, 12:553–62.
62. *PPA*, 12:553–62.

8. Victory, Roosevelt's Synthesis, and the Postwar World, 1944–1945

1. *PPA*, 13:31.
2. *PPA*, 13:32–42.
3. *PPA*, 13:32–42.
4. Memorandum, "Importance of Soviet Relationships and Suggestions for Improving Them," December 1, 1942, HLHP, Special Assistant to the President, Box 217, FDRL.
5. Forrest Davis, "What Really Happened at Teheran," *Saturday Evening Post*, May 13, 1944, 13.

6. Davis, "What Really Happened at Teheran," May 13, 1944, 13.
7. Davis, "What Really Happened at Teheran," May 13, 1944, 37.
8. Forrest Davis, "What Really Happened at Teheran," *Saturday Evening Post*, May 20, 1944, 48.
9. *PPA*, 13:147–52.
10. Roosevelt, "Reading Copy, D-Day Prayer," June 6, 1944, MSF, FDRL.
11. Roosevelt, "Reading Copy, D-Day Prayer," June 6, 1944, MSF, FDRL.
12. Roosevelt, "Reading Copy, D-Day Prayer," June 6, 1944, MSF, FDRL.
13. *PPA*, 13:160–63.
14. Butler, ed., *My Dear Mr. Stalin*, 237–38.
15. *PPA*, 13:172–77.
16. *PPA*, 13:179–80.
17. *PPA*, 13:232–34.
18. *PPA*, 13:326–27.
19. Department of State, *United Nations Monetary and Financial Conference: Bretton Woods, Final Act and Related Documents* (Washington, DC: United States Government Printing Office, 1944), 121.
20. Department of State, *United Nations Monetary and Financial Conference: Bretton Woods, Final Act and Related Documents* (Washington, DC: United States Government Printing Office, 1944), 121.
21. *PPA*, 13:197–98.
22. *PPA*, 13:201–6.
23. *PPA*, 13:254–55.
24. Stimson and Bundy, *On Active Service*, 448.
25. Stimson Diary, April 4, 1944, HLSD.
26. Stimson Diary, Memorandum, September 5, 1944, HLSD.
27. Stimson Diary, September 6, 1944 and September 9, 1944, HLSD.
28. Stimson Diary, Memorandum, September 15, 1944, HLSD.
29. Stimson and Bundy, *On Active Service*, 576–77, HLSD.
30. Stimson Diary, Memorandum, September 17, 1944, September 27, 1944, and October 3, 1944, HLSD.
31. Stimson Diary, Memorandum, September 17, 1944, September 27, 1944, and October 3, 1944, HLSD.
32. Department of State, *FRUS: The Conferences at Malta and Yalta 1945* (Washington, DC: United States Government Printing Office, 1955), 155 (hereafter *FRUS: Yalta* followed by page number).
33. *FRUS: Yalta*, 156–59.
34. *FRUS: Yalta*, 165–73 (emphasis in the original). See also *FRUS: Yalta*, 190–93.
35. Hyde Park Aide-Mémoire, "Tube Alloys," September 18, 1944, Map Room File, Naval Aide's File, Box 172, FDRL.
36. *PPA*, 13:284–92.
37. *PPA*, 13:317–24.
38. *PPA*, 13:337–39 (emphasis in the original).

39. *PPA*, 13:342–54.
40. *PPA*, 13:342–54 (emphasis in the original).
41. *PPA*, 13:356–66.
42. Daniels, *Franklin D. Roosevelt: The War Years, 1939–1945*, 448.
43. *PPA*, 13:507–17.
44. *PPA*, 13:507–17.
45. *PPA*, 13:507–17.
46. *PPA*, 13:523–25.
47. *PPA*, 13:523–25.
48. *FRUS: Yalta*, 217–18.
49. *FRUS: Yalta*, 221–23.
50. *FRUS: Yalta*, 224–25.
51. The best studies of the Crimea Conference are S. M. Plokhy, *Yalta: The Price of Peace* (New York: Viking, 2010), and Diane Shaver Clemens, *Yalta* (New York: Oxford University Press, 1970).
52. Sherwood, *Roosevelt and Hopkins*, 861–62. On the basis of this action, the Russians would later argue that this proved Roosevelt supported their position on reparations and the amount of $20 billion. This is certainly not what Hopkins or Roosevelt intended, and the president made no commitment to either reparations or a particular value.
53. *FRUS: Yalta*, 665–67.
54. In making his request to also have the opportunity for three votes, Roosevelt was going back to one of the objections raised about the League of Nations; some members of Congress insisted that the United States should not join any organization where any other nation had more votes than it did. In the end, the United States never made this request.
55. *FRUS: Yalta*, 667.
56. *FRUS: Yalta*, 727–28.
57. *FRUS: Yalta*, 780.
58. *FRUS: Yalta*, 792–93, 862–63, 846.
59. *FRUS: Yalta*, 968–75.
60. *FRUS: Yalta*, 968–75.
61. Sherwood, *Roosevelt and Hopkins*, 870 (emphasis in the original).
62. Edward R. Stettinius Jr., *Roosevelt and the Russians: The Yalta Conference* (Westport, CT: Greenwood, 1949), 322–23.
63. William Leahy, *I Was There: The Personal Story of the Chief of Staff to Presidents Roosevelt and Truman, Based on His Notes and Diaries at the Time* (New York: Whittlesey House, 1950), 315–16.
64. *PPA*, 13:548–54.
65. *PPA*, 13:548–54.
66. *PPA*, 13:548–54.
67. *The Aeneid of Virgil*, translation by Allen Mandelbaum (New York: Bantam Books, 1971), Book 6, 1136–137.

68. *PPA*, 13:556–64.
69. *PPA*, 13:570–86.
70. *PPA*, 13:570–86.
71. *PPA*, 13:570–86.
72. *PPA*, 13:570–86.
73. *PPA*, 13:570–86.
74. *PPA*, 13:570–86.
75. *PPA*, 13:570–86.
76. *PPA*, 13:570–86.
77. See Danya L. Barnes, *Architects of Occupation: American Experts and the Planning for Postwar Japan* (Ithaca, NY: Cornell University Press, 2017).
78. *PPA*, 13:607–11.
79. *PPA*, 13:570–86.
80. *PPA*, 13:607–11. Byelorussia and the Ukraine were admitted as original member states of the United Nations.
81. Butler, ed., *My Dear Mr. Stalin*, 310–12 (emphasis in the original).
82. Roosevelt to Stalin, March 24, 1945, March 31, 1945, and April 4, 1945, Map Room File, Box 28, FDRL.
83. Stalin to Roosevelt, March 29, 1945 and April 3, 1945, Map Room File, Box 28, FDRL.
84. Roosevelt to Stalin, April 4, 1945, Map Room File, Box 28, FDRL.
85. Stalin to Roosevelt, April 7, 1945, Map Room File, Box 28, FDRL.
86. Roosevelt to Stalin, April 11, 1945, Map Room File, Box 28, FDRL.
87. Warren F. Kimball, ed., *Churchill & Roosevelt: The Complete Correspondence*, vol. 3 (Princeton: Princeton University Press, 1984), 630.
88. Hopkins to Caffery, April 13, 1945, Map Room File, Box 13, FDRL.
89. Churchill to Hopkins, April 13, 1945, Hopkins to Churchill, April 13, 1945, and Hopkins to Stalin, April 13, 1945, Map Room File, Box 13, FDRL.
90. Hopkins to Chiang, April 13, 1945, HHP SC, Box 338, FDRL.

Conclusion

1. Roosevelt, "Undelivered Jefferson Day Address," April 13, 1945, MSF, FDRL.
2. Roosevelt, "Undelivered Jefferson Day Address," April 13, 1945, MSF, FDRL.
3. Roosevelt, "Undelivered Jefferson Day Address," April 13, 1945, MSF, FDRL.
4. *FRUS: Yalta*, 798.
5. Stettinius, *Roosevelt and the Russians*, 306, x.
6. Stimson Diary, April 15, 1945, HLSD.

Selected Bibliography

Primary Sources

Archives

Harvard University, Cambridge, MA

William Phillips Papers

Library of Congress, Washington, DC

Norman H. Davis Papers
Cordell Hull Papers (microfilm edition)

Franklin D. Roosevelt Presidential Library, Hyde Park, NY

Adolf A. Berle Papers
Francis Biddle Papers
Harry L. Hopkins Papers
Harry L. Hopkins Papers: Sherwood Collection
Franklin D. Roosevelt Papers
    Map Room File
    Master Speech File
    Official File
    President's Personal File
    President's Secretary File
James Rowe Papers
Grace Tully Collection: Marguerite A. ("Missy") LeHand Papers
Sumner Welles Papers

Yale University, New Haven, CT

Henry L. Stimson Diary and Papers

Published Documents

Baruch, Bernard. "Neutrality." *Current History* (June 1936): 44.

Blum, John Morton, ed. *From the Morgenthau Diaries: Years of Crisis, 1928–1938.* Boston: Houghton Mifflin, 1959.

Butler, Susan, ed. *My Dear Mr. Stalin: The Complete Correspondence between Franklin D. Roosevelt and Joseph V. Stalin.* New Haven: Yale University Press, 2005.

Cantril, Hadley, ed. *Public Opinion, 1935–1946.* Princeton: Princeton University Press, 1951.

Complete Presidential Press Conferences of Franklin D. Roosevelt, 1933–1945. 25 vols. New York: Da Capo, 1972.

Congressional Record

Department of State. *Foreign Relations of the United States 1933–1945.* Washington, DC: Government Printing Office, 1950–1969.

———. *Foreign Relations of the United States: Japan 1931–1941.* 2 vols. Washington, DC: Government Printing Office, 1943.

———. *Foreign Relations of the United States: The Conferences at Malta and Yalta.* Washington, DC: Government Printing Office, 1955.

———. *Foreign Relations of the United States: Conferences at Cairo and Tehran 1943.* Washington, DC: Government Printing Office, 1961.

———. *Foreign Relations of the United States: Conferences at Washington, 1941–1942, and Casablanca, 1943.* Washington, DC: Government Printing Office, 1968.

———. *Foreign Relations of the United States: Conferences at Washington and Quebec 1943.* Washington, DC: Government Printing Office, 1970.

———. *Foreign Relations of the United States: The Conference at Quebec 1944.* Washington, DC: Government Printing Office, 1972.

———. *United Nations Monetary and Financial Conference: Bretton Woods, Final Act and Related Documents.* Washington, DC: Government Printing Office, 1944.

———. *United States Statutes at Large: Public Laws and Reorganization Plans, 1940.* Washington, DC: Government Printing Office, 1941.

Gallup Poll: Public Opinion. Wilmington, DE: Scholarly Resources, 1972.

Kimball, Warren, ed. *Churchill & Roosevelt: The Complete Correspondence.* 3 vols. Princeton: Princeton University Press, 1984.

Kingdon, Frank. *As FDR Said: A Treasury of His Speeches, Conversations, and Writings.* New York: Duell, Sloan and Pearce, 1950.

McJimsey, George, ed. *Documentary History of the Franklin D. Roosevelt Presidency.* 33 vols. Bethesda, MD: University Publications of America, 2001–2006.

Nixon, Edgar B., ed. *Franklin D. Roosevelt and Foreign Affairs.* 3 vols. Cambridge: Belknap Press of Harvard University Press, 1969.

Roosevelt, Eleanor. *This I Remember.* New York: Harper and Brothers, 1949.

Roosevelt, Elliot, ed. *F.D.R.: His Personal Letters, 1928–1945.* 2 vols. New York: Duell, Sloan and Pearce, 1950.

Roosevelt, Franklin D. "The Future of the Submarine." *North American Review* 202, no. 4 (1915).
———. "Shall We Trust Japan?" *Asia* (July 1923): 475–78, 526–28.
———. *Whither Bound?* Boston: Houghton Mifflin, 1926.
———. "Our Foreign Policy: A Democratic View." *Foreign Affairs* 6 (July 1, 1928): 573–86.
Rosenman, Samuel, ed. *The Public Papers and Addresses of Franklin D. Roosevelt.* 13 vols. New York: Random House, 1938–1950.
Schewe, Donald B., ed. *Franklin D. Roosevelt and Foreign Affairs.* 11 vols. New York: Garland, 1979.
Stimson, Henry L. "The United States and the Other American Republics," February 6, 1931, Washington, DC: Government Printing Office, 1931.

Autobiographies and Memoirs

Bohlen, Charles. *Witness to History, 1929–1969.* New York: W. W. Norton & Company, 1973.
Hull, Cordell. *The Memoirs of Cordell Hull.* 2 vols. New York: Macmillan, 1948.
Ickes, Harold L. *The Secret Diary of Harold L. Ickes.* 3 vols. New York: Simon and Schuster, 1954–1955.
Leahy, William. *I Was There: The Personal Story of the Chief of Staff to Presidents Roosevelt and Truman, Based on His Notes and Diaries at the Time.* New York: Whittlesey House, 1950.
Perkins, Frances. *The Roosevelt I Knew.* New York: Viking, 1946.
Stettinius, Edward R., Jr. *Roosevelt and the Russians: The Yalta Conference.* Westport, CT: Greenwood, 1949.
Stimson, Henry L., and McGeorge Bundy. *On Active Service in Peace and War.* New York: Harper and Brothers, 1947.
Welles, Sumner. *The Time for Decision.* New York: Harper and Brothers, 1944.
———. *Seven Decisions That Shaped History.* New York: Harper and Brothers, 1950.

Secondary Sources

Barnes, Dayna L. *Architects of Occupation: American Experts and the Planning for Postwar Japan.* Ithaca, NY; Cornell University Press, 2017.
Barnhart, Michael. *Japan Prepares for Total War: The Search for Economic Security, 1919–1941.* Ithaca, NY: Cornell University Press, 1987.
Bennett, Edward M. *Franklin D. Roosevelt and the Search for Security: American-Soviet Relations, 1933–1939.* Wilmington, DE: Scholarly Resources, 1985.
———. *Franklin D. Roosevelt and the Search for Victory: American Soviet Relations, 1939–1945.* Wilmington, DE: Scholarly Resources, 1990.

Berinsky, Adam J., Eleanor Neff Powell, Eric Schickler, and Ian Brett Yohai. "Public Opinion in the 1930s and the 1940s." *PS: Political Science and Politics* 44, no. 3 (July 2011): 515–20.

Blower, Brooke L. "From Isolationism to Neutrality: A New Framework for Understanding American Political Culture, 1919–1941." *Diplomatic History* 38 (Spring 2014): 345–76.

Bolt, Ernest C., Jr. "Isolation, Expansion, and Peace: American Foreign Policy between the Wars," in Gerald K. Haines and Samuel Walker, eds., *American Foreign Relations: A Historiographical Review.* Westport, CT: Greenwood, 1981.

Borg, Dorothy. "Notes on Roosevelt's Quarantine Speech." *Political Science Quarterly* 72 (September 1957): 405–33.

Brands, H. W. *Traitor to His Class: The Privileged Life and Radical Presidency of Franklin Delano Roosevelt.* New York: Doubleday, 2008.

Breitman, Richard, and Allan J. Lichtman. *FDR and the Jews.* Cambridge, MA: The Belknap Press of Harvard University Press, 2013.

Butler, Susan. *Roosevelt and Stalin: Portrait of a Partnership.* New York: Knopf, 2015.

Carew, Michael G. *The Impact of the First World War on U.S. Policymakers: American Strategic and Foreign Policy Formulation, 1938–1942.* Lanham, MD: Lexington Books, 2014.

Carley, Michael Jabara. *1939: The Alliance That Never Was and the Coming of World War II.* Chicago: Ivan R. Dee, 1999.

Clemens, Diane Shaver. *Yalta.* New York: Oxford University Press, 1970.

Cole, Wayne S. *America First: The Battle against Intervention, 1940–1941.* Madison: University of Wisconsin Press, 1953.

———. *Roosevelt and the Isolationists, 1932–1945.* Lincoln: University of Nebraska Press, 1983.

Costigliola, Frank. *Roosevelt's Lost Alliances: How Personal Politics Helped Start the Cold War.* Princeton: Princeton University Press, 2012.

Cross, Graham. *The Diplomatic Education of Franklin D. Roosevelt, 1882–1933.* New York: Palgrave Macmillan, 2012.

Cross, Robert, *Sailor in the White House.* Annapolis, MD: Naval Institute Press, 2003.

Dallek, Robert. *Franklin D. Roosevelt and American Foreign Policy, 1932–1945.* New York: Oxford University Press, 1979.

Daniels, Roger. *Franklin D. Roosevelt: Road to the New Deal, 1882–1939.* Urbana: University of Illinois Press, 2015.

———. *Franklin D. Roosevelt: The War Years, 1939–1945.* Urbana: University of Illinois Press, 2016.

Davis, Forrest. "Roosevelt's World Blueprint." *Saturday Evening Post*, April 10, 1943, 20–21, 109–10.

———. "What Really Happened at Teheran," Part I, *Saturday Evening Post*, May 13, 1944, 12–13, 37–41.

———. "What Really Happened at Teheran," Part II, *Saturday Evening Post*, May 20, 1944, 22–23, 44–48.

Davis, Kenneth S. *FDR: The Beckoning of Destiny, 1882–1928*. New York: Random House, 1971.

———. *FDR: The New York Years, 1928–1933*. New York: Random House, 1985.

———. *FDR: The New Deal Year, 1933–1937*. New York: Random House, 1986.

———. *FDR: Into the Storm, 1937–1940*. New York: Random House, 1993.

———. *FDR: The War President, 1940–1943*. New York: Random House, 2000.

De Kay, James Tertius. *Roosevelt's Navy: The Education of a Warrior President, 1882–1920*. New York: Pegasus Books, 2012.

Divine, Robert. *The Illusion of Neutrality: Franklin D. Roosevelt and the Struggle over the Arms Embargo*. Chicago: University of Chicago Press, 1962.

———. *Second Chance: The Triumph of Internationalism during World War II*. New York: Atheneum, 1967.

———. *Roosevelt & World War II*. Baltimore: Johns Hopkins University Press, 1969.

———. *The Reluctant Belligerent: American Entry into World War II*. 2nd ed. New York: Wiley, 1972.

Doenecke, Justus D. *Storm on the Horizon: The Challenge to American Intervention, 1939–1941*. Lanham, MD: Rowman and Littlefield, 2000.

Dunn, Dennis J. *Caught between Roosevelt & Stalin: America's Ambassadors to Moscow*. Lexington: University of Kentucky Press, 1998.

Dunn, Susan. *1940: FDR, Willkie, Lindbergh, Hitler—The Election Amid the Storm*. New Haven: Yale University Press, 2013.

———. *A Blueprint for War: FDR and the Hundred Days that Mobilized America*. New Haven: Yale University Press, 2018.

Engel, Jeffrey A. *The Four Freedoms: Franklin D. Roosevelt and the Evolution of an American Idea*. New York: Oxford University Press, 2016.

Engelbrecht, Helmuth Carol, and Frank Cleary Hanighen. *Merchants of Death: A Study Of the International Armament Industry*. New York: Dodd, Mead & Company, 1934.

Farnham, Barbara Rearden. *Roosevelt and the Munich Crisis: A Study of Political Decision-Making*. Princeton: Princeton University Press, 1997.

Freidel, Frank. *Franklin D. Roosevelt: The Apprenticeship*. Boston: Little, Brown and Company, 1952.

———. *Franklin D. Roosevelt: The Ordeal*. Boston: Little, Brown and Company, 1954.

———. *Franklin D. Roosevelt: The Triumph*. Boston: Little, Brown and Company, 1956.

———. *Franklin D. Roosevelt: The Launching of the New Deal*. Boston: Little, Brown and Company, 1973.

———. *Franklin D. Roosevelt: A Rendezvous with Destiny*. Boston: Little, Brown and Company, 1990.

Friedman, Max Paul. *Nazis and Good Neighbors: The United States Campaign against Germany in Latin America in World War II*. New York: Cambridge University Press, 2003.

Gardner, Lloyd. *Economic Aspects of New Deal Diplomacy*. Boston: Beacon, 1971.

———. *Spheres of Influence: The Partition of Europe from Munich to Yalta*. Chicago: I. R. Dee, 1993.

Greenfield, Kent Roberts. *American Strategy in World War II: A Reconsideration*. Baltimore: Johns Hopkins University Press, 1963.

Hamby, Alonzo. *For the Survival of Democracy: Franklin Roosevelt and the World Crisis of the 1930s*. New York: Free Press, 2004.

———. *Man of Destiny: FDR and the Making of the American Century*. New York: Basic Books, 2015.

Harper, John L. *American Visions of Europe: Franklin D. Roosevelt, George F. Kennan, and Dean G. Acheson*. New York: Cambridge University Press, 1994.

Harris, Brice, Jr. *The United States and the Italo-Ethiopian Crisis*. Stanford, CA: Stanford University Press, 1964.

Hearden, Patrick J. *Roosevelt Confronts Hitler: America's Entry into World War II*. DeKalb: Northern Illinois University Press, 1987.

Heinrichs, Waldo. *Threshold of War: Franklin D. Roosevelt and American Entry into World War II*. New York: Oxford University Press, 1988.

———. "FDR and the Entry into World War II." *Prologue* (Fall 1994): 119–29.

Hoopes, Townsend, and Douglas Brinkley. *FDR and the Creation of the U.N.* New Haven: Yale University Press, 1997.

Iriye, Akira. *The Origins of the Second World War in Asia and the Pacific*. New York: Longman, 1987.

Johnstone, Andrew. *Against Immediate Evil: American Internationalists and the Four Freedoms on the Eve of World War II*. Ithaca, NY: Cornell University Press, 2014.

Jonas, Manfred. *Isolationism in America, 1935–1941*. Ithaca, NY: Cornell University Press, 1966.

Kaiser, David S. *No End Save Victory: How FDR Led the Nation into War*. New York: Basic Books, 2014.

Kennedy, David M. *Freedom from Fear: The American People in Depression and War, 1929–1945*. New York: Oxford University Press, 1999.

Kimball, Warren. *The Most Unsordid Act: Lend-Lease, 1939–1941*. Baltimore: Johns Hopkins University Press, 1969.

———. *The Juggler: Franklin Roosevelt as Wartime Statesman*. Princeton: Princeton University Press, 1991.

———. *Forged in War: Roosevelt, Churchill, and the Second World War*. New York: William Morrow, 1997.

———. "The Incredible Shrinking War." *Diplomatic History* 25 (Fall 2001): 347–65.

Langer, William L., and S. Everett Gleason. *The Challenge to Isolation: The World Crisis of 1937–1940 and American Foreign Policy*. 2 vols. New York: Harper and Row, 1952.

———. *The Undeclared War, 1940–1941*. New York: Harper and Row, 1953.

Lelyveld, Joseph. *His Final Battle: The Last Months of Franklin Roosevelt*. New York: Vintage, 2016.

Little, Douglas. *Malevolent Neutrality: The United States, Great Britain, and the Origins of the Spanish Civil War*. Ithaca, NY: Cornell University Press, 1985.
Luce, Henry. "The American Century." *Life*, February 17, 1941, 61–65.
MacDonald, C. A. *The United States, Britain and Appeasement, 1936–1939*. New York: St. Martin's, 1981.
Mahan, Alfred Thayer. *The Influence of Sea Power on History 1660–1773*. Boston: Little, Brown, and Co., 1890.
———. *The Interest of America in Sea Power, Present and Future*. Boston: Little, Brown, and Co., 1897.
Mandelbaum, Allen, translator. *The Aeneid of Virgil*. New York: Bantam, 1971.
Maney, Patrick J. *The Roosevelt Presence: A Biography of Franklin Delano Roosevelt*. New York: Twayne, 1992.
Moe, Richard. *Roosevelt's Second Act: The Election of 1940 and the Politics of War*. New York: Oxford University Press, 2013.
Moore, Michaela Hoenicke. *Know Your Enemy: The American Debate on Nazism, 1933–1945*. Cambridge: Cambridge University Press, 2010.
Norpath, Helmut. *Unsurpassed: The Popular Appeal of Franklin Roosevelt*. New York: Oxford University Press, 2018.
Offner, Arnold. *American Appeasement: United States Foreign Policy and Germany, 1933–1938*. New York: W. W. Norton, 1969.
O'Sullivan, Christopher D. *Harry Hopkins: FDR's Envoy to Churchill and Stalin*. Lanham, MD: Rowman & Littlefield, 2015.
Plokhy, S. M. *Yalta: The Price of Peace*. New York: Viking, 2010.
Preston, Andrew. "Monsters Everywhere: A Genealogy of National Security." *Diplomatic History* 38, no. 3 (2014): 477–500.
Reynolds, David. *From Munich to Pearl Harbor: Roosevelt's America and the Origins of the Second World War*. Chicago: Ivan R. Dee, 2001.
———. *The Creation of the Anglo-American Alliance, 1937–1941: A Study in Competitive Cooperation*. Chapel Hill: University of North Carolina Press, 1982.
Rock, William R. *Chamberlain and Roosevelt: British Foreign Policy and the United States, 1937–1940*. Columbus: Ohio State University Press, 1988.
Rofe, J. Simon. *Franklin Roosevelt's Foreign Policy and the Welles Mission*. New York: Palgrave Macmillan, 2007.
Roosevelt, Theodore. *The Naval War of 1812*. New York: G. P. Putnam's, 1882.
Rubinstein, William D. *The Myth of Rescue*. London: Routledge, 1997.
Schlesinger, Arthur M., Jr. *The Age of Roosevelt: The Crisis of the Old Order, 1919–1933*. Boston: Houghton Mifflin, 1957.
———. "The Man of the Century." *American Heritage* (May/June 1994): 83–93.
Schmitz, David F. *The United States and Fascist Italy, 1922–1940*. Chapel Hill: University of North Carolina Press, 1988.
———. *Thank God They're on Our Side: The United States and Right-Wing Dictatorships, 1922–1965*. Chapel Hill: University of North Carolina Press, 1999.

———. *Henry L. Stimson: The First Wise Man*. Wilmington, DE: Scholarly Resources, 2001.

Seldes, George. *Iron, Blood and Profits: An Exposure of the World-Wide Munitions Racket*. New York: Harper & Brothers, 1934.

Sherwood, Robert E. *Roosevelt and Hopkins: An Intimate History*. New York: Harper & Brothers, 1948.

Smith, Daniel M. *The Great Departure: The United States and World War I, 1914–1920*. New York: Wiley, 1965.

Smith, Gaddis. "Forty Months: Franklin D. Roosevelt as War Leader, 1941–1945." *Prologue* (Fall 1994): 131–39.

Thorne, Christopher. *The Approach of War, 1938–1939*. New York: St. Martin's, 1967.

Tierney, Dominic. *FDR and the Spanish Civil War*. Durham: Duke University Press, 2007.

Tugwell, Rexford. *The Democratic Roosevelt: A Biography of Franklin D. Roosevelt*. Garden City, NY: Doubleday, 1957.

Utley, Jonathan. *Going to War with Japan, 1937–1941*. Knoxville: University of Tennessee Press, 1985.

Winik, Jay. *1944: FDR and the Year that Changed History*. New York: Simon & Schuster, 2015.

Wood, Bryce. *The Making of the Good Neighbor Policy*. New York: Columbia University Press, 1961.

Woolner, David B., Warren F. Kimball, and David Reynolds, eds. *FDR's World: War, Peace, and Legacies*. New York: Palgrave Macmillan, 2008.

Wyman, David S. *The Abandonment of the Jews: American and the Holocaust, 1941–1945*. New York: Pantheon, 1984.

Young, Lowell T. "Franklin D. Roosevelt and the Expansion of the Monroe Doctrine." *North Dakota Quarterly* 42, no. 1 (Winter 1974): 23–32.

Index

About the Author

David F. Schmitz is the Robert Allen Skotheim Chair of History. He is the author of *Richard Nixon and the Vietnam War: The End of the American Century* (2014); *Brent Scowcroft: Internationalism and Post-Vietnam War American Foreign Policy* (2011); *The Triumph of Internationalism: Franklin D. Roosevelt and a World in Crisis, 1933–1941* (2007); *The United States and Right-Wing Dictatorships, 1965–1989* (2006); *The Tet Offensive: Politics, War, and Public Opinion* (2005); *Henry L. Stimson: The First Wise Man* (2001); *Thank God They're on Our Side: The United States and Right-Wing Dictatorships, 1921–1965* (1999); *The United States and Fascist Italy, 1922–1940* (1988); *Architects of the American Century: Individuals and Institutions in Twentieth-Century U.S. Foreign Policymaking* (edited with T. Christopher Jespersen, 2000); and *Appeasement in Europe: A Reassessment of U.S. Policies* (edited with Richard D. Challener, 1990). He is currently working on a study of the impact of the Vietnam War on American foreign policy from 1975 to the present and is writing the third volume of the history of Whitman College (1975–2015).

A specialist in twentieth-century U.S. history and American foreign policy, he teaches courses on U.S. foreign policy, America in Vietnam, twentieth-century U.S. history, the Iraq wars, and the history of rock 'n' roll. Professor Schmitz has received the Robert A. Fluno Award for Distinguished Teaching in Social Science, the G. Thomas Edwards Award for excellence in Teaching and Scholarship, Paul Garrett Fellowship, and Burlington Northern Foundation Faculty Achievement Award from Whitman College; the Arnold L. and Lois Graves Award in the Humanities from Pomona College; and grants from the National Endowment for the Humanities, Franklin D. Roosevelt Four Freedoms Foundation, and the Herbert Hoover Presidential Library Association. His scholarly contributions were recognized in a roundtable titled "The Scholarship, Influence, and Legacy of David F. Schmitz," *Pacific Historical Review* 88, no. 4 (Fall 2019): 659–714.

Studies in Conflict, Diplomacy, and Peace

Series Editors: George C. Herring, Andrew L. Johns, and Kathryn C. Statler

This series focuses on key moments of conflict, diplomacy, and peace from the eighteenth century to the present to explore their wider significance in the development of U.S. foreign relations. The series editors welcome new research in the form of original monographs, interpretive studies, biographies, and anthologies from historians, political scientists, journalists, and policymakers. A primary goal of the series is to examine the United States' engagement with the world, its evolving role in the international arena, and the ways in which the state, nonstate actors, individuals, and ideas have shaped and continue to influence history, both at home and abroad.

Advisory Board Members

David Anderson, California State University, Monterey Bay
Laura Belmonte, Oklahoma State University
Robert Brigham, Vassar College
Paul Chamberlin, Columbia University
Jessica Chapman, Williams College
Frank Costigliola, University of Connecticut
Michael C. Desch, University of Notre Dame
Kurk Dorsey, University of New Hampshire
John Ernst, Morehead State University
Joseph A. Fry, University of Nevada, Las Vegas
Ann Heiss, Kent State University
Sheyda Jahanbani, University of Kansas
Mark Lawrence, University of Texas
Mitchell Lerner, Ohio State University
Kyle Longley, LBJ Presidential Library
Robert McMahon, Ohio State University
Michaela Hoenicke Moore, University of Iowa
Lien-Hang T. Nguyen, Columbia University
Jason Parker, Texas A&M University
Andrew Preston, Cambridge University
Thomas Schwartz, Vanderbilt University
Salim Yaqub, University of California, Santa Barbara

Books in the Series

Truman, Congress, and Korea: The Politics of America's First Undeclared War
Larry Blomstedt

The Legacy of J. William Fulbright: Policy, Power, and Ideology
Edited by Alessandro Brogi, Giles Scott-Smith, and David J. Snyder

The Gulf: The Bush Presidencies and the Middle East
Michael F. Cairo

Reagan and the World: Leadership and National Security, 1981–1989
Edited by Bradley Lynn Coleman and Kyle Longley

American Justice in Taiwan: The 1957 Riots and Cold War Foreign Policy
Stephen G. Craft

Soccer Diplomacy: International Relations and Football since 1914
Edited by Heather L. Dichter

Diplomatic Games: Sport, Statecraft, and International Relations since 1945
Edited by Heather L. Dichter and Andrew L. Johns

Nothing Less Than War: A New History of America's Entry into World War I
Justus D. Doenecke

Aid under Fire: Nation Building and the Vietnam War
Jessica Elkind

Enemies to Allies: Cold War Germany and American Memory
Brian C. Etheridge

Grounded: The Case for Abolishing the United States Air Force
Robert M. Farley

Foreign Friends: Syngman Rhee, American Exceptionalism, and the Division of Korea
David P. Fields

The Myth of Triumphalism: Rethinking President Reagan's Cold War Legacy
Beth A. Fischer

The American South and the Vietnam War: Belligerence, Protest, and Agony in Dixie
Joseph A. Fry

Lincoln, Seward, and US Foreign Relations in the Civil War Era
Joseph A. Fry

The Turkish Arms Embargo: Drugs, Ethnic Lobbies, and US Domestic Politics
James F. Goode

Obama at War: Congress and the Imperial Presidency
Ryan C. Hendrickson

Fourteen Points for the Twenty-First Century: A Renewed Appeal for Cooperative Internationalism
Edited by Richard H. Immerman and Jeffrey A. Engel

The Cold War at Home and Abroad: Domestic Politics and US Foreign Policy since 1945
Edited by Andrew L. Johns and Mitchell B. Lerner

US Presidential Elections and Foreign Policy: Candidates, Campaigns, and Global Politics from FDR to Bill Clinton
Edited by Andrew Johnstone and Andrew Priest

Paving the Way for Reagan: The Influence of Conservative Media on US Foreign Policy
Laurence R. Jurdem

The Conversion of Senator Arthur H. Vandenberg: From Isolation to International Engagement
Lawrence S. Kaplan

Harold Stassen: Eisenhower, the Cold War, and the Pursuit of Nuclear Disarmament
Lawrence S. Kaplan

JFK and de Gaulle: How America and France Failed in Vietnam, 1961–1963
Sean J. McLaughlin

Nixon's Back Channel to Moscow: Confidential Diplomacy and Détente
Richard A. Moss

Breaking Protocol: America's First Female Ambassadors, 1933–1964
Philip Nash

Peacemakers: American Leadership and the End of Genocide in the Balkans
James W. Pardew

The Currents of War: A New History of American-Japanese Relations, 1899–1941
Sidney Pash

Eisenhower and Cambodia: Diplomacy, Covert Action, and the Origins of the Second Indochina War
William J. Rust

So Much to Lose: John F. Kennedy and American Policy in Laos
William J. Rust

The Sailor: Franklin D. Roosevelt and the Transformation of American Foreign Policy
David F. Schmitz

Foreign Policy at the Periphery: The Shifting Margins of US International Relations since World War II
Edited by Bevan Sewell and Maria Ryan

Lincoln Gordon: Architect of Cold War Foreign Policy
Bruce L. R. Smith

Thomas C. Mann: President Johnson, the Cold War, and the Restructuring of Latin American Foreign Policy
Thomas Tunstall Allcock